of
Prosperity

An Intentional Prayer Book

tonistone

Toni Stone

Wonder Works Studio
401 Buck Hollow Road
Fairfax, VT 05454

Copyright© 1996 by Toni Stone

All rights reserved. No part of this book may be reproduced without the permission in writing from the author, except by a reviewer who may quote brief passages or reproduce illustrations in a review with appropriate credit; nor may any part of this book be reproduced, stored in a retrieval system, or transmitted in any form or by any means – electronic, photocopying, recording, or other – without permission in writing from the publisher. This permission is easy enough to get. Write editor at Wonder Works Studio

Produced in the United States of America
by **Color PrePress Consulting**, Williston, Vermont

ISBN 0-942953-06-7

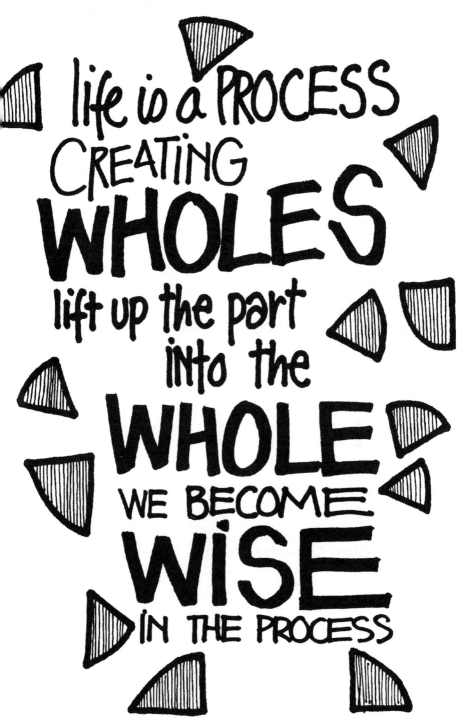

DEDICATION

This book
is dedicated to
my parents
ALICE and TONY FEDERICO.
Their partnership is an example of love
persistence
courage
commitment
in the face of all circumstance.

I thank them.
What they give is love.
Love is a practice.

INTENTIONAL PRAYER

Intentional prayer, goes hand-in-hand with more traditional forms of receptive beseeching prayer. Prayers of intention are purposeful, declarations. Aiming ideas to outcomes.

I think God means for us to be responsible, and responsive. Words, well-spoken and acted upon make the world work. When intentional prayer, in collaboration, with requesting, meditative and contemplative approaches, are practiced, there is steady inner/outer rhythm in our prayer life.

*This, I believe is fertile field
for appropriate futures
in the next century.*

Toni Stone

Seasons of Prosperity

ACKNOWLEDGEMENTS

*"dancing the circle is the most beautiful of life arts,
no more translation or abstraction....it is life itself."*
anonymous

sitting here in the foothills of buck mountain i see... a wide expanse of hills and mountains... it's spring..... my students have helped me, to understand prospering cycles. accomplishment is not linear, it is circular. i see it. i hear it . i feel it.
   i am grateful for all the contribution
                             they have been to
                             this collection.
   many helped ... the teaching learning group continues to promote life around us...
   special thanks to my wonderful spirited daughter Noelle for a strong stand in all seasons....in all her cycles, she helps things happen. for her dad, Lee Acker.... thanks to Rod Hunsaker, for emphasis on partnership.... thanks to Roberta Hamilton for a-friend-in-need.... to Marie Pappas for coaching to keep writing, and Janice Cummings for so much enthusiasm.
   thanks to Kathy Holmes, Donna Keith, Denise Greibel, who intended the best property and for continued friendship...thanks to Michael for helping me to relocate in the mountains, a most excellent idea. thanks to John + Jason Withitall for helping to start in Vermont, special thanks for the family feeling they brought when things seemed so cold. to David + Dana Brizendine, Paul + Katie Flynn, Markey Read, John Kesten for help to get established...for humor and heartfelt communications kept us all warm and able, during snowstorms. thanks to Bill Keith for keeping many things mobile, thanks to Murray Cohen, the Borglums, Barry Heerman and people from Ohio, for encouragement.
   thanks to twelve Teacher Trainings that kept the seasons. Entrepreneur Group tested, qualities for accomplishing, around the seasons. thanks to Ilene + Bob Elliott, Katherine Lavigne, Tim King, Katie Lessor and to Woman's and Men's Groups. thanks to Pelton and Gail Goudy. Thanks to Debb Sandlewood and her girls.
   thanks to work groups holding me accountable. thanks to the people of New Hampshire; Carol + Scott Stringham, Joanne + Dan Gingras, Joanne's mom, Jerry + Paula Glynn, Kathy + Dan Pouliot, Charlie Tyrell, Darrell Bradbury. thanks to Winter Writer's Weekends for quiet time set aside to work.

Seasons of Prosperity

appreciation to Ernie James for real start up encouragement showing his belief in Wonder Works Studio at an early, precarious, and crucial time twenty years ago. ....and to his daughter Judy St. James for all her help.

thanks to Gifford Booth, David Vincent, Paula Gifford, Laura Sheppard, Marc Rabinowitz , Frank Boros and Libby Bergamont for the backing of Manhattan's electrical energies always engaged. thanks to Stanley Bartlett for helping with Feng Shui. thanks to Michael Swaidner for the inspiration/technical back up, and good design to make this book real. thanks to Nira Harbin, Kevin Murray, Ruth Nager, and Angelo Colace.

gratitude to many teachers and friends at Unity School, Landmark Education, Consulting Services, Free Daist Community, Theosophical Society, the Wisdom Course in Montreal with Laine Mixer.

thanks to the wonderful work of Charles and Myrtle Fillmore, Mary Baker Eddy, Catherine Ponder, Buckminster Fuller, Ed Rabel, Albert Einstein, St. John of the Cross, Jack and Karen Boland, Rumi, Eric Butterworth, Brooke Medicine Eagle, Sig Lonegren, John Gray, Jean Houston, Theodore Schwenk, Sun Bear, Meister Eckhart, Matthew Fox, Mother Theresa, Clarissa Estes, Wabun Wind and Feather Anderson.

warm thanks to Rodney and Stephen for adding momentum. thanks to Lillian, Morris Newell, and Susan Reynolds in Boston who always helped and prayed for us. thanks to Meeks, Cronin, Colby and O'Malley for exceptional support. Robin Griffith and Eddie Amara, too.

thanks to Linda MacMillan, Pam Carlson and Ron Pallisco for always knowing what to do. thanks to my dear childhood friend Peggy Ywoskus who always encouraged my work and reminded me of just how old it really is. thanks to the people who went away to come back, and to all the folks who return. the circle is in action for teaching, learning, moving....so many people have supported this. I thank them all, especially Dave Davis and Ralph Malerba now also of Vermont.

thanks to my family who encouraged me a good long time. Anna Palacios and Virginia Hamilton were mentors of the highest. my grandmother Amelia for her love of the plant people. Aunt Polly for her incredible management abilities. my brothers Richard Federico and Michael Federico who have always stood by and contributed to me.

Introduction

deep appreciation to my husband, Steve Overton, who keeps purpose guiding us forward. i am grateful. give thanks for his mother, Susan Overton, who definitely got the job done!

... and with the financial assistance and goodwill of the patrons below that we are able to produce this book:

Noelle Acker
Gifford Booth
Pam Carlson
Joanne Casale
Connie Cervone
Alice Federico
Barbara & Doug Flack
Tom Flynn
Jerry Glynn
Sherry Gonnering
Pelton Goudy
Roberta Hamilton
Barry Heermann
Janice Heller
Delphos Herald, Inc.
Linda Susan Hill
Jeff Hull
Gail Igo
Beth Klarreich
Craig Lambert
John Linder
Linda MacMillan

Jeannie McBride
Howard & Glenna Morrison
Marie Pappas
Lynn Perrone
Richard Pratt
Markey Read
Susan Reynolds
Ayn Rose
Mary Hill Salinder
Laurie Sandler
Diana Segara-Mahoney
Don Slepian
Nancy Somers
Scott Stringham
Michael Swaidner
Dorothy Torrey
Peter Treska
Chuck Vassallo
Marie Walker
Dee Yorke
Peggy Ywoskus

with love
Toni Stone

Seasons of Prosperity

INTRODUCTION

"Four seasons fill the measure of the year;
there are four seasons in the mind of people."

John Keats

"...though i do not believe that a plant will spring up where no seed has been,
I have great faith in a seed. convince me that you have a seed there,
and I am prepared to expect wonders."

H.D. Thoreau

The process of life is a journey with nowhere to get to....
every year the same seasons appear as no surprise.....
yet they seem surprising and sometimes sudden.
The seeds of time gone bye; give rise to what is new.

Circular nature of circumstance is, undeniable. around
and around we go; beginning, working hard, developing,
growing, harvesting, saving seeds, gathering-in and freezing over,
welcoming the fallow field again, to rest........ everything has
beginning, middle, completion and rest. the resting stage sets
up seed for thrusting forward to produce again....

when i started working with circles it was, as a very young child.
i drew circle art all through grammar school. flowers, sun, moon,
planets, beach balls, fruit, and later on mandalas and medicine
wheels. Emerson remarks "THE EYE IS THE FIRST CIRCLE...
THROUGHOUT NATURE THIS PRIMARY FIGURE
IS REPEATED WITHOUT END."
St. Augustine had described once the nature of God
"AS A CIRCLE WHOSE CENTER WAS EVERYWHERE,
IT'S CIRCUMFERENCE NOWHERE".
circle is first form within wombs, before any other ...
every circle can have another around it.
the egg of what's next is within a circle of what's already been ...
children are circled by mothers before they know them.

circles are everywhere. life is circular.
permanence, in the world of particulars is.....a myth.
everything seen is fluid, moving in circular fashion.
Emerson comments,

Introduction

"....THAT WHICH BUILDS IS BETTER, THAN THAT WHICH IS BUILT...".
he reminds that everything looks permanent until it's
secret is known. the secret is it's circular nature.
the circular nature is constantly creating.

   the seasons of prosperity demand that we encounter and
master distinct ways of working... full circle way-of-living has
everything occur in appropriate timing for the overall pattern.
to be off key in any quadrant will affect harvest... therefore,
the way-of-working must be taught, in all generations.
life, all around us, reflects the seasonal nature of accomplishment...
who are we, to think we are not involved?
to learn and honor circle is the highest wisdom.

   these intentional prayers were written
for entrepreneurs-inventing-futures. the process made it
obvious that to honor the cyclical nature of accomplishment
was a form of wisdom... i've gathered together past pieces
with some new ones to take the form of a circle:

                    a time to begin   ...east is spring
                    a time to develop ...south is summer
                    a time to harvest   ...west is autumn
                    a time to rest   ...north is winter

   i have attempted to arrange pieces, to suit seasonal
rhythms.... may this work be a seed that helps you.

   conversation on the circular nature of experience,
follows this collection out into the world of people.
write to me and i'll tell you more about it.

                          love to you
                          and your circles,

                          Toni Stone

ISAIAH 43

"FEAR NOT
I AM WITH YOU

I WILL BRING SEED
FROM THE EAST

I WILL GATHER YOU
FROM THE WEST

I WILL SAY TO THE NORTH
GIVE UP
AND TO THE SOUTH
KEEP NOT BACK
...SHOW US FORMER THINGS...
THEY MAY BE JUSTIFIED...
IT IS TRUTH."

Table of Contents

BE, Start
SPRING . . .
The Season of EAST ....1 – 77

DO, Work On
SUMMER . . .
The Seasons of SOUTH ....79 – 145

HAVE, Finish
AUTUMN . . .
The Season of WEST ....147 – 217

REST, Get Ready
WINTER . . .
The Season of NORTH ....219 – 295

To Pray for the Earth . . .
Random Intentions for the World ....297 – 313

Index
by Subject ....315 – 317

Index
by Intentional Prayer ....319 – 326

Seasons of Prosperity

The Season of EAST ....Pages 1 – 77

Category	Intentional Prayer	Page
Introduction	Direction of the East	2
	standing in the East	5
	East is a time of	6
	spring-East	6
	East thinking	8
	i have what it takes in the spring	8
	spring equinox	9
	qualities to call forth in the East	9
attention to results	getting back to work	10
	i work effectively	10
	today is the day	11
	i begin now in the East	12
	expecting good	15
	about results	15
	in the East this is how i work	16
	attention to successful results	16
expansiveness	about communicating	18
	beauty is expressed	19
	order is apparent	19
	goodwill	20
	i am expansive	20
	expansiveness	21
	renewed: we seek to draw new circles	22
	being pregnant is a happy experience	22
	Dana's birth declarations	23
	parents daycare treatment	24
	i am open and receptive to miracles	24
	action begins today	27
	to go beyond limits	27
	sunshine morning	28
	i enjoy animating happiness right now while beginning	29
accepting challenge	i am willing to act quickly	29
	about challenges	30
	i am willing to think further than i've been before	32
	i say yes to good	32
	without fear	35
	about breakthroughs	36
	myself: a hero	36
	heros are just like us	37
	breakthrough to beginnings	37
	purposefulness	38
	i am determined	39
purposefulness	goals are achieved	40
	about good use of time	40
	i am purposeful	41
	purposefulness: gathering power in risking	41
	i am decisive	43
	appearances are powerless over me	43

The Table of Contents

	beginning today everything insures my success 44
	i know what to do and i do it 45
	gathering power in risking 45
	new affirmations 46
	i accomplish despite appearances 46
	God is greater than chaos 48
	practicing transcendence 48
	extending beyond 49
	i am transcendence 49
	monday declarations 50
	alive and alert each morning 50
	wednesday declarations 50
	day of transcendence 51
	providing power is always with me 52
	i must be what i was created to be 52
	East: i accept plenty of help 52
	we are the same as heros: the author's breakfast 53
confidence	we celebrate this year 54
	about winning 54
	my speaking resolves breakdowns 55
	to truly dare 55
	more affirmations for the city 56
	i assess myself as competent 56
	affirmations for today in the city 57
	beginning in confidence 58
	esteem 58
	it takes many new actions 61
releasing the past	courage: we are no longer avoiding what is new 62
	i release the past to move forward now 62
	being fully beginning 63
	i move in new ways 63
	celebrating life with my family 64
bye bye worry	goodbye to fear 64
	goodbye to fear of the future 65
	about leaving worry behind 66
	goodbye worry 66
	there are no mistakes 66
safety	safety prevails 67
	safety: i move in good sequence 68
	we give thanks for protection 69
	traveling declaration 69
	what is in error in unreal 70
	the circumstance of this car is safety 70
spring sun signs	aries declaration 73
	taurus declaration 74
	gemini declarations 75

how to write a mind treatment and affirmations
          affirmation: conscious creative speaking makes things real ..76
          mind treatment: we are already connected with perfection ..76

Seasons of Prosperity

The Season of SOUTH .... Pages 79 – 145

Category	Intentional Prayer	Page
introduction	Direction of the South	80
	standing in the south	83
	oh South spirit	84
	South is a time of	84
	summer-South	85
	i have what it takes in integrity	86
	summer in the spirit of the circle	86
	qualities to call forth in the South	87
working	i am determination	87
	i know how to work	88
	a declaration for the work place	89
	entrepreneurial affirmations	90
	goodbye obstructions to getting the job done	91
	i have entrepreneurial spirit	92
	i am working hard, no matter what	92
	i work hard today	94
truth telling and integrity		
	i am integrity	94
	saying no	94
	being responsible	95
	prosperous doing	96
	i create congruence	97
	we have authentic speaking	97
	stay coherent	98
	integrity is congruence	99
	the serious thing	100
	i speak true. i take a stand on myself	100
	life is no longer a popularity contest	101
	my heart is true	101
leadership	achieving leadership	103
	it' s possible	103
	committed	104
	this is completely good	105
	powerful purpose is mine	105
	what's mine to do is done today	106
	true satisfaction of together	106
caring and commitment		
	practicing love in everyday life	109
	partnership	110
	our activities together help us know ourselves	111
	commitment	112
	love: affirmations and denials	112
	partnerships help me serve my purpose	114

The Table of Contents

	partnerships serve human community:	
	declarations for partnership	115
	wedding convocation	116
	we give thanks for this marriage day	117
well being	health today	118
	dealing with disorder in body	119
	life is good	120
	physical well being	121
	beauty is expressed	122
	well being decree	122
	decree of perpetual health	124
	healthy thinking is mine	124
	healing is always available	125
communicating	complaining is a thing of the past	126
	about relationships	126
	beauty is a way of looking	127
	about enrolling	127
	i know how to be with people	128
	thinking language	128
	i communicate breaks in my sense of integrity	129
redirecting	reactive responses no longer run me	130
	i am awake and fully conscious now	130
	saturday goodbye tensions	131
	this body is in perfect submission to Universal Intelligence	132
	i am of God therefore sustaining perfect partnership	133
	growing to more good	134
	i live as a success story today	134
goodbye anger	goodbye anger	135
	patience for today	135
	the litany of dissappointment	137
discipline	i know what to do and i do it	138
	i am discipline	139
	about bad habits	140
	i complete what i start	141
summer signs in the South		
	cancer declarations	142
	leo declarations	142
	virgo declarations	143

Seasons of Prosperity

The Season of WEST ....Pages 147 – 217

Category	Intentional Prayer	Page
introduction	Direction of the West	148
	standing in the West	151
	autumn – West	152
	West thinking	152
	here approaches autumn of the circle	153
	i have what it takes in the autumn	154
	West is a time of......	154
	qualities to call forth in the West	155
forgiving	prelude to forgiveness	155
	an ancient proclamation of forgiveness from China	156
	goodbye to enemies	156
	freely and happily i forgive	157
	peace with my parents	158
	end the old: autumn process	159
letting go of suffering	i let go of problems	159
	i recognize and release resistance to changing	160
	release decree	160
	intimate with everything	161
	the buck hollow declaration for surrender	163
	goodbye self-pity	163
	giving up being afraid and conflicted	165
	i know when to hold and when to fold	165
	relinquishment	165
	mighty presence of God within	166
	nothing is where everything comes from	166
	thursday: self concern gives way	166
	goodbye: remember me as loving you	167
prospering	about the flow of money	168
	abundant thinking	169
	prosperity attitudes	170
	prosperous thinking	170
	prosperous declaration	171
	more money affirmations	172
	i leave behind, i accept and i am willing	173
	prosperity mind treatment	173
	i let go	174
	i am leaving behind	174
	i see	174
	i know	175
	i realize	175
	i establish certitude of plenty	176
	friday going forward	176
	waiter/waitress affirmations	177
	always there is increase	177
	i am free to prosper in my business	179
	prosperity prevails	179

The Table of Contents

giving	my giving makes me rich	180
	i give up scare scarce thinking by giving	183
	increasing income	183
	i tithe effortlessly and i prosper	184
	generosity affirmations	186
	increasing generosity	187
	men affirmations	188
receiving	i am willing to be contributed to	188
	i trust that everybody prospers me	189
	life is created with thought	190
	prosperous provision has been made	190
	change is the heart of my being	191
	sunday in an opulent universe	191
	changing continues to bless me	192
	ready to relocate declaration	192
	pumpkin harvest	193
	prosperity teacher covenant	194
	declaration for prosperity teachers	195
	prayer of a dedicated teaching life in the company of others	196
	self-talk for an advisor..	197
	teacher's proclamation	197
	i am a prosperity teacher	198
	i promise today....	199
	teaching affirmations	199
	leadership	200
being supportable	i choose changing	200
	about being supportable	203
	supportability looks like this	204
	i am associating with people who empower me	204
	about friends	205
	i work successfully with others helping me	205
celebrating	blessing all people	206
	i express praise easily	206
	holiday declaration	207
	start out with thanksgiving	208
	holiday times together are events of celebration	208
	we give thanks for life	209
creating	creativity	210
	i speak prosperous results	211
	about creativity	212
	true creativity	213
	i have a clear space to work	213
autumn sun signs	libra declarations	214
	scorpio declarations	215
	sagittarius declarations	216

Seasons of Prosperity

The Season of NORTH ....Pages 219 – 295

Category	Intentional Prayer	Page
introduction	Direction of the North	220
	standing in the North	223
	North is a time of	224
	i have what it takes in the winter	224
	winter - North	225
	qualities to call forth in the North	226
being quiet	the decision for quietness	226
	the great way isn't difficult	227
	i am loved and appreciated	227
	listening	228
	i choose prayer as a foundation	228
	listening to life	231
	thoughts like i want to have...	231
	i grow in closeness with God	232
	don't worry no matter what anything looks like	232
	the power mightily with me....of perfect pattern	233
	conditions for intentional prayer	233
	life always responds	233
	reflection	233
	to practice death	234
	prayer of peace	234
	on death	234
	perpetual light - declaration for the dead	235
	treatment for a peaceful passing	235
	dealing with death	236
	letting go	236
	constantly remember death	237
	Jason's best thought	237
expectancy	what's eternal?	238
	expansiveness	239
	truth song	239
	attraction increase decree	240
	new year mind treatment	240
	expectancy treatment	241
	good will for all, wherever we are	242
	today: i accept good	242
	good is certain	243
	good is assured	243
	my own nature can be heard in quiet	244
decisiveness	i am guided to go forward	244
	declaration: to command a thing to be so	245
	decisive, i choose my next plan of action	245
	order perfectly outworking	245
	declaration of divine order	246
	prayer treatment for divine guidance	246

The Table of Contents

	prayer of appropriate choices	247
	renunciation decree	247
	something new is beginning	248
magnanimity	bodhisattva vow	248
	a human being is part of the whole	248
	we have a healthy, peopled, peaceful world	249
	God great spirit, i see you with my heart	250
	i am a universe creature	250
	goodbye small world	251
	my heart reveals love, i surrender	251
	God is God....is God is	252
	the high laws	252
	i thank God	253
	universal prayer	253
	up,up, and away: broken open	253
living happily with questions		
	living the mystery	254
	answers are always available	254
	all conditions change and pass	255
	move to natural world	255
	pattern seen everywhere	255
	the impulse of love designs my future	256
	universal mind....	257
	i follow a high calling	257
	waiting with patience	258
happiness	life extension	259
	happy words are my choice	259
	declarations for enlightened beings	260
	freedom is already mine	260
	candlemas: light in the darkness is a happy event	261
	winter happiness	261
the natural world is my world		
	i have a new friendship with the natural world	262
	weather storm declaration	262
	we keep earthwaters sustaining life	263
	blessing for flowers	264
	happy celebrating nothing	264
	declarations for a tree	264
	human beings are a viable species	267
	sioux prayer	267
	sacred site declarations	268
	this body is a field of transformations	268
	blessing for seeds	269
	blessing for the birds	270
	natural law	270
	thank God for animals	271
	streams come alive again and fill with fish	271
	the animal blessing	272

Seasons of Prosperity

The Season of NORTH (con't) ....Pages 219 – 295

Category	Intentional Prayer	Page
community	communities rebuilding	272
	divine universal family declaration	273
	today i am a citizen of earth	273
	on earth today	274
	we have peace prevailing on earth	274
	for earth the time is now	277
	we declare that peace is prevailing on earth	278
	the community prayer	281
	emergency community affirmations	282
	awake to the nation	282
celebration: the light is brigher now	blessed be	285
	being free of unworkable ways	285
	God is the companion of my heart	286
	merry making at the winter solstice	286
	thanksgiving: we give thanks to creation for all this	289
	we yield to the leading edge of divine will	289
	responsive yule rite	290
expectancy	expectation is in place	295
	merry days are behind and in front	295
winter sun signs	capricorn declarations	292
	aquarius declarations	293
	pisces declaration	294

Intentions for all Seasons ....Pages 297 – 313

world intentions	To pray for the earth	297
	Intentions for children	298
	Intentions for all people	299
	Intentions for elders	300
	Intentions for people health	301
	Intentions for Americans	303
	Intentions for nations	303
	Intentions for world leaders	305
	Intentions for business	305
	Intentions for the green world	307
	Intentions for the weather	308
	Intentions for the ecology department	308
	Intentions for the ocean & waters	309
	Intentions for animals	309
	Intentions for the earth world	310
	Intentions for the future	310
	Intentions for the universe	312

Introduction

Direction of The East

we honor
powers of the East
green is East. green is vitality.
East is where the day break star
                 of knowledge appears.
East is the rising sun
bringing everyone . . . . .the new day of
                     new experiences
                     new possibilities
thanks to Great Spirit, for each day
we walk on this Mother Earth planet.
from beginnings spring wisdom and goodness.
                 we are thankful ongoingly for
       knowledge beginning in this direction,
becomes peace and understanding later in the circle.
the power of starting is vitalizing in the spring.

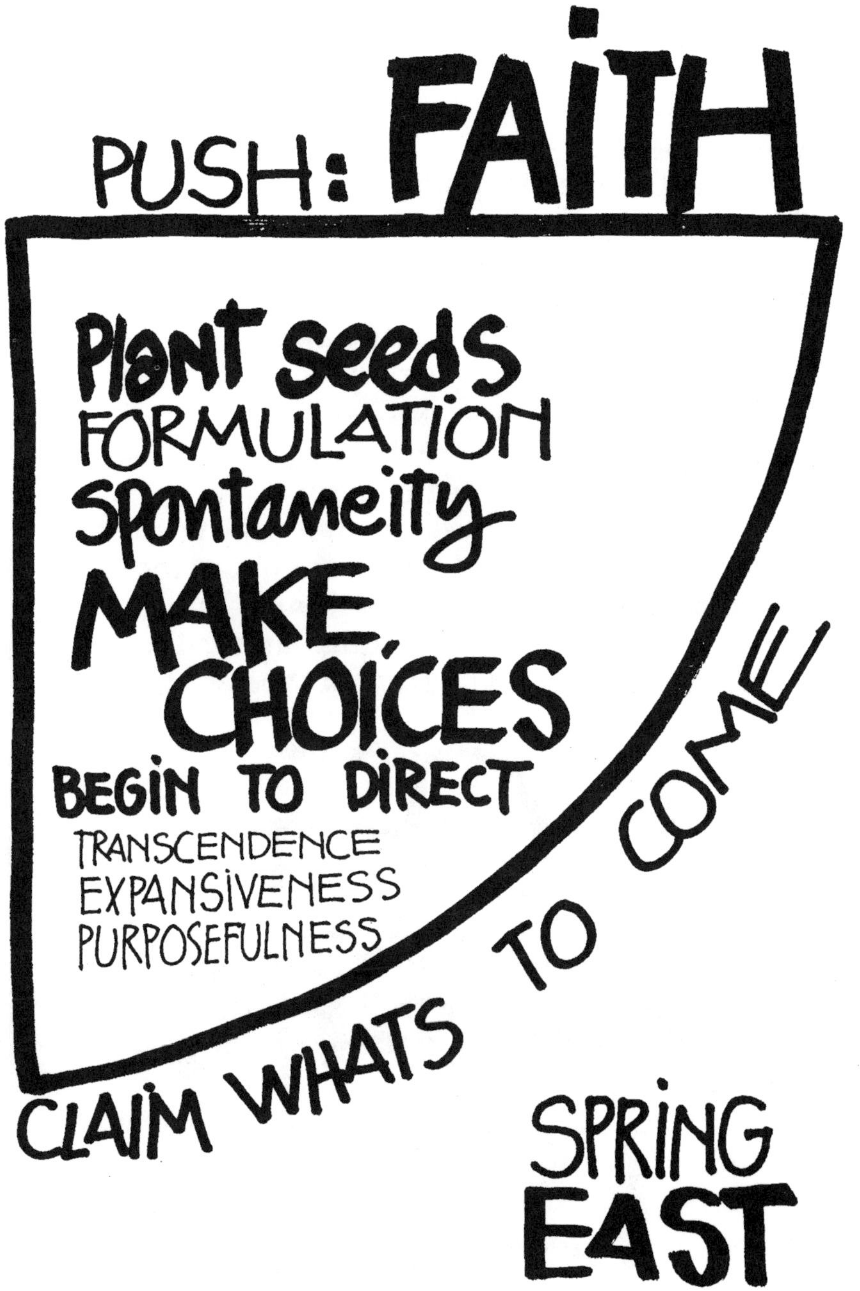

The Direction of East

PUSH: FAITH

- Plant seeds
- FORMULATION
- Spontaneity
- MAKE CHOICES
- BEGIN TO DIRECT
- TRANSCENDENCE
- EXPANSIVENESS
- PURPOSEFULNESS

CLAIM WHATS TO COME

SPRING EAST

BLESSED BE THE LORD WHO DAILY LOADETH US WITH BENEFITS
PS. 68:19

©toni acker 82

The Direction of

STANDING IN THE EAST
i give great thanks for Healing
        provided by the
        Archangel Raphael
This is where i increase my ability to believe in the unseen
i am grateful for all the people
        all the circumstances
        all the events
        that have brought me to the
        EAST
As i continually move in the circle of cycles
i am starting to arouse movement, these are new beginnings for me
i am empowered by truthfulness and courage
i am formulating and articulating the Journey
i am renewed by the warmth of spirit - i hear the fire
                                                      i hear the thunder
i trust this process that has already begun to
        produce new ideas
i feel vulnerable in the face of what
                is so new i can hardly
                speak it.....
                i am awake
                being prepared.
                there is great joy in the EAST
with discovery
with beginnings
with illumination from within
this is the start of new light
an interruption, of that which normally has continued.
the agitation of telling truth, confessing and revealing
facilitates new actions for everyone around me.
the action of "setting free" and "being set free" is present here.
actions of parting, keeping apart and going apart for awhile
are happening and i let them without fear or grasping.....
it's okay to withdraw and make new discernments
the process of analysis and extraction happens here in the EAST.
i distinguish appropriate boundaries clearly and quickly.
i know change must be part of beginnings and discoveries.
clarity comes, wisdom prevails
inner illumination reveals appropriate movements.
i gladly reach beyond former boundaries.
i will go beyond my old self here in the EAST.
in the EAST i ask:
    what new actions, new choices, new blendings to dedicate to?
    how to feel secure as the old dissolves and change takes place?
    how can i stay above the opinions around me?
    what am i really going away from? -what am i going towards?
    can i allow for something being produced thru me?
    how to devote myself to serving others?
    what is leadership really?

Seasons of Prosperity

EAST IS A TIME OF

- ♥ joy in beginnings
- ♥ courage to get going
- ♥ quick starts
- ♥ birth, rebirth, childhood
- ♥ growing love that is uncritical
- ♥ able to see through complex, to make it simple
- ♥ guiding and leading others into action
- ♥ leadership, devotion to the service of others
- ♥ trusting the vision received in the winter
- ♥ renewal, faith, illumination
- ♥ spontaneity, vulnerability, trust
- ♥ truthfulness, purity in speaking
- ♥ declarations for a future
- ♥ increasing light
- ♥ focus of attention on the task-to-be-done now
- ♥ putting into words what's-to-be-done

SPRING - EAST

using the model of four season's in nature... the sun seems to come up in the East. East is the direction of starting... the season is spring and this time symbolizes beginnings.

thaw starts a beginning... all beginnings have previous fuel. East portrays where <u>what's new is finally noticed</u>. outward action now thrusts forth... we dash forward to do in the East what was given to us to do way back in the autumn. when the pumpkins occurred on the vine, <u>within them</u>, were seeds which are now being planted in the East!! every direction is intimately related to the others. what begins in spring, ends in autumn .
what ends in autumn carries the seed forward to spring.

East reflects fertility, new life, birth, beginnings and <u>going outside with it</u>. freedom, excitement-to-begin-at-last, all these are seen in the East direction... maple syrup, animal babies, bird babies. all kinds of revitalization and regeneration are typified by East.

The Direction of East

spring equinox is a time when night and day are finally equal in length. <u>light is growing steadily longer</u>, winter is behind. eggs are ritually eaten, after being colored to celebrate "rebirth" of the sun in spring.
the ancients noticed, eggs of fowls, began to-be-laid, when the eye of a hen was stimulated by more than 12 hours of light each day. this connection between eggs and the shift of darkness, for more light, was the basis of spring ritual eggs. magical signs, drawn on eggs are a practice of rich EASTER meaning, each year.

eggs colored in the Ukraine as red, yellow and orange were eaten to celebrate the rebirth of the sun and return of the seasons of plenty. In Italy colored eggs are baked into breads. natural colors for eggs are obtained by boiling onion skins with eggs for soft orange. half teaspoon of tumeric for yellow. beet juice and vinegar for pink. boiling eggs with vinegar and outer leaves of red cabbage allowing the whole mixture to cool overnight produces robin's egg blue.

the thought was these "charms" helped the sun gain strength and power over the darkness of winter. geometric shapes, plants and creatures are drawn on eggs already colored.

the EASTER egg rabbit tradition is derived from the hare's fertility as an expression of spring's life renewal. the upsurge of life in springtime brings new growth to all kingdoms of nature.

in the beginning direction of our projects and lives, the demand is that we work quickly and imperfectly, putting in correction as we move. this style of East, takes a certain greatness of spirit to declare what's-not-yet-been when there's no evidence of it's manifestation yet. <u>what's-to-come must be claimed</u> by naming it. this is the direction, to <u>take plenty of new actions</u> .
merging total being with the activity at hand will produce something. concentration, purposefulness and true dedication are called for here.
<u>a way to describe the new desired result</u> must be put together.
new affiliations, to back the emerging outcome will be required...
breaking away from the old, dashing to the new...
choices set up the summer of blooming which will come next.

transcendence; means ending the trance of what stopped us.
East outpictures, quickly dashing forward...new life growing in wombs doesn't come down delicately...it bursts forward, full-force...

    spring stands for quickening and risky action,
        taken to promote future outcomes
            that were planned seasons ago.

EAST THINKING

- ♥ i now declare what hasn't been done before by me,
  i take on what "seemed" impossible.
- ♥ unproven i dash forward risking.
- ♥ i take action to produce results today.
  my viewpoint about the future and how i put myself in it,
  has expanded.
- ♥ everyday i produce something.
- ♥ i find experts to advise my tasks and projects
  i do what trusted advisors recommend
  and establish accountabilities for myself.
- ♥ new actions help me to resolve issues i take new actions each day.
- ♥ i learn to measure results
  and take appropriate actions to keep results
- ♥ i am producing something, rather than thinking it over.
- ♥ i am quick to discover what impedes progress.
  i move in a productive way instead of becoming bogged down.
- ♥ here is where i change things
- ♥ i keep on changing things to get the results required.
- ♥ elimination, getting down to the "bones" of the matter is required here.
- ♥ i quit a lot of talk: what's the request? what's the promise?
  when will it be finished by? i cut out the fluff here.
- ♥ i am "set free"... now, unbound, i have broken chains of inertia.
- ♥ something is left behind to get started.
- ♥ i dash forward to get to work quickly.

I HAVE WHAT IT TAKES IN THE SPRING

- ♥ i demonstrate transcendence in all my working today.
- ♥ i am beyond opinions.
- ♥ i have a posture of assurance enabling me to act quickly for what's next.
- ♥ i am expansive today, in all my undertakings.
- ♥ i am willing to have more, be more, give more, and i do.
- ♥ i keep jumping-out making new choices. i focus.
- ♥ i am willing to change things, creating new affinities
  and wider communications all around me.
- ♥ i am purposeful, willing to act now, for what's next.
- ♥ i am dedicated, to what i am called to do...
- ♥ i act intentionally with boldness and efficiency today.
- ♥ i have what it takes to call something forward.

QUALITIES TO CALL FORTH IN THE EAST:

♥ **transcendence**

a way of being beyond opinions that results in a posture of assured quick action.

♥ **expansiveness**

a way of willing to have more, be more, give more ... making new choices creating new affinities and wider communications ... natural compilations.

♥ **purposefulness**

knowing your mission, willing to act for what's next ... "going towards" and being dedicated to, what you are called to do ...

SPRING EQUINOX

is known as the vernal equinox. It occurs approximately March 21. this time is when night and day are equal in length. the light is about to grow stronger now. this is the time and place to put winter behind us. seeds can now be blessed for planting. these seeds have laid dormant through the dark cycle and are now ready to begin the renewal of life with the increased outpouring of life forces, from the sun. each day gets longer. every bud, blossom and leaf of spring owes its existence to the sun's forces. the colors in the world are coming alive, rendered increasingly visible by more sunlight. the major dynamic of vernal equinox is fertility renewal. the awakening, re-arising life of springtime calls attention to manifestation in the physical realms. the ecclesiastical Easter festivals call attention to the triumph of spirit over matter. thrusting forward is happening everywhere at spring equinox.

I WORK EFFECTIVELY

- i produce much.
- i stay on purpose today.
- i give up, what only distracts me.
- i take on, what brings me where i'm headed.
- i refuse to use what's inappropriate for me.
- i move into patterns of action that keep me productive.
- my actions are aligned with results i desire.
- at this point, i overcome all odds, on my path.
- i am grateful for ability to work hard.

GETTING BACK TO WORK

- i am empowered to begin again.
- l accomplish visions with ease.
- i overcome obstacles to accomplishment.
- barriers disappear daily as i move quickly.
- i bring vision into action, step by step.
- no longer do i stress and strain.
- i am satisfied to be a beginner.
- i am expanding my ability by learning as i work now.
- everyday, in every way, things are getting better and better for me now.
- i dare to be magnificent and give full effort.
- i am grateful for all the good continuing to come my way.
- i am open and receptive to life, receiving prospers projects too.
- understanding forwards me in all work. i trust intuition.
- i leave behind worry and take on enthusiasm
- what used to seem impossible is now possible and effortless.
- i get all the facts i need, to do the work that's expected of me.
- my work is excellent. corrective influences guide me.
- all acknowledgements empower me to take future risks.
- i surpass all previous performance as i dare more ...
- i am learning and remembering at a very fast rate.
- people are pleased with my progress. i am fulfilling promises.
- i use all tools necessary to do what needs to be done by me.
- i know what to do and i do it quickly and thankfully.

The Direction of East

TODAY IS THE DAY

♥ We...have an enthusiastic outlook.
>produce the results we desire.
>are moved to successful outcomes.
>move steadily without doubt.

♥ We...can be counted on to enable others.
>contribute in a big way.
>are full participants.
>are not sidetracked.

♥ We...avoid too much time with complainers.
>refuse to waste energy on what doesn't matter.
>show up vital, lively, and effective.
>are moving forward quickly on purpose.

♥ We...attract miracles.
>demonstrate winning.
>focus on what's intended.
>create what's possible.

Seasons of Prosperity

i BEGIN NOW, IN THE EAST

- i trust in my vision. images are important.
- i trust the good ideas i've accepted.
- i advance to accomplish , i do something great.
- spontaneity and joy increase my trust in the future of good ideas.
- i say goodbye to thoughts of waiting until later.
- i call forth the courage to create ability.
- despite any evidence around me, i speak solutions, before they are seen.
- i dash forward to claim a day of getting to work.
- i see complex situations clearly in perspective.
- i have the ability to focus attention on present tasks to make a workable future for good ideas.
- i find out what's required to head things in necessary directions.
- truthfulness, warmth of spirit and a great capacity to believe in the as-yet unseen help me to move quickly forward, working fast and putting in corrections, as i progress.
- i announce new beginnings cheerfully. there is creation intensification.
- i make measurements and new language for results to occur.
- i take many new actions to produce something.
- success is found in serving people, i start now.
- i establish accountabilities. i have people helping me.
- i resolve challanges quickly with determination.
- i get lots of advice from experts.
- i have the humility required to get help.
- new blendings of people, places and activities spur me on.
- my whole being is involved in the activities at hand.
- i leave behind withholding full effort.
- i develop the dazzling full power of will.
- i let go of what impedes progress.
- my will to get into action is improving.
- i let people know what i can be counted on for ...
- i have a posture of assurance. i take action.
- i am making choices easily. new ideas keep bubbling up.
- i change things. i put productions together.
- i break away from some things and go towards other things.
- i get rid of what's no longer useful.
- i have new ways of being. . . purposeful and dedicated.

– LUKE 9:62

NO ONE ★ HAVING PUT A HAND TO THE PLOUGH ★ and looking back IS FIT FOR THE KINGDOM OF GOD.

©toni acker 82

I STOP WAITING AROUND for something to happen....
I MAKE SOMETHING HAPPEN
I STEP OUT INTO ACTION

EXPECTING GOOD

- i expect good.
- i reflect good.
- good is what i expect.
- good is what i reflect.
- i expect good and i get it.
- expectation is conscious with me.
- expecting and getting outcomes involves more than luck.
- today, i direct my thinking/feeling process.
- i notice as i think, believe and act, it is done exactly how i expect.
- i see what is useful to think and believe.
- i know the specific direction of my expectations.
- i expect solutions to all problems.
- i expect freedom from all difficulties today.
- i expect questions to be answered.
- i expect guidance in all confusions.

ABOUT RESULTS

In this year...

- i set priorities and commit myself to fully live forward into them
- work is directed and effective.
- i produce more results in less time...
- the quality of my work increases.
- good Results are abundant!!!!!
- i am no longer: distracted. instead i AM assured.
                    worried. instead i AM focused.
                    disorganized. instead i AM certain and orderly.
                    unsatisfied. instead i AM satisfied.
                    confused. instead i AM decisive.
- ...in this year i have less stress
- i produce good results easily.
- high energy and effectiveness are simply present.

IN THE EAST THIS IS HOW I WORK

♥ i make public announcements about what i am going to be doing next.
♥ the essence of true success is serving people.
♥ i move quickly and keep putting in corrections.
  cleaning things up, as i go forward.
♥ i have the humility to get coaches and i do...
♥ i set up communication, in a network so i can be known.
♥ i find out what's required to produce results.
♥ i keep on taking new actions to produce results.
♥ i surrender fully to the job-at-hand.
♥ i am developing the power-of-will, to get results.
♥ i separate myself from what doesn't work.
♥ i get rid of old stuff. i change things. i work quickly ...
♥ i am above opinions-of-doubt and confusion.
♥ on-purpose i expand to cover more territory daily.

ATTENTION TO SUCCESSFUL RESULTS

♥ i declare ancient and powerful practices enable me to enter the domain of noticing where i put my attention.
♥ the power of attention cannot be underestimated for developing cycles to greatest results.
♥ i come into harmony with whatever my attention is focused upon. i focus on results.
♥ intelligence is operative with me, as the power to conceive and perceive successful results in all my projects.
♥ my wise use of attention puts me in the position of aiming successfully, for desired results.

Seasons of Prosperity

ABOUT COMMUNICATING

- i have effective communications
- ...in my communicating i both speak and listen.
- my ability to communicate is transforming.
- i experience more and more good results from my communications...
- i have effective communications.
- communications are a vehicle for producing results
- i express power in communicating. i give as well as receive.
- ability to listen is transforming all communications.
- i experience more and more good results from my listening...
- i listen and hear effectively.
- i get what people are really communicating and i respond to that information.
- listening is a vehicle for producing results.
- i express understanding in listening
- ...i have effective communications ...i listen and hear effectively.
- i produce results with my ability to communicate.
- i produce results everywhere i am by communicating and by participating fully in what's going on around me.
- in my communications i tell the truth...
- how it is to be me, how i am experiencing life.
- i leave out my: advice, opinions, criticisms, judgments
- instead i give people my: feelings, experience, sharing.
- i share more of me and less of what i think.
- my communications make a difference.
- i have effective communications.
- i am listening and hearing in a way that makes a difference.
- i am exercising power in producing results today.
- i produce results with what i do.
- i produce results with what i say.
- i produce results with how i am.
- i transcend all barriers to true communications.
- my self expression is no longer within the confines of my childhood experience.
- i am breaking thru all barriers to communication
- my power to communicate fully is expanding.
- i awaken new insights...new inspiration...new expression.
- i express all that i am.
- i am continually committed to producing results.
- i keep on keeping on, even when it looks like i don't like what's happening.
- giving up is a thing of the past. i have effective communicating.

The Direction of East

BEAUTY IS EXPRESSED PART ONE

- ♥ beauty is easy to express.
- ♥ order is Heaven's first Law.
- ♥ now and always beauty is called forth.
- ♥ perfect balance, auspicious sequence.
  and inevitable consequence are here.
- ♥ i celebrate what is beautiful all around me.
- ♥ i create beautiful life in all surroundings.
- ♥ i live day-to-day in wonderful designs and patterns.
- ♥ i give thanks, for all evidence of continual beauty,
  with me, around me and beyond me.
- ♥ beauty is easy to express and experience today.
- ♥ i acknowledge the Law of Beauty and Order,
  which always shows up in life, over and over again.
- ♥ whatever i praise and appreciate, multiplies around me.
- ♥ today i praise and appreciate, the many forms
  and function of beauty everywhere present.

ORDER IS APPARENT TODAY

There in One Power
        One Intelligence
           One Knowing
everyone is part of that One... united and included.
divine ORDER is what's apparent today all around everywhere.
perfect UNION is at work. good is present, active and felt.
humility and understanding exist in perfect right timing.
reliance on error is given up and vanquished.
convenient alliances of deceit are dissolved and disowned.
avoiding issues, rationalizing lies, inappropriate actions disappear.
the spirit of truth prevails. truth becomes evident now.
the still small voice for good is heard, it's counsel is accepted.
divine UNIONS are already revitalized. ORDER establishes equanimity.
integrity reigns. commitment continues.....
patterns of good prevail. divine DESIGN directs all events.
THANKS today is given for perfect right ORDER!
ORDER is apparent in all outcomes today. so it is!

GOODWILL

- i am a powerful force for good.
- it is natural for me to express good.
- i am good.
- i introduce good wherever i am.
- i heal small-mindedness.
- i focus attention on what works, what heals, and what brings people together.
- i bring light and delight everywhere i go.
- my presence dissolves blame and negativity.
- natural harmony happens around me, i am a peace maker.
- i provide looking that disappears problems.
- i apply ideas lovingly and with good humor.
- problems move naturally to solutions when i am present.
- i express truth, beauty, goodness, love.
- my sense of humor is refreshing and vital.
- all cynicism and pessimism are left behind now.
- i radiate good will, all around me.

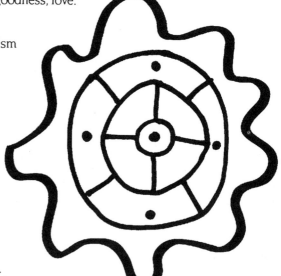

I AM EXPANSIVE

- i affirm all of life with actions and thinking.
- i no longer live only between my own elbows.
- i initiate views that include everyone.
- i see for all in ever widening ways.
- i value new ideas, new options, new views.
- i allow continuing forward motion.
- i am willingness to experience satisfaction.
- i am willingness to feel grateful and thankful.

EXPANSIVENESS

- ♥ i have a winning way of being. i look at life in a friendly fashion every day.
- ♥ i encourage and support winning for all others.
- ♥ i work for the good of all people.
- i am an expert at deprogramming complaints.
- ♥ i creatively move forward out of fixed positions.
- ♥ i am straightforward in offering and requesting services.
- ♥ i am willing to accomplish results by being invisible, functioning outside the spotlight.
- ♥ i am willing to accomplish results by being in the spotlight.
- ♥ i have a natural attribute, ability, and inclination to call what's next.
- ♥ i let go all boundaries, distinctions, and ideas which limit.
- ♥ i allow new actions now.
- ♥ i am spontaneously forming new ideas.
- ♥ i incorporate ideas that relax limiting boundaries today.
- ♥ i interrupt what normally continues, to presence good that's new!!!
- ♥ i am willing to create the unknown, where familiar used-to-be.
- ♥ i am constantly going out further ... miracles abound.
- ♥ i am a constant rolling forward at full expansion, pressing-out.
- ♥ profuse, lavish, generous, good results are everywhere today.
- ♥ i have increasing willingness to experience unusual circumstances that bring good.
- ♥ i continue to create value with everyone and everything.
- ♥ being expansive works for me now.

Seasons of Prosperity

RENEWED: WE SEEK TO DRAW NEW CIRCLES

- ♥ new circles of wider experience are setting up now.
- ♥ in nature every moment is new
  past is gone before, the future is coming up.
- ♥ life is a series of surprises: i am glad, cheerful to begin.
- ♥ much is possible that hasn't been thought of yet...
- ♥ there is new power in expansiveness.
- ♥ new courage to make new roads is what's present now.
- ♥ bold actions break down old structures.
- ♥ life, transition, and moving into action is what's so now.
- ♥ wherever i am, possibilities for new circles exist.
- ♥ this is a cheerful, determined time to move forward.
- ♥ i am happy to be circling in wider ways now.
- ♥ building up into new circles is happening.
- ♥ all energies of the past, help presence what's next.
- ♥ i am renewed with universal possibilities.
- ♥ this is a new moment, a beginning.
- ♥ i draw a wide circle today with new ways.
- ♥ i am convinced, the way of life is wonderful.
- ♥ the forward motion of life, calls forth new circles for me.
- ♥ i sing, dance, and think possibilities.
- ♥ what's new is always calling for attention.

BEING PREGNANT IS A HAPPY EXPERIENCE

- ♥ i expect good results. i am patient and happy.
- ♥ right action prevails in this pregnancy with me.
- ♥ i make intelligent assessments and choices.
- ♥ the great law of creation is operative.
- ♥ i am aligned and in harmony with great universal order.
- ♥ i accept perfect results easily, effortlessly.
- ♥ i am participating in heartful disciplines
- ♥ i am happy today being pregnant.
- ♥ the systems of my body function in appropriate order.
- ♥ i am always going forward... i expect the best.
- ♥ waiting is a fruitful experience.
- ♥ i am in the disposition of health and happiness today.

DANA'S BIRTH DECLARATIONS
with thanks to Dana Brizendine

- ♥ i surrender to the process of healthy, happy childbirth.
- ♥ this baby develops in perfect well-being in a timely way.
- ♥ we do not rush the readiness of this child.
- ♥ having a baby is a normal process of nature.
- ♥ childbirth is not a medical problem...
  it's a natural state of womanhood.
- ♥ my body knows how to deliver a baby.
- ♥ i cooperate effortlessly with changes in physical body for motherhood.
- ♥ i rest knowing Divine guidance is at work in this pregnancy.
- ♥ in due time, this baby comes effortlessly
  through the birth canal and emerges confidently.
- ♥ life itself as perfect intelligence is in complete control
  during the delivery of this baby.
- ♥ i am perfectly capable of delivering this baby free of drugs
  and other interventions and i do...
- ♥ we are open and receptive to cosmic forces
  instructing the delivery of this baby.
- ♥ husband, child, and i work together as a team during birth.
- ♥ the life energy of creation is strong with us, i know i can depend on it.
- ♥ we have been perfect parents since the moment of conception.
- ♥ baby receives all the required information
  about the environment he or she will emerge into.
- ♥ we are giving birth to a being who can handle new life in this world.
- ♥ this baby will express being in full potential.
- ♥ this baby knows and understands everything that is happening.
- ♥ this baby will easily understand the language of this local space.
- ♥ We are grateful to host new life on earth, we know our own
  self-transcendence is available in our sacrifice to serve this child.
- ♥ life moves in perfect ways with us.

Seasons of Prosperity

PARENT'S DAYCARE TREATMENT
- with thanks to Patrick and Deb Webb

all wonders of the Universe stem from a single perfect source of power.
    this power cannot be stopped or thwarted.
i am of that power and i inhere in that power.
my child realizes when i have him at daycare
    that i love him and will return soon. my child is strong and patient...
he likes daycare better each day. he is happy and well-served spending time
at daycare. he is making good friends and looks forward
to seeing them each day. gratitude abounds..
children care about each other at this daycare.
    teachers are kind and understanding.
i am grateful for my expanded ability
while he makes this adjustment. change blesses us today. change is good.
i see good in changing situations. i am a satisfied parent. i am a fine patient
    parent. tension and blame are gone now. we are all growing wiser each day.
    our humor is refreshing and timely. we enjoy our time apart.
we enjoy our time together. we express love and good cheer easily. we continue
    to know each day the truth of being, we are never apart from Divine love.
we are never separated from our good no matter what anything looks like.
we release these powerful words of truth
    they do their work in good form, we allow good.
        this is now so.

I AM OPEN AND RECEPTIVE TO MIRACLES

- ♥ miracles happen everyday, everywhere...
- ♥ miracles are events that demonstrate a higher law unknown to present thought.
- ♥ all true action is governed by Universal law.
- ♥ mighty things have been experienced in the past by people who let "blind faith" guide them.
- ♥ i am willing to be guided beyond reasons today.
- ♥ i am open to miraculous movement in my life.
- ♥ i receive universal blessings thru miracles now.
- ♥ today i assume the thinking that allows great good to occur.
- ♥ i rearrange my perceptions today, i undo the constricted thinking that binds outcomes.
- ♥ divine dynamics are at work with me now.
- ♥ my thinking is light and feathery today, joyous expectations.
- ♥ no matter what appearance may present itself i am able to expect miracles, and i do.

- ♥ the mechanism of miracles are thoughts given to me...
- ♥ instead of insisting on old thinking today i hear what is new thinking.
- ♥ i escape from dark thoughts by remembering what is good and true.
- ♥ everything i have comes from Divine.
- ♥ today i know i was never isolated or deprived nor will i be...
- ♥ God brings good, God is always with me.
- ♥ today i am released from an unmiraculous existence.
- ♥ i am ready and willing for miracles in this day.

YOU'LL WALK ★ ON WATER
YOU'LL GET THRU YOUR PROBLEMS
YOU'LL MAKE IT...
GOD WILL HELP YOU DO IT.

©TONI ACKER 82

ACTION BEGINS TODAY

- ♥ a new idea lights the way for leaping ahead.
- ♥ i am getting started...
- ♥ i produce results now, with action.
- ♥ my action-oriented choices involve insight and sensitivity.
- ♥ risks are taken, the action begins today.
- ♥ what my mind can conceive, will be achieved. i break habits of doubt.
- ♥ new explorations abound.
- ♥ new patterns are emerging.
- ♥ new ways of seeing are present now.
- ♥ new perspectives build bridges.

TO GO BEYOND LIMITS

- ♥ i initiate actions.
- ♥ i have transcendence within me.
- ♥ i have an expansive attitude.
- ♥ i am intelligence, operating within intelligent systems.
- ♥ my mental determinations are templates,
  patterns for possibility which i supply, in mind and feeling.
- ♥ i am playing the game-of-life, full-out, pushing forward fearlessly.
- ♥ today i participate consciously, in Universal designs
  by deliberately putting attention where i am aiming to go...
  i am able to rise above limits and old boundaries.
- ♥ inner assurance, replaces doubt, with conviction.
- ♥ assurance produces new actions to be taken.
- ♥ i am set free to make choices.
- ♥ i see that all opportunities are valuable.
  i produce continuing forward motion.
- ♥ in dedication and purposefulness,
  i break away from the old and dash to the new with good speed.
- ♥ i have a new way of being, beyond limits.
- ♥ new options interest me.
- ♥ doing "the impossible" looks easy to me now.
- ♥ i affirm all-of-life with actions today.
- ♥ i am inspired to act on new ideas.
- ♥ i willingly move quickly to win.
- ♥ goals and plans excite me. i am enrolled in acting for results.
  i am happy to be in action for a future, that's wonderful.

Seasons of Prosperity

SUNSHINE MORNING

TODAY
THE
SOURCE
OF ALL POWER,
LIGHTING ALL WORLDS,
IS ILLUMINATING ALSO
MY HEART, SO, MY HEART
DOES THE WORK, OF THIS
WHOLE WORLD. TODAY.

>this is an excellent, auspicious very wonderful good morning.

ABUNDANT GOOD MORNING

>i arise today
>with the strength of heavens
>which was in my ancestors
>it is a very good morning
>
>i arise today
>with the light of sun
>it is a very good morning
>
>i arise today
>with swiftness of wind
>it is a very good morning
>
>i arise today
>with speed of lightening into this good morning
>with stability of earth into this good morning
>with certainty of stone into this good morning
>
>i arise today
>in strength
>with conviction of my revelations
>it is a very wonderful morning
>i stand as <u>a creator in creation</u>
>...i extend intelligence.
>i know nothing of lack. this is an abundant good morning.

I ENJOY ANIMATING HAPPINESS RIGHT NOW, WHILE BEGINNING

- ♥ with a spirit of reverence and courage i begin.
- ♥ life always provides what's required.
- ♥ i adapt to beginning in my living today.
- ♥ the me-of-tomorrow has left the me-of-yesterday behind.
- ♥ to begin, i give up holding on to who i was.......
- ♥ every moment is a moment of true feeling today.
- ♥ self-possessed motivations give way to true service in the realm i have chosen to begin.
- ♥ everything about beginning is new and transforming.
- ♥ all service is direct service to God, through others ...
- ♥ i accept the transformation of beginning, i am happy in it.....
- ♥ radiance pervades my being as i love and serve others.
- ♥ my sacrifice of self-possessed reactive emotions leads me into feeling happiness each day.
- ♥ i am active in beginning, free of concern today.
- ♥ i am surrendered to transformation of becoming in each beginning.

I AM WILLING TO ACT QUICKLY

"It is when we all play safe that we create a world of utmost insecurity"
                                                                      - Dag Hammerskjold

    life itself, as intelligence, is ever present with ME. i can go anywhere and do anything that's ever been done.... i am adaptable.

    Fear of failure is really the fear of "being wrong". Today i am willing to act quickly. i risk making errors. i don't have to wait for the "right time" the appropriate time is <u>right now today</u>. i am willing to be transformed, by taking action on my own behalf. i can deal with stress. i can innovate. i can find friends to help me. i can correct mistakes. i can improve performance. i can afford to look foolish. i am willing to exercise corrections. i am willing to go ahead producing results, in the real world. Life expands ahead, producing results, in the real world. Life expands in the face of my courage today. i give up trying-to-reduce-the-risk-that-life-is. i give up thinking thoughts that scare me. Learning is acting. i act for what i intend quickly . i turn to account, all opportunities ...called upon, to do extraordinary things,
    i insist on saying YES. YES i will. YES i do...
    That's what's so today. YES quickly.

Seasons of Prosperity

ABOUT CHALLENGES

- i welcome challenge that life is.
- i no longer shrink from the opportunity of it.
- i am willing to get to work in life powerfully.
- i am now surrounding myself with allies to my commitment.
- my purpose is clear and directive.
- in the face of risk, i am empowered and strengthened.
- i remember Intelligence guides and directs.
- i make a difference everywhere i show up.
- possibilities for being abound wherever i am.
- my agreement is to forward projects, action and thinking.
- who i am is the stand i take. i am bold, taking on what's new next.
- declarations begin the action.
- i am being...i am intelligence.
- all good is here available to me.
- i create possibility equal to my commitment.
- i bring myself forth in profoundly creative relationship.
- i am clear for full expressions of Being.
- i deepen my ability to access Being.
- i bring power and impact to bear on work, relationships, and commitments in my life and in all people's lives.
- i work on what's up in front of me. i master challenges.
- i make happen what once seemed impossible.
- real results in projects are achievable.
- i have freedom and opportunity to produce results.
- i do not have to "work hard" or do lots of things to get my job done daily.
- i am bringing about breakthrough in the possibility of Being.
- what i intend is happening with or without a lot of effort.
- i live at full participation to midnight each day... what is wanted comes to me.
- i let go limits on productivity.
- moods, feelings, and thoughts support highest purpose.
- i am uncovering new opportunities for producing results.
- i engage in life, in fresh ways, to create satisfaction for others and myself.
- i am expanding ability to get the job done in life.

Seasons of Prosperity

I SAY YES TO GOOD...

my life is a state of consciousness...

- ♥ use of consciousness changes outcomes...
- ♥ thinking forms pictures in space/time.
- ♥ expressing creates experiencing.
- ♥ in reality i have the power of being, to stand free of circumstance.
- ♥ universe is abundant, i am a system of powerful ideas for GOOD. even now, i access GOOD ideas.

i am willing to think further than i've been, before...

- ♥ i recall that i reflect evolution of all life.
- ♥ i leave behind small personal identity.
- ♥ there is great assurance that i can do "the impossible".
- ♥ there resides with me, potential to do, whatever is next to do.

...there resides, potential to do,
    whatever is next to do!!!

I AM WILLING TO THINK FURTHER THAN I'VE BEEN BEFORE...

- ♥ i am being active, thinking beyond boundries ...

- ♥ i am extroverted and very active in taking actions for new ideas. i make things happen. i get results.

- ♥ energy is applied to the world and people around me. change happens. results occur. outcomes are manifesting.

- ♥ effort is put toward the future today. i think past the borders that used to hold me back.

- ♥ i travel at a high level of motion, working with futures and plotting futures.

- ♥ i am very active on behalf of the future, which is calling me forward now.

- ♥ i go out, past the boundaries of my mind.

evil is stripped of it's (seeming) POWER in the presence of the SPIRIT

— ST. BASIL

WITHOUT FEAR

when circumstance looks bad, it's time to start thinking and declaring good:
                      in mind
                      in heart
                      in partnerships
                      in groups
speak out loud the good behind any appearance, speak powerfully:

i AM WITHOUT FEAR,
i BELIEVE IN UNLIMITED GOOD
        FEAR HAS NO ATTRACTION FOR ME.
        i SEE WHAT THERE IS TO DO, SPEAK, FEEL...
        i KNOW WHAT TO DO AND i DO IT
        i PARTICIPATE WITH INTENTION IN WHAT'S REQUIRED NEXT:

- ♥ BRIDGES BETWEEN PEOPLE
- ♥ CONSTRUCTIVE APPROACHES
- ♥ SOLUTIONS TO PROBLEMS
- ♥ BREAKING LIMITATIONS
- ♥ HEALING CONDITIONS
- ♥ INSPIRING, UPLIFTING
    AND BRINGING OUT THE GOOD.

    i AM WITHOUT FEAR
    i BELIEVE IN UNLIMITED GOOD.
    i KNOW WHAT TO DO
            AND i DO THAT NOW

Seasons of Prosperity

ABOUT BREAKTHROUGHS

- ♥ i break through rather than break down.
- ♥ all my troubles are only ways of looking.
- ♥ i am committed to looking through what used to stop me.
- ♥ i give up, giving up, right now and i'm glad for that.
- ♥ i now see what encourages me to go further forward to achieve my purpose and goals.
- ♥ my purpose in life is a high calling.
- ♥ i am aware of the possibility that life is.
- ♥ i give up the idea that risk can stop me.
- ♥ i give up the idea that barriers have power.
- ♥ i give up the idea that circumstances dictate what can happen.
- ♥ when in doubt, i move forward.
- ♥ i no longer build shrines to doubt.
- ♥ i am the intention to be victorious.
- ♥ i am a winner, doing winning
- ♥ i know what to do and i do it.

MYSELF: A HERO

- ♥ i declare myself a hero...
- ♥ i am willing to encounter all doubts without drama.
- ♥ i live as the main character in my daily life.
- ♥ i encounter. i endure.
- ♥ i transcend.
  i push past being comfortable.
- ♥ i see beyond what appears.
  i master challenges.
- ♥ there is always providing power behind, and with right action.
- ♥ i am guided to right action. i accept inner instructions.
- ♥ it's possible to look beyond whatever seems to be the case.
- ♥ good is always available. good never runs out
- ♥ the qualities to be expressed never run out, in any circumstance.
- ♥ i am able to call forth what's necessary by knowing that it's possible.
- ♥ tendencies to feel good is not available, are now left behind!
- ♥ qualities required, to enable me in overcoming obstacles, are already with me, waiting to be called forth...

The Direction of East

- i push past, discomfort.
- congruent thinking, speaking and feeling, match my goals.
- today i take, my ability to see beyond barriers to heroic proportions... i defy current evidence.
- i consistently act for the outcomes i've envisioned even when they appear impossible.
- today i take, my language, beyond the barriers of current evidence. i am heroic... i speak beyond what's seen.
- i am awake to what's possible. i see opportunity.
- i act for what's possible.
- possibility rules in my world.

BREAKTHROUGH TO BEGINNINGS

- i am challenged and excited to begin.
- i am committed to generating possibilities.
- i represent the capacity to: create, generate, invent, design
- from nothing, i have the power to create distinctions for what is possible next...
- what i create is original, innovative and effective.
- i consistently produce unique, powerful, miraculous results with my work.
- the work i set out to do, helps life to work for everyone.
- well-being, self-expression, accountability and integrity are extending into today's world from the work i start.
- i serve others. i contribute to others.
- i foster the contribution of others.
- my work helps to establish a viable, nurturing humankind.
- i have limitless opportunity today, available in beginning.
- i am grateful, joyous and vitalized as i breakthrough in beginning.

HEROES ARE JUST LIKE US

"Courage consists in equality to the problem before us."
   – R.W. *Emerson*

If we think heroes who risk are different from us, we will be less able.
Everyone who's accomplished great deeds has mastered fear in the process.
Risk is a big step. Following "yes" with action, moves circumstances.
Taking risk starts a resounding reaction of possible conclusions.
Choices then surface. Heroes are people who live through their fears to win.

PURPOSEFULNESS

- i am open to the future...
- i no longer look for authority from the past.
- i know that the creation-of-what's-next comes in the now moment.
- i am willing to have ideas i never had before...
  hesitation is left to the past.
- i dash forward to do the things that are meant for me to do...
- i predominate all hesitation with intention.
- my mind is now very willing to be guided by intention.
- i am glad to be free of hesitation...
- i move "fast forward" doing actions that produce intended outcomes.
- i have strategic vision which gives me magnetic direction forward.
  i have an organizing focus.
- all my thinking is retrained easily for successful outcomes.
- i serve higher and higher purposes with time and resources.
- i am clear and responsible for my intentions in life.
- i have thinking, feeling and actions that are consistent with my goals.
- i always think, feel and act so that desired outcomes are achieved.
- i see results, even before evidence is apparent...i live as my vision.
- i allow massive opportunities to exist, i invite and accept them today.
- i do more and more of what forwards motion in life for everyone.
  i live with an attitude of increasing joy .
- i have more experiences and less evaluations.
- i see everything as an opportunity, rather than as a problem.
- i am willing to investigate often, the new and mysterious.
- i am willing to behave spontaneously more and more often.
  i go in rather than stay out...
- i include myself rather than withdraw...
- i create value with all experiences.
- all opportunities call forth further abilities for me.
- i trust life, to bring me exactly what's needed and wanted next...
  i have an ever increasing willingness
  to learn from every experience and outcome.
- everything that appears to be happening is for my highest good.
- all seeming problems are really extraordinary opportunities.
  i have a new power to recreate circumstances ...
- i easily establish new interpretations which empower, rather than restrict.
- now, i initiate actions beyond previous boundaries.
- i create and establish new motions, where old habits bred stagnation.
- creating wider opportunities is for me now.
- established conditions give way
  for wider opportunity.
- i accept the invitation to a new future, to a new possibility.

The Direction of East

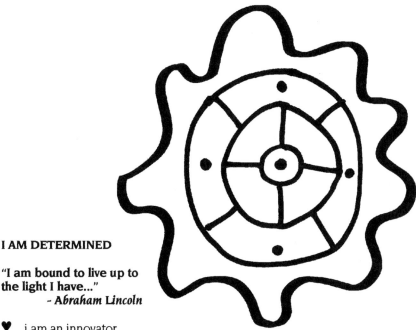

I AM DETERMINED

"I am bound to live up to the light I have..."
- Abraham Lincoln

- i am an innovator.
- i am determined.
- i have enormous amounts of energy today, being determined clears the way.
- i learn what's mine to learn now.
- i have a purposeful sense-of-drive today.
- at all points, i make the appropriate choice for results.
- clarity helps me to cause innovations.
- i freely say what's mine to say.
- i easily do what's mine to do.
- i create the forms required for me to operate in...
- i define my work structures.
- i pursue what is consistent for goals.
- i study and work tirelessly to develop my range of skills.
- i walk past fears, in courage, to create new results and satisfactions.
-     i take in, the world around me, forwards results.
- my inner core energies are congruent with outer actions.
- what i am doing is an expression of who i am being.
- rich satisfaction continues, i affirm determinations.

Seasons of Prosperity

GOALS ARE ACHIEVED...

stability, consistency and performance is what's required to achieve goals.
these qualities are elements
> of consciousness...
> they keep us on purpose...
> vital and independent of the feelings
> and thoughts that would keep us in bondage.
>> to dissatisfaction.

PROBLEMS MOVE OUT OF OUR
EXPERIENCE TODAY
> we stay in-action to make intentions into OUTCOMES.
> endless creativity and effective RESULTS are everywhere present.

ABOUT GOOD USE OF TIME

- ♥ i have enough time to do the work that energizes and empowers me and all others.
- ♥ every night i have the perfect amount of sleep.
- ♥ i am in the right place at the right time.
- ♥ time moves to suit my needs.
- ♥ with little time, i make more money.
- ♥ i have ideas that i've never had before...
- ♥ the less i do the more money i make, it's wonderful.
- ♥ Time is my servant, it waits for me.
- ♥ i finish my tasks ahead of time.
- ♥ i know what to do and i do it.
- ♥ completing tasks energizes me to do still more.
- ♥ now is the perfect time to start and finish projects.
- ♥ everything i start i complete quickly.
- ♥ money rushes in to fill all requests and needs.
- ♥ i no longer need pressure to motivate me.
- ♥ i love to work quickly and completely.
- ♥ i do that more often.
- ♥ completing and finishing projects is easy and effortless.
- ♥ i do everything as soon as i have the idea or i delegate it immediately.
- ♥ i use time the way that produces the most desired results.
- ♥ the faster i do things the more time slows down to allow me to do more.
- ♥ i throw away or give away everything that i no longer use or need.
- ♥ there's no need to hurry anymore.
- ♥ i have all time necessary.

The Direction of East

- ♥ there is no lack of time. Time is unlimited.
- ♥ i use time, time doesn't run me anymore.
- ♥ i get more done on time than ever before...
- ♥ i have no limits on productivity.
- ♥ "wasting time" contributes to results.
- ♥ time expands so that work allotted gets completed.
- ♥ more fun is happening in time.
- ♥ time is no longer serious for me.

PURPOSEFULNESS: GATHERING POWER IN RISKING

- ♥ commitment is now determined.
- ♥ i am picking up speed.
- ♥ there is no return to the old position for me now. good-bye to fear and doubt.
- ♥ i am leaving the familiar behind.
- ♥ i accelerate action.
- ♥ now there is resolution.
- ♥ courage of convictions, supports me now.
- ♥ friends help me win. they give support. i am grateful.
- ♥ i have courage to keep moving ahead risking.
- ♥ i seek a high goal, with all the energy available, for me to achieve it in perfect timing.

I AM PURPOSEFUL

- ♥ i know how to start and begin things.
- ♥ i know how to be specific and name what has to be done.
- ♥ i have strategic vision and the power to create vision.
- ♥ i see how to put in place what's been missing.
- ♥ i am prone to action with optimism.
- ♥ i predict outcomes before they occur.
- ♥ i keep saying yes no matter what happens.

I AM DECISIVE

♥ i move with sure speed and certainy.
　i act for what's next... i think this thought BE NOT AFRAID
　i am in motion for what's to be achieved... i am certain.
　i do not waste time with doubt now... i am decisive.
　make my views known... demands never exceed abilities.
　people know what i am standing for...
　people help me stack-up ways to win now.
　i act effectively... to be in action for decisions.
♥ intuition is clear, pointing me forward...
　reactive-mind-making-me-wrong has no power now...
　trying-to-be-safe has no power now...
　doubting-others has no power now.
　i think, i talk, i speak, i feel, i act with true direction.
♥ what people think, is no longer stopping me...
　since talking alters my reality... i talk about what i intend.
　i talk into and as, directed intention. on the difficult and
　intricate path, i think this thought: BE NOT AFRAID

APPEARANCES ARE POWERLESS OVER ME

"... to come into possession of what you do not have,
　　you must go where now you have nothing."
　　　　　　　　　　　　　　　　　　　　　- *John of the Cross*

　　GOD IS ALL IN ALL... the only power acting. i am at one with all that acts. i am awake to true being. i SUBMIT TO GOOD. i am steadfast, persistent in seeing only good... in yielding to God's control i expect things to go right. my being is an affirmation of good... everything needed or wanted already exists within me as a good idea.
　　BY THE PRINCIPLE OF GOOD. i use creative mind energy to stay awake to TRUTH. Evil is no power, it is only nothingness.
　　i defeat danger and obstacle now.
　　　　　　evil is not more powerful than good.
　　　　　　GOD is omnipotent, all present and good.
　　　　　　nothing can be more powerful than good...
　　　　　　nothing is everlasting but God and spiritual creation, all good.
　　GUARDING and GUIDING are always in effect. i am listening and watching to think, speak and act good. i am always bringing BLESSING.. in the middle of anything i show up as good outcoming. no matter what seems inevitable or threatens, no real harm comes. appearances are powerless over principle... solutions are ever created in any challenge. good persists, good prevails. i GIVE THANKS that i rely on intuition to TRANSFORM APPEARANCES with appropriate action and ideas. this is what's true... Appearances Are Powerless Over Me.

Seasons of Prosperity

BEGINNING TODAY EVERYTHING INSURES MY SUCCESS

- ♥ Aptitude insures my success.
- ♥ Abundant resource insures my success.
- ♥ Appreciation insures my success.
- ♥ Appreciation of diversity insures my success.
- ♥ Declaration insures my success.
  Decisiveness insures my success.
  Determination insures my success.
- ♥ Efficiency insures my success.
- ♥ Excellence insures my success.
- ♥ Great speed insures my success.
- ♥ Growing insures my success.
- ♥ Goodness insures my success.
  Gladness insures my success.
  Goodwill insures my success.
- ♥ Communication insures my success.
  Encouragement insures my success.
  Endurance insures my success.
  Enthusiasm insures my success.
  Exhilaration insures my success.
- ♥ Experience insures my success.
  Exuberance insures my success.
  Evolution insures by success.
- ♥ Reliability insures my success.
- ♥ Responding quickly insures my success.
- ♥ Pioneering insures my success.
- ♥ Teachability insures my success.
  Toughness insures my success.
  Thankfulness insures my success.
- ♥ Trustworthiness insures my success.
- ♥ Tenacity insures my success.
  The way-it-looks insures my success.
  The way-it-doesn't-look insures my success.

GATHERING POWER IN RISKING

- ♥ i am intuitive
- ♥ i am as intuitive as i can be. my intuitive capacity
helps me select the risks that work well.
i have an exuberant day today. taking on new things to think and do.
human beings have intuitive capacity. inertia can be overcome.
risks can be accepted. i overcome inertia. i accept risks.
- ♥ my style of thinking is intuitive today.
- ♥ fear and doubtful hesitance are replaced with assurance and joy.
- ♥ i have chosen to follow a vision. i make things happen.
obstacles are opportunities.
i listen to intuition guiding me when i am taking a risk.
intuitive capabilities are developing even stronger influence.
- ♥ i act on what i am convinced of...
i am in action, about new accomplishment.
i gather power, as i go about risking...
- ♥ intuition brings me a day of insights as i take chances.
intuition brings me a day of perception as i say "yes".
intuition brings me a day of liberation as i accept guidance.
the creating power of mind, gathers power, with me, in risking now.

I KNOW WHAT TO DO AND I DO IT

i declare
that
from
this moment
forward
    my life will be
    significantly
    different.
i choose to make
a decision
to be in charge of
my life and go forth
to do what has to be done
by me.

Seasons of Prosperity

NEW AFFIRMATIONS

- ♥ a new beginning is at hand.
- ♥ i set a direction to freedom and it works.
- ♥ i can now have what i used to dream about.
- ♥ my progress is more certain than it has been before... new adventure and renewed strength is now available to me.
- ♥ i have new certainty and stability that allows me
  to handle new obstacles
  with equanimity.
- ♥ what was holding me back is gone now.
- ♥ i have regained power over circumstances.
- ♥ new life is mine. i choose what to think.
- ♥ incredible accomplishment now happens.
  i'm free to win without reservation.
- ♥ life is simple and in affinity, i notice it.
- ♥ attention, intention and awareness are now aimed to goals.
- ♥ i plan in terms of decades, not years.
  my ability to have is increased.
  my ability to give is increased.
  my ability to serve and be served has increased.
- ♥ this new beginning is a wonderful one.

i accomplish despite appearances

> "when we fail in our purpose, we have let side issues
>   distract us and rob us of energy allocated to our purpose."
> - *j. sig paulson*

- ♥ when there doesn't appear to be progress, i accomplish.
- ♥ when people are not helping me, i accomplish.
- ♥ success happens, i make failure impossible.
- ♥ i am productive in the face of my own unproductive behaviors.
  in the face of lack of acknowledgement, i accomplish.
  when it doesn't seem like i thought it would be, i accomplish.
- ♥ when i feel like everything is a bother, i accomplish.
- ♥ when it's boring, i still accomplish. . . . .
- ♥ even when i feel like taking my self away, i stay engaged
  in what i said i would do...i accomplish.
  i have courage of accomplishing in the face of all circumstance.
- ♥ i accomplish and i see it.

PRACTICING TRANSCENDENCE

- ♥ i am willing to be practicing consistent discipline with myself.
- ♥ i am now open to ever growing wisdom of practice.
- ♥ i am willing to encounter boredom and bear it,
  to encounter discomfort and express it.
- ♥ i am willing to encounter all doubts without drama and display,
  to have windows open in my self enclosed life today.
- ♥ today i see the mechanism of attention and how i use it.
- ♥ today i see the mechanism of attention
                  and how it uses me.
- ♥ i encounter.
  i endure.
  i transcend.
- ♥ i break mental traps.
  i see beyond static
  representation.

GOD IS GREATER THAN CHAOS

- ♥ today i look forward to changes.
- ♥ during changes, taking a true
  view of things is vitalizing.
- ♥ when undergoing great changes
  i remember...
  good is dominant as i watch all the changing around me.
  i can always, and do always expect good.
  i see Divine intelligence always at work.
- ♥ change is always positive in the long run.
- ♥ intelligence, joy and love are always present.
- ♥ today i refrain from accepting only an outward sense of things.
  the effectiveness of great intention is apparent
                            in small and large circumstances.
- ♥ today i have a true view of things.
- ♥ i trust in life's direction.
- ♥ intelligence is everywhere present... we represent and reflect intelligence.
  the power of good is certain...
                          the power of good is greatness...
                          the power of good is victory.
- ♥ strength is available to us all.
- ♥ safety and protection are real.

EXTENDING BEYOND

    We are transcendent beings... We have the power and ability to extend beyond whatever happens. We can feel through it and be undiminished by it, no matter how tragic we think it is... this power, this ability, it is what we are...
There is always a brightness of face, a lightness of heart
that is ours when we remember the power to extend beyond circumstance.

The question: Are we willing to give up unhappiness?
...the "poor me" racket?
...complaining?
...sadness?
...resentment?
...blame or guilt?
...worry and fear?

    As long as we indulge in unhappiness, we cannot extend beyond appearances, or circumstance. When we are finished with long and ancient sufferings, we build new emotional responses to life, right where the old ones used to be.
It takes practice... it takes being willing to be some vulnerable new ways.
Leaving behind old emotional responses fuels new patterns of happiness.
Just as an acorn has within it the makings of a tree...
We have the power of extending beyond, within us.
It's just a new state of references, other marking places,
a different window of viewing waiting to be accessed.

I AM TRANSCENDENCE

♥ i see what scares me as only a shadow.
♥ i accomplish and envision in the midst of challenge.
♥ i am the ability to be unmoved by circumstance.
♥ i am above opinion, i am assured.
♥ i know that i am already related with everything.
♥ i allow being intuitive to guide me.
♥ i know how to be without opinions.
♥ i allow "feeling into" situations.
♥ i rise above past histories and old conditionings.

Seasons of Prosperity

ALIVE AND ALERT EACH MORNING
- Sabrina Milbury, **Vermont**

- ♥ i eagerly arise in joy each morning.
- ♥ i am grateful for new mornings.
- ♥ morning is a welcome invitation to participate.
- ♥ Each morning i've had exactly the perfect amount of sleep.
- ♥ i reaffirm commitments each morning.
- ♥ new opportunity abounds with each day. i welcome it.
- ♥ i love getting out of bed ready to start, alive to possibility.
- ♥ i am truly energized by appropriate thinking.
- ♥ starting the new day is refreshing. every morning i am ready for action.
- ♥ enthusiasm marks mornings now.
- ♥ i give up tired, exhausted, complaint thinking.
- ♥ i take on zestful, energized speaking in the morning.
- ♥ i sing and dance to the shower with great humor.
- ♥ In the shower i recreate myself with true enthusiasm.
- ♥ i get up each morning ready for everything. i greet days with delight.

MONDAY DECLARATIONS

today the living Spirit of Truth is my very active on-going teacher...
this whole day is a continued intention for good... even when talking with people
   or doing physical work, the active presence of all pervasive Wisdom
      Intelligence is ever guiding all thoughts, words, and deeds forward.
all day today, i see clearly what is good and appropriate.
i make those choices which bless me and all those around me.
i see, hear, and feel the answers i've been intending to receive...
i rediscover today that the Divine does exist and is responsive
   to the call of my Heart.
there is great good in store for me on mondays.

WEDNESDAY DECLARATIONS

today, great Divine Power propels me
   through a day of transcendence.
i do not examine the past critically.
i do not dash ahead to the future in worry.
i do not scheme for today.
i am not running from what is feared.
i am living for what i love each wednesday.
i am the action expressing Divine design
       and intuitive Truth.

The Direction of East

DAY OF TRANSCENDENCE

- ♥ my power of feeling is in agreement with what i intend.
- ♥ i am easily above opinions everyday.
- ♥ my power of action is in agreement with my aims for today.
- ♥ i have a posture of assurance.
- ♥ i stand as a winner, even when winning is still being formulated.

   i am master of circumstances. i know what to think.
   my power of perception agrees with what i intend to see,
       i am able to see it, even before
       it seems to happen outwardly.
       i hold the vision of what's being created.
- ♥ i am enabled to act quickly for what's next.

   i leave behind withdrawal habits, i stay engaged until the outcome occurs.
   i no longer give up. i stay committed.
- ♥ i am aligned in the direction of my intentions.
- ♥ i know that my vision is real possibility.
- ♥ there is nowhere where possibility is missing.
- ♥ all possibility is with me, wherever i am today.

   i transcend all appearances.

I HAVE A NEW FRIENDSHIP WITH THE NATURAL WORLD

- ♥ everywhere is the green of new growth happening now.
- ♥ everything flows, everything grows, prosperity abounds.
- ♥ there are amazing sightings of renewal everywhere
- ♥ prosperity abounds, everything flows... all around me.
- ♥ everywhere and always birdsongs, bushes, bendings, blendings,
       beautiful trees and ancient lively waters...
- ♥ energies of life are everpresent, vitalizing, empowering.
- ♥ i dash forward to do what's mine to do today.
- ♥ i touch life.
- ♥ i am touched by life.
- ♥ i know life.
- ♥ i am known by life.
- ♥ i love life.
- ♥ i am loved by life.
- ♥ body, mind and spirit have new rhythm
       revitalization comes to me, thru me and life
       is recreated in me today...i give thanks for new life.

Seasons of Prosperity

PROVIDING POWER IS ALWAYS WITH ME

Universe is self-sustaining.
The same law that sustains ALL, "watches over" me, i am a part
of all-there-is...i claim my identity. There was never a time
when i was without what i needed...anytime i didn't have something
important to my life, i got it. I feel assured in depending on abundance.
Life itself always provides what is required. i rest in that knowledge.
i am grateful to be dependably cared for. i act out of certainty and assurance.
    Providing power is always with me
    equilibrium is established by law.
- i dare to do something new even when others have given up.
- Behind appropriate action, Providing power
is always at work making clear the way.
- i call forth qualities in me to meet challenges.
- By knowing all things are possible, i call forth what's necessary next.
- Providing power is always with me.

I MUST BE WHAT I WAS CREATED TO BE

- there is a duty to become what should be.
- i always have what's required to be who i am in life.
- approval does not dictate my way.
- i have the courage of my convictions.
- i let-go looking "to-be-liked".
- i have the courage of my purpose.
- i leave behind being out of integrity with myself.
- i have the courage of my revelations.
- compromises are no longer watering-down my stand.
- i am who i know myself to be.

recognizing the truth of my own being, i act congruently.
i am what i was created to be.

EAST: I ACCEPT PLENTY-OF-HELP

As the cycle turns
from winter to spring...
in the East i am renewed!
i leave behind old encumbrances
Reborn into new, decisive actions now.
   ...in swirling energy of much-to-do-today, i give up desire to
control and tightly manage each segment...I work quickly and loosely in the East.
It takes courage to dare. It takes humility to dare. i call forth appropriate faculties.
   Finding someone who's been on this way, i access them and ask for
coaching. i accept plenty-of-help
from experts while i am in the East.

WE ARE THE SAME AS HEROS:
THE AUTHOR'S BREAKFAST

*"It is not the critic who counts; not the person who points out
how the strong stumbled or the doer-of-deeds could have done better.
The credit belongs to the one who is actually in the arena, whose face is marred with dust and
sweat and blood; who knows the great enthusiasms,
the great devotion; who spends themselves in a worthy cause;
who at the best knows the triumph of high achievement,
and at the worst, at least, fails while daring greatly."*

- Theodore Roosevelt

I had been under the impression that authors were other than me. Authors were better. Authors were brighter, more concise. Authors were together, accomplished and they knew everything. Authors were nothing like how I was. I was confused. I didn't know how to start writing, work on writing and get writing finished. I didn't know how to talk in front of groups, etc.

When we moved to Hyannis on Cape Cod, I was privileged to meet Ruth Goldrossen at Charthouse Books. She was the owner. Each Spring she set up breakfast events where authors would come to speak about their books to a small breakfast audience.

At these events I was confronted over and over again with real life authors in all their peculiar and wonderful ways of being. They were confused, nervous, remote, silly, uninformed, uncoordinated and not always good-looking. They spilled coffee, flubbed their lines, made mistakes, told stupid jokes and acted arrogant or self-concerned... they acted in all the ways I acted, ways that I felt disqualified me, from being an author.

They were also wise, funny, personable and very, very human. Some of them worked on a book seven years or more; some wrote a book based on a dream; some wrote books in the kitchen overnight. These authors represented all manner of accomplishment, making it finally possible for me, to see me published too.

I am always grateful for the opportunity to see real life heroes, teachers, authors and spokespersons of great ideals up close...That they allow themselves to be known wakes me up to understanding that we are not so different after all. We are the same.

The biggest drawback to accomplishment is to think i am different from the heroes and true achievers...when this is seen, the excuse for withholding has ended. Life is no dress rehearsal.

The work of the world has rested always on very few shoulders...we have for too long thought that to affect the thinking of many was the work of archangels... The more we rub up against heroes,
the more we see, we are them. We are the same.

Seasons of Prosperity

ABOUT WINNING

- i am winning now.
- i am truly motivated.
- i push through all barriers as a natural winner.
- i do what produces results each day.
- i know what to do and i do it.
- i am inspired from within.
- i continue to take risks necessary to produce results.
- i have resources to keep motivated...
- when fear comes up i keep taking forward steps.
- i have productive communication skills.
- i have courage to do what works over and over again.
- when people don't like what i do it's okay with me.
- i keep on no matter what happens... i see beyond appearances.
- i allow people space to be in disagreement and i keep on doing what needs to be done.
- i am no longer stopped by invalidation.
- i image what i want and live from those pictures.
- i am successful and so are the people around me.
- success is a process; i am in it, i keep on, i am a natural winner.

WE CELEBRATE THIS YEAR

- creative and productive we look forward...
- with eagerness we greet this new year.
- we are grateful for being here. thanks is everpresent.
- fresh starts are everywhere now.
- there is new resolve to follow through...
- planning, envisioning bright starts happens now.
- nothing is inevitable where possibility exists.
- we are renewed from the inside out...
- refreshed minds and hearts work easily now.
- life is infinite and good news is true...
- we celebrate life today all over the place.
- we refuse to be time-bound and limited.
- experiencing endless creativity is our privilege this year.
- perpetual blooming, healthy laughter, increasing humor happens.
- usual routines open up to serendipity surprises.
- disheartening perspectives dissolve.
- ever-colorful life is ours. inspiration and spontaneity are everpresent. we celebrate possibility here.

The Direction of East

TO TRULY DARE

"You can't build a reputation on what you're going to do."
— Henry Ford

- ♥ goodbye to standing still now.
- ♥ I turn toward courage today with vital strength.
- ♥ it is my mission to express all that I can be.
- ♥ expanding perspective, calls me forward to future possibilities.
- ♥ the more experiments I make, the better my actions are....
- ♥ i am willing to make mistakes and correct them.
- ♥ the future calls me forward, my heart trusts the future.
- ♥ i live with fear, and I am not afraid.
- ♥ i join the adventurers who accomplish great things.
- ♥ inner knowledge comes forward to guide me. things change....
- ♥ i participate deliberately in the design, around me.
- ♥ the dynamics of courage are at work with me today.

MY SPEAKING RESOLVES BREAKDOWNS

- ♥ when i speak action happens.
- ♥ my speaking forwards the action.
- ♥ my words and way of being with people call for their cooperation and committed action.
- ♥ whenever i am around problems are resolved.
- ♥ whenever i am around goals are realized.
- ♥ whenever i am around new possibilities occur...
- ♥ i initiate actions that are completed and fulfilled.
- ♥ my speaking puts shape on what's possible in the world.
- ♥ my speaking enables others.
- ♥ my speaking penetrates unworkable situations.
- ♥ my speaking represents the highest order of intelligence for which i am capable now.
- ♥ my speaking resolves breakdowns.
- ♥ my speaking empowers others to perform beyond former levels of skill.

Seasons of Prosperity

I ASSESS MYSELF AS COMPETENT

"God is a good Judge because knowing all the facts God does not Judge..."
— The KORAN

- ♥ plans for fulfilling futures are set in place.
- ♥ i establish choices and leave opinions behind.
- ♥ i end controversy and confusion with choices.
- ♥ i renounce conflict and choose peace.
- ♥ living in a problem no more, i live as a solution
- ♥ i intuitively know when to hold and when to fold.
- ♥ i give up judgment which is the source of all stress.
- ♥ i am flexible. i am accomplishing outcomes.
- ♥ i call forth in myself and others ways that make things work...
- ♥ i maximize energy available to attain outcomes.
- ♥ i am vital and lively. i speak true. i am competent.
- ♥ with linguistic surgery i cut-out speaking that slows progress.
- ♥ what is required is always present...
- ♥ who i am, (in any matter i take on), is always more than who i "think" i am.. i am grateful.
- ♥ sustaining enthusiasm nurtures courage.
- ♥ i shift "self-instruction" whenever appropriate to produce outcomes.
- ♥ fully present, fully revealed, i move steadily from where i am to where i'm going...
- ♥ i can be counted on to enable everyone around me.
  i always get instructions required.
  In every moment i assess myself as competent.

MORE AFFIRMATIONS FOR THE CITY
— *Mark Rabinowitz,*
Prosperity Teacher, New York City

- ♥ in my city, or any city,
  i greet each day with love.
- ♥ everywhere i am, i choose to see and express love in this city.
- ♥ always i am free to choose what i see ...
- ♥ the more love i give, the more love i receive.

The Direction of East

- ♥ love produces many miracles in this city.
- ♥ the more i serve people, the more i am served.
- ♥ love and service prosper all... i am free to accept and give love.
- ♥ i live this day in love and service in this city.
  i am free to express love today.
- ♥ love is the powerful force in this city. love moves in and thru this city.
- ♥ love is a prospering peaceful force in this city.
- ♥ all battles, grudges and misunderstandings are cleared up today.
- ♥ people peacefully and happily help each other here.
  no one is withholding love anymore.
  projects to improve life are implemented.
- ♥ people freely reveal their hearts, and care about each other here..
- ♥ the power of love is at work.
- ♥ people in this city practice love, express love, and experience love,
  they are free to ACT and move in love.
  this city is love. this city is loving. this city is loved.
  plans for successful fulfilling futures are set in place
  for the people of this city now.

AFFIRMATIONS FOR TODAY IN THE CITY
— KIP, New York City

- ♥ my natural generosity keeps expanding...
- ♥ today i feel and show love. i am generous.
- ♥ today, i give and receive everything i intend.
- ♥ as i give today i am strengthened by giving.
- ♥ i allow heartfelt emotions in relations with everyone.
- ♥ i acknowledge the great contribution that people constantly are to me.
- ♥ today, i touch someone's world and improve it forever...
- ♥ people are demonstrating love and compassion everywhere.
- ♥ today i see all the love in this city as i praise the good i see,
  it magnifies and multiplies abundantly.
- ♥ people helping people are everywhere in this city.
- ♥ i am grateful for a city that works for everybody with no one left out today.
- ♥ everyone here is an ambassador of goodwill.

Seasons of Prosperity

SELF-ESTEEM

- i pass my own criteria of goodness. i have integrity i do what i say i will do.
- i am learning to love myself more each day.
- i have esteem for myself and for others.
- i like myself. i know i do the best i can do each day.
- i like myself even when others do not.
- each day i practice good. i discern what is for good.
    > i have love
    > i feel it...i show it...
    > i know good
    > i depend on the good
    > i praise the good
- now that i have self love. i experience my own abilities for changing. i experience the love of others. i experience the love for others. the more i love myself... and others.
    > the more others love me.
- i practice giving. love is everywhere with everyone.

BEGINNING IN CONFIDENCE

- i am becoming responsible for my intentions in life.
- i am giving up passive-waiting and hope.
- consistently i think, speak, act from what i intend. results occur.
- i begin to have success. i am happy to report results.
- i grow in confidence and assurance. i am glad.
- i look for evidence that i am succeeding. i see it.
- i see evidence that success is inevitable now.
- i call forth bigger, riskier goals... i see them to fruition.
- confidence follows from taking-a-stand-on-myself instead of on circumstances.
- failure fades away like a conversation. no longer useful.
- the confident stand i've taken influences me to further happiness and productivity.
  i envision results.
  i take a stand for results.
  i perceive results, and more good results.
- i language up my future in terms of the results. i see are possible.
- i find results are on the way. i "see" results before they occur ...
- i know what's next is success.
- i am confidently ready to succeed.

YOUR **HEAVENLY FATHER** KNOWETH... YOU HAVE NEED OF ALL THESE THINGS

— MATT. 6:32

© toni acker 82

LIGHTEN UP...

...and the LORD said "let there be light" and there was light.

—GENESIS 1:3

The Direction of East

I TAKE MANY NEW ACTIONS

- i begin now, **in the east**
- i trust vision. i trust good ideas i've accepted.
- i advance to accomplish today.
- spontaneity and joy increase my trust in the future.
- i say goodbye to thoughts of waiting until later.
- i call forth the courage to create.
- despite any evidence around me i speak solutions, before they are seen...
- i dash forward quickly to claim a day of getting to work.
- i see complex situations clearly and in perspective.
- i have the ability to focus attention on present tasks.
- i find out what's required to head things in necessary directions.
- i announce new beginnings.
- i make measurements for results...
- i take many new actions to produce results.
- i have the humility required to get help.
- success is found in serving people. i am serving people now.
- i establish accountabilities for future outcomes.
- i have people helping me,
  i have people hearing me,
    and holding my promises with me.
- i resolve issues quickly with determination.
- new blendings of people, places and activities spur me on . . .
- my whole being is actively involved in activities at hand.
  i leave behind withholding full effort.
- i am developing full power in all endeavors.
- i let go of what impedes progress quickly now.
- willingness to get into action is improving everyday.
- i have a posture of assurance and action.
- i am making decisive choices easily.
- i am purposeful and dedicated in many new actions.

Seasons of Prosperity

I RELEASE THE PAST TO MOVE FORWARD NOW

- ♥ today i make room for future in my thinking.
- ♥ i am pioneering a world of possibility. i act for intentions ...
- ♥ a sense of expectancy urges me onward. i cast myself into new roles ...
- ♥ i alter the nature of what's been before...
- ♥ i dedicate myself to what's next, all that is good occurs...
- ♥ i am free of the past. i release the past. i am grateful.
- ♥ i develop new capacities for redefining a future of unseen possibilities.
- ♥ i am thinking and feeling beyond old limits now. i pursue new goals.
- ♥ i leave behind complacency, resignation and cynicism.
- ♥ i am stepping beyond what's been usual, for me.
  i am free of past encumbrances. i accomplish. i apply new skills.
- ♥ greater possibilities call me continually forward.
- ♥ i see abundant resources ahead of me. i expand horizons.
  i accept the constant renewal of dynamic actions.
- ♥ i grow and prosper in gracious circumstances.
- ♥ i generate ground-breaking thinking that honors the ancient ways.
- ♥ i attract people, events and positions which bless me.
- ♥ i am a blessing to those around me, as i move forward inventing and designing new horizons.
- ♥ i like what i am thinking.
  i have complete confidence.

COURAGE:
WE ARE NO LONGER AVOIDING WHAT IS NEW

- ♥ We no longer run from what we don't like.
- ♥ We no longer escape. We are encouraged. We are empowered.
- ♥ We are no longer avoiding what is new. We are supported in being successful.
- ♥ Our ancestral programming and primitive notions have lost their grip.
  we are free to choose what works. Old programs that no longer suit us are now invalid, ineffective, and dissolved. We are free to choose EXPANSION. We deliver results. We accomplish courageously.
  We appreciate attainment. We acknowledge accomplishment.

The Direction of East

I MOVE IN NEW WAYS

The truth is that there is but One power and that power is God. i am that power individualized, and all that God is i am. My good already is... This truth sets me free to prosper and expand good!
RIGHT ACTION GOVERNS ALL DECISIONS.
MY FUTURE CALLS ME FORWARD.
Infinite Intelligence is always guiding. i bless all who are in my consciousness. My good and their good already is... This truth sets us free.
GOOD ALREADY IS...GOOD ALREADY IS... I HAVE A HAPPY OUTLOOK.
There is no challenge i cannot meet. The stream of life carries with it the change and cycles necessary for renewal. i move in new ways. RIGHT ACTION GOVERNS ALL CHOICES AND COMMITMENTS. SUPERB DECISIONS ARE SO ... i increase in wisdom...appropriate doors open for me. i move forward creating more good. THE GOOD I ACCEPT FOR MYSELF, I ACCEPT FOR EVERYONE.
And because Being, establishes me
in exactly what i accept as accomplished...
i accept this as accomplished now. so it is... that's what's so.
i move in new ways.i have already acheived a flourishing mode of being.

BEING FULLY BEGINNING

Today i enjoy being human. i do not try to escape.
i move fully human, fully expressed. Saints did not live in caves, they lived, with people, in towns, they were known ...
i know how to choose. Between withdrawal and participation..
i choose wisely.. i do not look for what is easier. i assume difficulty with boldness.. i look toward what will serve for this season of beginnings.
i turn energy to important work for starting. Sometimes it is easier to withdraw from the world than to live in it... Today, i live in the world.
i participate in rebirth. Sometimes it is more comfortable,
to repress emotion than to feel...i express emotions.
To communicate in a group is more difficult than to be noble and meditate for hours alone. Today i risk feeling and looking dumb. i feel through all emotions, i feel through sadness to happy... i can no longer afford narrow definitions. My fullest expression is to animate happiness in all seasons, all cycles, all directions.
To be a bender, to be a shaper, to be a wise person, is not laid back, mellow, safe and comfortable nor is it a guarantee of peace of mind. i have courage, i work hard and i am capable of repose and rest. i go deep down
for this full living authentically. It requires openness and vulnerability in each minute, not sometimes. Each day there are no answers, only more problems, i am happy in the middle of this... Tasks to be done, positions to be left behind, more questions to consider. Wisdom is a function of experience...
Beginning is not an event it is a process.
    i am fully alive today.
    i enjoy adventures of being fully human today.
    i enjoy animating happiness right now, while i am beginning...

CELEBRATING LIFE WITH MY FAMILY

- ♥ i look forward to celebrating life with my family.
- ♥ i am no longer at effect of my family.
- ♥ i am now confronting issues that used to stop my participation with my family.
- ♥ i am free to be who and how i really am with my family.
- ♥ i no longer withhold communications in certain circumstances.
- ♥ i laugh, speak, and listen from the heart everywhere.
- ♥ i no longer have "certain ways to be" with special people.
- ♥ i am the way i be, with everyone, and it works to be true.
- ♥ if people do not like or approve of actions, speaking, or thinking... it's okay with me.
- ♥ i no longer demand approval from my family.
- ♥ what others "think" of me is no longer my business. it's okay.
- ♥ i am open and receptive to the living spirit of truth, in all circumstances.
- ♥ i accept people for the way they are...and the way they aren't.
- ♥ peace begins with me. things are as they should be ...
- ♥ i cheerfully and lovingly appreciate and acknowledge the people in my family.
- ♥ i display great generosity in all family circumstances.

GOODBYE TO FEAR

- ♥ i declare fear has no power over me.
- ♥ constructive possibilities outnumber all fears.
- ♥ i never run away from what scares me.
- ♥ i squarely face what i fear, i turn toward it.
- ♥ fears are illusions, they lose power as i walk into them.
- ♥ i train myself to stop thinking thoughts that frighten me.
- ♥ when i am tempted to become fearful i find an ally to my commitments to speak to me.
- ♥ i share and dissolve what i dread.
- ♥ i no longer listen for long amounts of time to fears of others.
- ♥ i direct conversations to constructive possibilities.
- ♥ i control attention and direct my mind.
- ♥ Since feelings follow thought, directing thought directs feelings.
- ♥ i let go anxiety and worried thought.
- ♥ i transform fear to an opportunity for aimed thinking.
- ♥ Attention directs my feelings. feelings follow attention.

The Direction of East

- ♥ i think about what i intend rather than what i fear.
- ♥ i put attention on freedom and possibility today.
- ♥ i use the wise thinking process to create patterns and attitudes of great satisfaction.
- ♥ fear no longer has any power with me, i am free.

GOODBYE TO FEAR OF THE FUTURE

- ♥ i have deeper trust in the process of life.
- ♥ today, i experience being without hesitance.
- ♥ fear fades progressively from consciousness now.
- ♥ i declare i am guided and guarded always in an excellent manner.
- ♥ every good gift comes to me through new ideas. i permit new ideas.
  new ideas are unending forever.
- ♥ goodbye to: lack
  loneliness
  dissatisfaction
  and disability.
- ♥ good is natural, ever-available and eternally present.
- ♥ the changeless nature of principle enables me
  to expect permanent good even though its
  form is ever changing.
- ♥ good is dependable, present now, not far off...
- ♥ today i find no fear in my thoughts about the future.
- ♥ life supplies every requirement, right on time.
- ♥ now and always, i evolve in wisdom.
- ♥ i grow in understanding. i take steps to acheive outcomes.
- ♥ I am willing to touch the realm of multiple realities.
- ♥ I no longer repress insights that contradict old belief systems.
- ♥ i have happily lost any future fear.

GOODBYE WORRY

- God is all there is... life is God in action. The universe of form is the living expression of Divine Intelligence... We are all God activity in motion, in manifestation. The process is perfect.
- Universe abounds in love...
  Universe abounds in whatever is required...
  All form is from ONE INFINITE INTELLIGENCE in action.
- Today, i dismiss my tendency to judge life
  according to the appearances i determine...
  Today i see further than a chronic state of tension...
  Mental concerns that possessed me are now gone...
  i relax and feel beyond reacting...
  remember i am part of a perfect process.
- Now i am living in a co-operative circumstance called life...This realization demands i transcend small self and doubts. Today i do that. Life all around me is ongoing, changing and rearranging...It's fine, i live life happily, radiantly, expansively, in the spirit of absolute freedom.

THERE ARE NO MISTAKES

There are no mistakes, only misunderstood experiences.
To realize that there are no mistakes restores and revitalizes everything...
Harmony and restoration then abound.
Emerson reminds us: OUR STRENGTHS GROW OUT OF OUR WEAKNESSES, every evil to which we do not give in becomes a benefactor. If we appear to lose any good, more is gained somewhere else. No one ever had a defect that was not made useful to them. For every apparent failure, there is
an equal success as long as we stay on the road.
PERFECT equity adjusts its balance
in all parts of life...
Life always resumes balance
no matter what anything looks like.
everything works for good ...
Today we declare that LIFE is good
and good is victorious.

ABOUT LEAVING WORRY BEHIND

- my world is transformed
  from complaints to possibilities.
- i know that Intelligence is always guiding my way.
- in all circumstances i see that greater good is being brought forth.
- no matter what things look like,
  i expect good results to come forth and they do.

The Direction of East

- ♥ the power of my thinking is transcendent.
- ♥ now i leave negative assumptions behind.
- ♥ i calm racing thoughts easily.
- ♥ i know what to do and i do it/i know what to do and i do it!
- ♥ i have a bright outlook...
- ♥ i have orderly ways and intuitive ways to do what needs doing today.
- ♥ i trust myself to tell truth, and live the truth.
- ♥ everything works out perfectly whenever i show up.
- ♥ my life is becoming more harmonious and peace-filled.
- ♥ i make the highest choices in all situations and circumstances.
- ♥ there is no limit to the good that can be expressed through me.
- ♥ guidance and direction are always clear.
- ♥ thank God i am now free to be making choices and seeing clearly.
- ♥ turbulent emotions are a thing of the past.
- ♥ Regardless of appearances, i am a harmonizer all the time now.
- ♥ i empty my mind of all worries easily, today.
- ♥ i meet each day in a positive way. i am relaxed, i feel relaxed.
- ♥ everyday and every way things are getting better and better for me now.
- ♥ i am directed, encouraged, supported and enlightened in every possible way... i am leaving all worry behind me now...
free from tension, stress, and strain.

SAFETY PREVAILS

We recognize
the ever presence of CREATIVE INTELLIGENCE
there is no where, where it isn't reigning..............
the SOURCE OF ALL LIFE is eternally maintaining
        what's to be relied upon.
Guidance is provided. We gladly follow intuition.
Right directions are accepted, in timely fashion.
Thoughts are filled with certitude, assurance,
      peace, and plenty.
      negatives are filtered-out.
What's positive is reinforced. Safety is certain
The stress and storms of experience
have no power to slow us down today.
Any thoughts to-the-contrary are now erased
      from consciousness.
We are lively, energetic and we embody a-feeling-of-protection.
JOURNEYS ARE COMPLETED IN ABSOLUTE SAFETY.
Every event, condition and situation is directed Divinely.
Thanks is everpresent. Safety is certain.
    ......So it is now.

Seasons of Prosperity

SAFETY: I MOVE IN GOOD SEQUENCE

i am a part of the circle of life.
i celebrate the cycles of life that i inhere in.
i am relaxed and safe in life's changing pattern.
i see changes each calendar year, as the wheel of seasons turns.
                      i am moving onward.
                            i have a promise of each season to come,
knowing, understanding and recognizing the governing forces
    of the season's power to affect me...

this helps me to be in proper interface with what's so in my world.

planting a garden on-the-edge-of-winter, i don't expect results
for a good many months...planting a garden on-the-edge-of-spring,
i will see results, in a very short time, understanding IS power.
understanding is power.

i represent understanding-of-seasons and cycles.

when i take into account wisdom of the obvious cycles,
my development and success of projects is empowered.

i know when to move and when to rest...

i grow and blossom in perfect timing
in harmony with the seasons

the wheel of life is turning all around me...
month by month, minute by minute, the seasons change, inside and out.

i am liberated by understanding the nature of changing.
the seeds from harvest past, go with me to each new spring.
time turns the wheel-of-life,
in universal harmony.

i move certain and sure of what's next...

i am safe and relaxed for traveling
in life's cycles of time and place.

i move in good sequence.

The Direction of East

WE GIVE THANKS FOR PROTECTION

God is with us now,
in trust and thankfulness.
we inhere in God's care, nothing can harm us,
                      neither tangible forces of the material world,
                      nor fear of things unseen.
God's love protects us.
God's love surrounds us.
we know and express divine justice.
we are sustained and strengthened.
we enjoy clearness of vision,
       strength of limb,
       soundness of mind,
       balance of body.
God's wholeness is within us. We are at peace.
path's open to us where we couldn't see them before.
we are kept from harm and confusion.
those who are with us are uplifted also.
God's love is wide.
God's power is eternal.
we walk confidently.

TRAVELING DECLARATION

♥   In the state of non-obstruction, we begin.

♥   On this trip, in all directions, the force of joy abounds.

♥   On this trip, we move in happiness and humor.
     All challenges are subdued.
     The force of light bright prosperity is everywhere.

     Wherever we are, what occurs is forward motion
                             good will is all around us.
     Firmly rooted miseries dissolve. The sea of afflictions evaporates.

♥   We speak auspicious language.
     Miraculous events happen whenever we show up.
     We accomplish what we said we would accomplish.
     Effectiveness and wisdom are everywhere we go.
     We perform appropriate deeds and make good choices...
                             happy joy abounds.
     Great gratitude occurs on this trip.
     Broad and vast understanding prevails.
     All beings are benefited on this trip.

Seasons of Prosperity

THE CIRCUMSTANCE OF THIS CAR IS SAFETY

with one heart and one mind we call forth blessing
    for this car, its drivers and passengers.
those who are separated can be brought together with transportation.
we give thanks for the usefulness of this car.

bless those whose work made this car.
bless those who ride in it.
bless everyone who encounters it.

bridges, highways, small streets, avenues, and parking lots are cleared for this car.
journeys in this car are peaceful, happy, and purposeful.
drivers in this car care for the safety of others. this is certain.
those who make use of this car listen to the words
    of intuition and spirit guiding them always in safety.

all trips bring people in this car, safely to their destinations.
in God we live and move and have our being.
we reflect the good movement of all life in this car, and with this car.

WHAT IS IN ERROR IS UNREAL

What's real is what reflects God....
Matter is non-intelligent (of its own accord) its guidance is of mind...
People are expressionsof Spirit everywhere
PEOPLE HAVE A POWER TO DECLARE DIVINE ORDER
and they use it everywhere they are today
    Real being is forever
    Freedom...we can be free and we are free
    Harmony...we let go of what is disharmonius now!

<u>Harmonious action</u> proceeds from God, even as we speak, everywhere
inharmony has no principle of organization. Disharmony is entrophic.
Its action is in error.
It has no guidance,
    no course-of-action for a future.
    Error conversations disappear today
    Syntrophy prevails

Whatever is not of God disappears today.
Sin, sickness and death fade away
They vanish before the reality of good. Good prevails.

Today we choose good as reality! This is ours to say.
People are tributary to God, Spirit and to nothing else.
Today we remember and recall often what is real reflects God.
And we are grateful for this truth.

ARIES DECLARATION

i declare that ...
   through the power and mighty presence of the Divine within,
   i am a great contribution to the people around me...
   i take initiative. i am happy to forge ahead even when others hesitate. i love to be first.. the great Divine power of creative energy empowers me and provides dependable regenerative ability to meet all requirements. my refusal to admit defeat brings vitality,
   stamina and strength to overcome all obstacles.
   i AM A NATURAL LEADER.

i am successfully learning:

- ♥ tolerance
- ♥ cooperation
- ♥ patience and restraint
- ♥ to wait for others
- ♥ discerning what's really important
- ♥ attentiveness with others
- ♥ to listen to what people have to say
- ♥ to reach out to include others
- ♥ to follow up on details to completion.

i am leaving behind:

- ♥ unwise risks and rash actions
- ♥ feelings of competition
- ♥ imposing my convictions
- ♥ being wrapped up in my own concerns
- ♥ reprimanding the opinions of others
- ♥ using force to get a point across
- ♥ refusing to compromise
- ♥ being quick to anger
- ♥ walking away in an argument.

TAURUS DECLARATIONS

i declare ...
    that through the power and mighty presence of the Divine within, i am a great contribution to the people around me. i am very patient and persistent. i work carefully. i have practical, real results. i can be depended on to complete things that i start...power is expressed when i stand for something. i achieve mastery over physical matters. i go to great extents for others. nothing interferes with what i want. my loyalty makes me a very great companion. my strong willpower enables me to make plans from a distance. success follows my plans without exception. i embody determination. I AM NATURALLY PRACTICAL.

i am successfully learning:
- ♥ to have a spiritual practice
- ♥ to welcome the unconventional
- ♥ to push ahead when i want to slow down
- ♥ pleasure is short-lived as a goal
- ♥ to calm down easily when upset
- ♥ material acquisitions are not so important
- ♥ to feel vulnerable and safe in groups
- ♥ people's affection for me is not my property
- ♥ others have methods which are useful, too
- ♥ to accept help from others

i am leaving behind:
- ♥ complaining
- ♥ being dictatorial
- ♥ great desires for comfort
- ♥ the "problems" of my friends
- ♥ being intensely jealous
- ♥ low-grade companions
- ♥ obsessions with material goods
- ♥ avoiding "strenuous" situations
- ♥ calculated generosity
- ♥ fears of being "out-of-control"
- ♥ reluctance to what's new

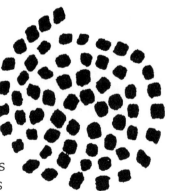

GEMINI DECLARATIONS

i declare ...
  that through the power and mighty presence of the Divine within, i am a great contribution to the people around me...
  i am truly versatile. i identify, classify and imaginatively invent. speech is the framework for my activities. i have a highly developed learning capacity. i bring intuitive unsuspected solutions to emergencies.
  i am most happy when my hands are busy giving form to my plentiful ideas. i love changes of atmosphere and constantly being on my way to "somewhere". my versatility adds excitement wherever i go... i represent nonconformity.
  I AM A NATURAL COMMUNICATOR.

i am successfully learning:

- ♥ calmness of mind
- ♥ to let people really know me
- ♥ everything doesn't have to be my way
- ♥ intellectual tranquillity
- ♥ cooperation is necessary to happiness
- ♥ to conform sometimes
- ♥ to be "pinned down" and like it
- ♥ to yield and be disciplined

i am leaving behind:

- ♥ depression
- ♥ impatience with people
- ♥ the attitude that "i already know"
- ♥ tense energies unexpressed
- ♥ running away from long term relatedness
- ♥ directing myself only by mood of the moment
- ♥ intense curiosity and questioning
- ♥ rebelling and resisting authority

MIND TREATMENT:
WE ARE ALREADY CONNECTED WITH PERFECTION

What is a mind treatment?
- ♥ An act of purposeful perception
- ♥ Speaking what's required for a condition to be resolved.
- ♥ Deliberate thinking of a situation into a possible future.
- ♥ An assemblage of words declaring what's desired

What use is a mind treatment?
at the center of things intelligence responds to situations in the exact manner of our thinking. With mind treatments we lead our expectation to desired outcomes, by choosing thoughts.

How can I write my own treatments?
HOW TO WRITE A MIND TREATMENT
1. Recognize One power in all the Universe at the beginning.
2. Recognize that the One power and you are united.
3. Affirm the ideal that you intend as already so.
4. Deny the opposing appearance.
5. Re-affirm the intention, recognize that it's true now.
6. Give thanks for the outworking of the intention in manifestation.
7. Release the treatment to do its work,
   i.e. ("...and so it is", "These words are the truth about me", etc.).

CONSCIOUS CREATIVE SPEAKING MAKES THINGS REAL

What is an affirmation?
- ♥ Exercising the yes action of mind...
- ♥ A positive statement of ideal.
- ♥ A mental act that asserts the best in any appearance.
- ♥ The persistent movement of appropriate thinking.
- ♥ That which raises consciousness and perception to ideals.
- ♥ Bringing ideas into form to aim in a preferred direction.

How can I use affirmations?
The use of affirmations trains thinking in useful directions, rather than having habitual attention on concerns. Mental affirmations are "far stronger than the strongest (visible) thing in the world", someone once said. The discipline of appropriate thought is a good step erasing reactive response. A famous teacher remarked that to "change your thinking"
changes your life.

effective
RICH
ENERGETIC
RESOURCEFUL
RESILIENT...ENDURING
Resolute
REMARKABLE encouraged
EXCELLENT
RESPONSIBLE

Direction of the South

we honor
powers of the South
red is the South. red is strength.
South is where earth gives us our growth.
> what sustains us
> the multitude of plants
> and herbs that heal us
> are strengthened with the
> bright sunshine of this
> southern direction.

South is growth, strength and empowerment. . . . .
many processes happening at once. . . . . .
> skills
> will and discipline
> are called for here.

thanks to Great Spirit, for activity
that we invest ourselves in, to bring about bounty.
. . . from hard work, comes fruit of our labors.
we are thankful for the integrity
of all systems working together for good.
commitment becomes the beginning
of dependable harvests.

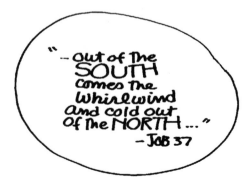

"...out of the SOUTH comes the whirlwind and cold out of the NORTH..."
— JOB 37

standing in the SOUTH

i give thanks for beauty and teachings
                    provided by
                    Archangel Uriel
this is where i concentrate on development
            i work hard in the SOUTH
i am grateful for all the people
            all the circumstances
            all the events
            that have brought me to the SOUTH

as i continually move in the circle of cycles
i am unfolding a theme, expanding potentialities of a greater state.
manifesting begins here...
i am setting up a language for distinguishing accomplishment.
i am empowered by the ability to express feelings.
i am renewed by music and growing things.
i trust my gracefulness as i move from simple to complex
            in all my working in the SOUTH.
i demonstrate discrimination and adaptability in devotion.
i feel building momentum of being consistent in thought,
                            speaking and action.
i am deeply moved to do work and i allow myself to work and be accountable.
i unite in responsible alliances
      that keep me habitually on purpose with reliable patterns of character.
clearly i accomplish completions
            finalizations
            and negotiations that work.
i have integrity, discipline and commitment in all my working.
the process of maturing relationships evolves appropriately
                        as i take responsibility for my idealism
i encourage explicit honesty in all those around me.
my loyalty and compassion increases as i continue
                    to take courage, and realize goals.
my love is deep, solid, dependable.
i know what do to and i continuously do it.
union comes, cohesion is happening.
i gladly refrain from impulses that distract me
                    i crystallize vision
                    into a solid state,
                    here in the SOUTH.
in the SOUTH
i ask:
    what promotes fidelity?
    can development be made durable?
    does process have struggle innate in it?
    do i get distracted from doing?

Seasons of Prosperity

oh south spirit

South spirit give us
the brightest, longest light
to help us work hard in the warmth of production.
With it commitment and discipline
brings us dedication and true accomplishment.
Our consistency in word and deed is established.
The integrity of reliable patterns is made apparent.
Touching South teaches concentration to complete projects.
New ability to work hard and not demand retribution is available here.
We have good relationships with all things in summer,
heartful actions occur in appropriate timing.
Fixed certainties open up to new ideas.

The South cycle of the four directions
is a very popular part of the circle.
It is masculine in style.
Working-hard, bouncing a lot of balls in-the-air,
seeing good results, establishing the disciplines required
to bring about blossoms and fruits of labors,
the flag says work-hard! Work on!
There's plenty of busy activity in the
Southern direction.

south is a time of

- ♥ adolescence, idealism
- ♥ determination
- ♥ anger at justice
- ♥ the heart and compassion
- ♥ kindnesses, noble passions
- ♥ appreciating beauty and art
- ♥ loyalty, partnerships
- ♥ working hard, learning to share
- ♥ physical discipline, goals established
- ♥ developing the art of caring for another
- ♥ passionate involvement in the world
- ♥ development of gracefulness, listening to music
- ♥ balanced development of aspects of the self
- ♥ ability to express hurt as well as joy
- ♥ feelings to be refined, developed, and controlled
- ♥ ability to set aside feelings to serve others

The Direction of South

summer - south

using the model of four season's in nature...we notice, at noon, sun appears to be in the South, the brightest section of day, is used to represent the season of summer, the brightest season of four seasons.
summer represents South. South is development.
when our lives, or projects are in the South direction, it is not time for rest or vacation. it is <u>a time of concentrated focus on getting results</u>...on getting tasks completed...on getting communications urgently responded to...on getting whatever's required done immediately. South is an act-fast direction... for blooming. days are longer. life looks very good in South of the circle. we can easily be fooled away from our tasks by thinking, ease, is the banner of the time, but it isn't. summer is where almost anything you put in the ground will come to fruition. remember like all the other seasons, it is only a quarter of the circle...even tho it seems long and forever, it's just as brief
                                  as each other season.

    South is <u>to be committed to what you said you would do</u>. the temptation will be to change focus, change your mind, change task. this is time to tell truth, not say what you think they want to hear, or tell just part of what's so, hoping no one will guess the rest. it's time to keep discipline, tight,
even tho you'd rather sit in the sun or go to a beach, or take long vacations.

    when you are in a circle's southern section, work you do there determines autumn's harvest, which will bring you thru the winter.
the<u> labor of summer provides for the impending cold season</u>.
working hard for no immediate reward may not sound sensational,
                                                     in hot sunshine,
however in the icy frost the abundance from this time,
                        well-invested, will carry you over to spring.

    the evermore active life processes of summer, when fruition is maximal, is <u>time to work smart and hard</u>. predominance of warmth and light will grow all work to its best blossoming.
there is no other time like this, in the circle.
seeds for next year are formed in the outbreath of summer.

    South is popular. hard work is masculine in style,
bouncing lots-of-balls-in-the-air,
seeing good results firms up disciplines required, to bring fruits later.
this is development time.
production calls for commitment, no waving, no wavering

Seasons of Prosperity

summer in the spirit of the circle

- ♥ the circle serves an important function
  of understanding the coming in, and going out, of life.

- ♥ i push when it's time to push
  attention to the urgent details of life bring me the results i desire...

- ♥ no longer do i avoid
  working hard in this aspect of the circle.

- ♥ i discover regularities and repetitions,
  that help me keep Divine Order.

- ♥ everything <u>works together for good</u> when i stay engaged,
  speak true and give-up trying to be popular

- ♥ i get the results required by planning ahead,
  doing what i said, i would do...
  and acting quickly in issues that are urgent.

- ♥ i leave behind waiting until later, i seize the day

i have what it takes in integrity

- ♥ i have integrity. i live how i talk. my position is true.
- ♥ i am consistent in thinking, speaking and doing.
- ♥ i am fully accountable for who i am and what i said ...
- ♥ reliable patterns in character are mine today.
- ♥ discipline is easy for me. i do what i said i would do.
- ♥ i am consistently & habitually-on-purpose.
- ♥ i do away with what doesn't aim toward the goal.
- ♥ i demonstrate the ability to renounce and eliminate
  what doesn't work, to bring about successful completions.
- ♥ i am capable of commitment. i live true.
- ♥ i am being deeply moved to work.
- ♥ i have a response that accounts for what i am devoted to ... each day.
- ♥ i produce unions and collaborations wherever i go.
- ♥ i give full percent thrust to what i've committed.

The Direction of South

qualities to call forth in the south:

♥ **integrity**
a way of being consistent in thinking, speaking and doing,
which makes full accountability for what was said...
reliable patterns in character.

♥ **discipline**
being habitually-on-purpose, by doing away with what doesn't aim toward
goals. the ability to renounce and eliminate obstacles,
to bring about successful completion.

♥ **commitment**
being deeply moved to work, a posture and response
that has devotion ...
this produces some union
where there wasn't one

i am determined

♥   With eagerness i greet each day.
♥   i am deeply moved to do work.
♥   my dedication produces
    true accomplishment.
♥   i know that i know, no matter what's happening around me.
♥   i let go of data and let my heartfelt instinct keep me
    directed and standing for authenticity.
♥   i resolve to follow through on important work.
♥   i represent determination for results.
♥   i am letting heart knowledge replace head knowledge.
♥   i am refreshed and renewed in my work each day.
♥   i let go disheartening perspectives, gladly.
♥   commitment consciousness reshapes my life thinking now.
♥   higher ideas keep me from stale thinking and stagnant views.
♥   i am accomplishing all the time, now.

Seasons of Prosperity

i know how to work

"There is no greater mistake than to suppose one is
                too good for the work called upon to do..."

- ♥ light of life is what i represent in working.
- ♥ i have pure methods and supreme insights in all work.
- ♥ i understand that i am not separated in any way from Divine Order.
- ♥ my projects are successful beyond what i imagine... prospects improve.
- ♥ each day i sincerely contemplate what i am doing. i am happy doing it.
- ♥ all my doing reflects a process of right timing.
- ♥ i am directed and guided in all projects.
- ♥ all fear (and confusions) are quickly dissolved.
- ♥ my associates are clear and committed.
- ♥ my communications are clear and committed.
- ♥ i respond to intuition in the marketplace.
- ♥ i am seeing and hearing in undistorted ways.
- ♥ i work in cooperation with dedicated others to expand visions and make heartfelt goals real.
- ♥ projects are inspired and inspiring.
- ♥ life changes as a result of my working.
- ♥ Ideal influence is actively at work with me.
- ♥ the light that illuminates our true nature reveals my way.
- ♥ failure is temporary always. i know how to work.
- ♥ i know how to work without compulsive mental activity.
- ♥ doing little things well is a step toward doing big things excellently.
- ♥ my work is for a world that works. i allow good ideas to direct work.
- ♥ i forever remain guided in all planning and collaboration.
- ♥ finishing plans in good order is happening.
- ♥ all working is a fine experience for me. i know how to work!
- ♥ i am expressing gratitude and magnanimity in all working.
- ♥ i am able to finish projects in good order and start them appropriately.
- ♥ when i am only working, where "i-already-know-it-works"
                i am not working enough.

The Direction of South

a declaration for the work place

> All that's past
> is free to leave.
> We move with sure speed
> and certainty
> into what's next.

In this business,
whatever is not of true value fades away now.
>   People are true, loyal and loving.
Wisdom lives in these alliances at work.
Previous errors are cleared up easily, fully.
Lies dissolve quickly around here.
Truth is uncovered, apparent.
There is clean-clear-speaking here...
discriminations are purposeful.
Wisdom, directed and effective,
is working here.

This work contributes to many.
Knowing what to do is easy with
    minds rested in peace.
In this work place we care
    about people,
    people care about us.

Wealth is the condition
of this work.
The well-being of all those
involved in this work
is assured.
We move with certainty
into what's next.

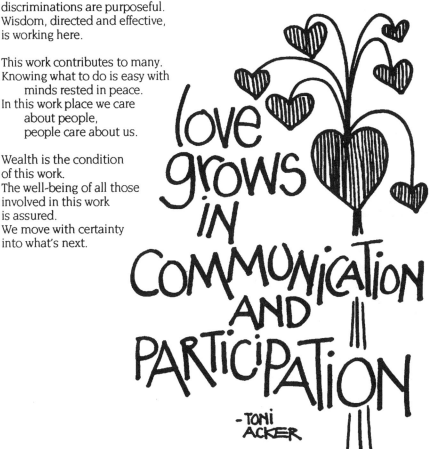

love grows in COMMUNICATION AND PARTICIPATION

— TONI ACKER

Seasons of Prosperity

entrepreneurial affirmations

- i have an ever present, inspiring vision which keeps me motivated and productive.
- i go past all "seeming" problems by making them into opportunities.
- i have the power to take my vision into action in such a way that true results are the outcome.
- each day i put old ideas into new uses and develop plans that are successful.
- upsets are a thing of the past for me, i keep going despite appearances.
- my commitment is fully expressed, recognized and fulfilled.
- the strength of my dedication moves everything into beneficial accord.
- i coordinate my efforts with those of other people, we all prosper.
- the work in which i am engaged attracts partnerships, affiliation and association with a network of allies.
- i have plenty of allies to my commitment. my work prospers.
- every outcome is a stepping stone to further success.
- i easily re-direct and transform my usual ways of being into success attitudes.
- i assimilate only ideas around me that keep me moving in profitable directions.
- i focus my attention on forward-moving ideas...i put them easily into action.
- i am discovering more talents, abilities, and skills each day in myself and all those around me.
- my clear communication opens opportunities and possibilities everywhere i am.
- every day in every way, i have a true sense of accomplishment.
- i love and appreciate all the people who are empowering.
- my success and excellence as an entrepreneur are already established.
- i release full power, full participation now.
- energy is restored and energized. i have full freedom to act.
- i expand without reservation in financial income.
- i let go all false purposes, i expand work miraculously.
- i have a new high level of certain basic purpose.
- i operate directly at full speed
    at full strength
        on my purposes
- with laser precision i push through completely what ever obstacles occur.
- i am restored to create purpose.
- actions and thinking clear the way to financial freedom.
- increased power restores truth .

The Direction of South

GOODBYE OBSTRUCTIONS TO GETTING THE JOB DONE

- ♥ i forge ahead to a future of auspicious outcomes.
- ♥ i have a new life, a new avenue of good outcomes.
- ♥ power is now available to achieve completion and resolution.
- ♥ i move, live and work in my perfect place.
- ♥ all that is good and gracious helps me win.
- ♥ i free myself from habits that hinder me.
- ♥ i free myself from relationships that hold me back.
- ♥ people, events and circumstances that have slowed me down are now gone from consciousness.
- ♥ i loosen burdensome patterns and partners.
- ♥ i let go activities that no longer suit the new me.
- ♥ my space is cleared of all unwanted influences.
- ♥ i am led out of all danger safely. i emerge from the closed chrysalis state.
- ♥ i am glad, good-willed and glowing.
- ♥ i am released from tensions. i am released from uncertainty.
- ♥ i resolve and clear away the old. i experience a release.
- ♥ i am looking forward to even more challenges.
- ♥ i attract to my life people who bless me.
- ♥ i attract to my life events that prosper all.
- ♥ i attract circumstances that bring results.
- ♥ i give attention to all that's required today.
- ♥ i give without expectation of return.
-    i am set free.
- ♥ i enjoy meeting people who help me stay committed to my goals.
- ♥ i am gallant, generous and genuine.
- ♥ with calm certainty, i open to the highest good.

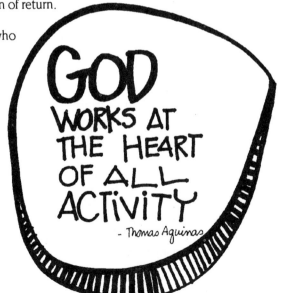

GOD WORKS AT THE HEART OF ALL ACTIVITY
— Thomas Aquinas

Seasons of Prosperity

i am working hard, no matter what

- today goals are achieved.
- i have stability and consistency in all actions.
- my performance is reliable. people count on me.
- i continue to make contact with people, places and things that help me complete work.
- i have the skills required to motivate myself and others to the aims named.
- i concentrate major strengths on the center of planned actions.
- i am independent of the feelings that would keep me from achieving.
- problems move out of experience, obstacles dissolve.
- i measure and am accounting for the ongoing success of results.
- i am free of thoughts that cause complaints.
- i stay in action, making intentions into outcomes.
- i am working smart and effectively to cause results.
- i make plans that assure outcomes, manifest goals.
- i carve out contemplation time to think where my plans are going and how they can go better.
- conversations involve others in getting results to happen.
- goals are achieved as i continue to invent the future.
- i create and take advantage of all future opportunities to have results.
- endless creativity and effective results are everywhere present today.

i have entrepreneurial spirit

- i proclaim i intuitively know when to do the right thing at the right time.
- i make things happen easily today. i concentrate easily.
- successfully starting each day i remind myself of how grateful i am for the-help-of-others.
- i am in constant communication and affinity with allies to my commitments everyday.
- resentment has dissolved... i ask for what i want and get it quickly.
- mysterious help comes my way, i accept it, with gratitude.
- i am willing to let people help me too.
- corrective actions are applied immediately when required.
- i see clearly what works and what doesn't work.

The Direction of South

- ♥ i practice boundless faith, gut instinct, and generous giving in all my interactions each day.
- ♥ staying clear of doubt, anger and fear; many forces come to my rescue.
- ♥ i remain constant in my inner equilibrium to push forward today.
- ♥ trusted advisors hold me accountable for desired results.
- ♥ each day i acquire more knowledge and skill with experience and study.
- ♥ i keep alert and everything happens to right advantage.
- ♥ incredible discrimination is mine today in every decision i make or participate in... i am happy and grateful ongoingly...
- ♥ i relinquish comfort happily to achieve results quickly.
- ♥ i continue each day to do what is appropriate in a cheerful manner.
- ♥ plenty of people in the world are helping me to succeed.
- ♥ i continue perseveringly on the path with strength, no matter what happens.
- ♥ i do not need to know all the answers in advance.
- ♥ i renew my determination to persevere whenever obstructions appear. obstacles disappear quickly today.
- ♥ i go forward with integrity and full commitment.
- ♥ entrepreneurial spirit guides me

"... all actions take place in time by the interweaving of the forces of NATURE but the person lost in selfish delusion thinks that he himself is the actor."
— BHAGAVAD GITA

Seasons of Prosperity

i work hard today

- i produce much.
- i stay on purpose today.
- i give up, what only distracts me.
- i take on, what brings me where i'm headed.
- i refuse to use what's inappropriate for me.
- i move into patterns of action that keep me aimed and productive.
- my actions are aligned with the results i desire.
- at this point, in time, i overcome all odds, in my path.
- i am grateful for the ability to work hard.

i am integrity

- what i think, what i say, and what i do are congruent and cohesive.
- i am consistent in thought, word and deed.
- i am dependable. i have reliable patterns.
- my "feelings-of-the-moment" do not direct me.
- when i say i will do something, i do it.
- i have coagulative power... i have staying power.
- there is right relationship in my actions, feelings and thoughts.
- i am consciously connected in all the fields that i am moving in ease and good sequence.
- proper processing is at work with me.
- appropriate regard generates my motions.
- i know where to say "yes" and when to say "no".

saying no

- i have the courage to say "no" appropriately.
- i no longer say "no" falsely to delay what's next.
- being able to say "no" is a valuable skill.
- i work discovering my true "yes" and "no" today.
- saying "no" when it's true now, is appropriate.
- i resolutely turn away from temptations to say "yes" when "no" is my real response.
- i am able to live convictions today.
- resentment is no longer real for me.
- the confusion of doubt and decisiveness is apparent to me today. i act boldly and decisively.
- intelligence is governing what it creates.
- i am willing to speak honestly today.
- i act with full integrity today.

The Direction of South

being responsible

♥ i have chosen everything
about me
both consciously and
unconsciously

♥ i take responsibility for
        all that i do
        all that i don't do
        what i think
        what i feel
        the images i hold in my mind
        what i expect in the future
        all my anger and frustration
        all my love and excitement
        all my joy and happiness
        all my sadness and depression
        the words that i say
        the songs i sing
        the dreams and goals i have
        the sound of my voice
        all my actions
        my fears
        my successes
        my mistakes

♥ because i am honest about what i am claiming,
i can really know myself, appreciate myself, and even though i don't
always like all the things i do...i can love me!

♥ i am doing the best i can do...i feel loving towards myself.

Seasons of Prosperity

prosperous doing

- ♥ i agree to do only the things i intend to do.
- ♥ i do all the things i have agreed to do.
- ♥ i am a responsible person. it works for me to have money.
- ♥ i do what i say i will do, my speaking is true.
- ♥ i am noticing the things i really like doing.
- ♥ i am noticing what i really don't like doing.
- ♥ i make wise choices about what to do.
- ♥ i am in order. all around me is in order.
- ♥ the world reflects good feelings back to me.
- ♥ i act for what's next. i am making positive changes.
- ♥ each day i get more and more enthusiasm for life.
- ♥ my attitude is one of joy, i am in high spirits.
- ♥ i am letting my light shine. i am grateful.
- ♥ i look to what i like. i describe what i desire more of ...
- ♥ i choose to think about it. i write and speak what i praise.
- ♥ i have an attitude of gratitude for all good changes.
- ♥ i voice my appreciation often. i praise all the help i have had ...
- ♥ my attitude of gratitude brings more good into my life.
- ♥ i give thanks often and out loud. i let people know how much i love them.
- ♥ i am expressing magnanimity in my thanksgiving.
- ♥ it works fo me to have money.
- ♥ it works for people around me when i have money.
- ♥ money enables me in places where i used to hold back.
- ♥ i now press out instead of holding back.

The Direction of South

we have authentic speaking

- ♥ We communicate and make ourselves known today gladly.
- ♥ In our partnerships we stay fresh, revealed and real with each other.
- ♥ We leave behind safe, contracted, careful positioning.
- ♥ Genuine disclosure helps us to know and serve each other easily.
- ♥ We tell, discover and divulge truth about ourselves.
- ♥ We are no longer fearful to be known by each other.
- ♥ Speaking and showing, plainly and clearly, how we are feeling is a fine way for us to have intimacy.
- ♥ We speak directly, distinctly, and explicitly.
- ♥ We are leaving behind ambiguous, dubious communications.
- ♥ Rather than imply or infer, we say exactly what we mean.
- ♥ Delivered without delay, we admit and acknowledge errors as well as put in corrections.
- ♥ Talking straight tells us who we are counting on and how we are doing.
- ♥ Concealments are confessed and opened to view.
- ♥ We are listening to each other and speaking to make ourselves and our loving clear.
- ♥ We enjoy certainty of being loved and accepted
  - as we really are...
  - instead of how we
  - imagine we are imagined.
- ♥ Loving kindness lives each day in our being together.
- ♥ Our power to communicate fully is expanding.

i create congruence

- ♥ today i look further... to create futures.
- ♥ i go beyond the outward appearance today ... my life is inspired and revitalized.
- ♥ i am not disoriented by events or circumstances.
- ♥ i have strength to stay with intended outcomes, a purpose to serve the future
- ♥ i repeatedly confront disorder, chaos, discord, endings, and conflict to bring about order, peaceful harmony, good results, and new beginnings.
- ♥ i create congruence with intention and action.
- ♥ i demonstrate persistence and courage.

stay coherent

Stay in coherence with the call of your heart even when it looks:
>unlinear
>illogical
>stupid
>wrong
>incongruent.
>even when it looks like you
>are dancing against what you want.

The Direction of South

Integrity is congruence

"HUMAN INTEGRITY *is the uncompromising courage of self-determining whether or not to take initiative to support or cooperate with others, in-accord with* ALL THE TRUTH AND NOTHING BUT THE TRUTH *as it is conceived by the* Divine Mind *always present in each individual*"

— Buckminister Fuller

♥ integrity is congruence.
♥ integrity is doing what i said i would do. people can count on me.
♥ integrity means showing up as who i am. . . . i am what i say i am.
♥ whenever i violate my ideals i don't allow my life to work. . . .
today i take out pretense. today, i put in being true.
♥ whenever i "sit" with pain or sadness,
i can move through by representing where i am . . . .
when i speak true, i move past obstacles.
i move past obstacles by speaking true today.
♥ i give up illusion, concealment and all pretense today.
♥ i keep my ideals intact even when it's uncomfortable.
♥ i say yes when it's yes. i say no when it's not. i tell the truth
when it's inconvenient.
♥ integrity is congruence.
when i lack integrity i am missing what's required to be myself.
i live as my ethical values and ideals today.
♥ i take a stand for what i represent.
♥ i am clear and public about my ethics.
♥ my inner drive and outer drive are aligned.
♥ i am honest and authentic in all that i say, feel, think and do. . . .
♥ i have an unwavering sense of authenticity.
i operate with ruthless compassion.
♥ i am author of the beliefs that advise my occupations.
♥ i am willing to be accountable for all that i do.
♥ i operate as a tight ship. i do complete work.
♥ i am sound, upright, honest. i have the sincerity essential to being.
♥ integrity is congruence is what i am . . .

Seasons of Prosperity

i speak true. i take a stand on myself

"if anything creative is going to show up in our lives and in the lives of those around us. . .not as an accident. . .not as a strategy but as real action, it will only show up by the stand one takes for its possibility."
— Werner Erhard

- ♥ i know what's so. i tell truth. i say what's so ...
- ♥ my confidence comes from taking a stand on myself rather than on circumstances.
- ♥ i say what's so, up front and clear.
- ♥ i go beyond compromising and adjusting truth to be popular.
- ♥ i am willing to confess withholds, deceits and betrayals.
- ♥ i see what's so and say what's so.
- ♥ i am willing to forgive, therefore i can be forgiven. . . .
- ♥ the people around me, remind me to be clear in all speaking.
- ♥ i let go of allowing failures to influence the stand i've taken on myself.
- ♥ i know the difference in what's so and, what i wish were so . . . i talk straight.
- ♥ i am capable of fulfilling my purpose by being true and staying true each day in every way.
- ♥ i serve high purpose with time and resources today.
- ♥ i tell truth. i live in true ways today. I say what's so ...

the serious thing

"The challenge is to keep searching for our values, to examine our own judgments of excellence and see how we can honor them."
— Anonymous

- ♥ the serious thing i recall today, is that every crime against my-own-nature, will record itself in my own unconscious and disempower me.
- ♥ i am as good as my word. i direct life based on my ideals.
- ♥ today i remember the value of a simple, good life.
- ♥ i show up each day with less pretense and more compassion.
- ♥ my heart beats in response to noble ideals
  i am willing to speak in coherence with what i know to be true.
- ♥ i no longer try to please everyone else. i am as good as my word.
- ♥ i take initiative and cooperate with others, in agreement, with what i know to be true...
- ♥ i am faithful to my own value system.
- ♥ i am doing with my life all that i know i can do.
  i'm happy to be feeling honest, fine and good.

The Direction of South

life is no longer a popularity contest
Prayer of a Consultant or Advisor

*"Every real thought on every real subject knocks the wind
out of somebody, or other."*
— Oliver Wendall Holmes

God, the contribution i am to people
is not always compatible
with the wish i have
        to be admired
        to be liked
        to be thought well-of.
This does not determine my range of interaction.
What determines my interactions
is the highest good possible
in each given situation.

my heart is true
        — *adapted from* Psalm 26

i have trusted in life.
i walk in integrity.
my heart is true.
i do not join in, with those who take life apart.
i can be counted on to keep putting life together
with the voice of thanksgiving   .
i tell everyone, about wondrous works
        and miracles i have seen.
i walk in peace with good humor.
my life is used for good works and honor.
i walk past the company of the arrogant
        and those who are not
             standing in an even place.
i bless life.
i bless creatures.
in groups of people
i am not afraid to be
known as i am.

achieving leadership

- ♥ i am a stand for the success of others
- ♥ i earn the responsibility of leading, by serving.
- ♥ i understand to lead is to follow the call, of serving others.
- ♥ serving others is my spiritual practice
- ♥ my life makes a difference in lives around me.
- ♥ everything achieved, i am willing to share...
- ♥ people give permission to lead, because they are served.
  i can only lead in circumstances, where permission is given.
- ♥ my leadership comes from the permission of those around me.
  leaders are the same as everybody.
- ♥ serving others is uncomfortable and demanding.
- ♥ it's more important that people's lives work
  than it is for me to be "popular" in every moment with them.
- ♥ i see that everyone demonstrates
  my own admired, and disowned qualities.
- ♥ i am willing to do what i said i would do.
- ♥ i am willing to have others do what they said they would do.
- ♥ i take actions that are answers. i dash forward to do what's mine to do.
- ♥ i learn from those who give me permission to lead...

it's possible

- ♥ it's possible, all good is possible, yes, it's possible.
- ♥ **there is no situation, situated outside of possibilities.**
- ♥ apparent discords come undone, in the face of possibility.
- ♥ thinking about situations in terms of good, is my right and privilege.
- ♥ impossible things happen everyday.
- ♥ i move from discouragement to expectation.
- ♥ i move from hopelessness to certainty.
- ♥ in the vast patterns of harmony and happiness
  small pockets of resignation, have limited power.
- ♥ ample proof is plenteous that Infinite Possibility exists.
- ♥ i shift my point of view, to remind me
  of the promise, **that all things are possible**.
- ♥ the law of good is always at work.
  i can choose good thoughts of possibility, and progress.
- ♥ possibility depends on what i am thinking and feeling...
- ♥ happy resolution is always possible.

committed

Until committed
there is, still a chance, to withdraw,
to take myself away.
> **today i put in commitment.**

In acts of initiative (and creation)
i commit myself, to a "named result".
Providence moves too, on my behalf...
> **today i put in commitment.**

All sorts of things occur to help me when i commit myself.
A whole stream of events issues from my promise,
raising all manner of meetings and junctions of possibility.
My declarations of commitment, empower outcomes.
Whatever i can do, i begin it now...
My boldness has genius, plus power to move life
in the direction it was already headed.
i commit myself unconditionally today.
This is good.

powerful purpose is mine

- ♥ i have a new way of being consistent
  and congruent in thought, word ,and deed.
- ♥ my actions match my speaking.
- ♥ my speaking is in affinity with what i feel.
- ♥ i have a posture of being accountable.
- ♥ people can count on me, to be the way i said i would be.
- ♥ i have reliable patterns of character.
- ♥ i keep my word. i do what i said i would.
- ♥ i am in the habit of being on purpose.
- ♥ random feelings, do not direct my day.
- ♥ i am willing to eliminate what doesn't work.
- ♥ i quickly rid myself of obstacles to achievement.
- ♥ i renounce old habits
  that are obstacles to new accomplishment.
- ♥ powerful purpose advises all my actions today.
- ♥ i am successful in all outcomes.

... EVER READY HAPPY

this is completely good

- ♥ i express life everything around me expresses life.
- ♥ my styles and patterns, of looking at patterns,
  tell me what it is i see! today i see good.
- ♥ i am the judge and jury on what i see.
- ♥ **whatever i say i see, is what i see.**
- ♥ **only i, can say, what it is that i see.**
- ♥ **i am the author of what i say i see.**
- ♥ no one else can tell me what, i have to see.
- ♥ i see, only what i desire to see, in all experiences.
- ♥ what i see, emanates from me.
- ♥ i call the shots, on what i am perceiving.
- ♥ what a wonderful day this is...this is completely good.
- ♥ today i say that   everything i see is good
                       everything i see has good
                       everything i see provides good
                       everything i see restores good
                       everything i see assures good
- ♥ it is possible to reinvent whatever i see as i am seeing it.

Seasons of Prosperity

true satisfaction of together

- ♥ together is all there ever always was or is....
- ♥ there are no solitary creatures, interdependence is the law.
- ♥ life is a collaboration
  i am part of, and inhere in, collaboration.
- ♥ everything is an accommodation.
- ♥ everything gives with and to, everything else.
- ♥ all of life is exchange.
  exchanging is all that's ever going on,
  i am part of and inhere in, that exchanging.
- ♥ everything is on-going-conversation.
  i am part of, and inhere in, that conversation,
  all fused into consortiums of colors and patterns
  ...everything is ongoing patterns.
  i am part of, and inhere in, that patterning
- ♥ real satisfaction is a satisfaction of <u>usefulness</u>...
  to the degree that "my life" is useful to,
  or makes a difference in the life of others...
  there is true satisfaction.
  anything else is a dream of hope...
  that entangles me in self concern.

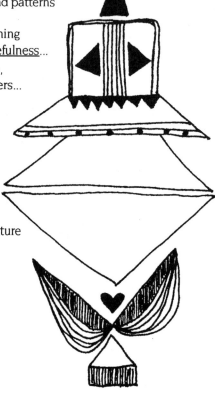

what's mine to do is done today

- ♥ i complete what i start. yes i do.
- ♥ my disciplines are crisp and offer structure
  to the plans for a productive day.
- ♥ life, is to do, what's mine to do.
- ♥ each day i create further energy
  by finishing things i started.
- ♥ work is wrapped up fast,
  purposefully and with rigorous cheer.
- ♥ i am capable to respond
  to what needs doing...
  i am responsible.
- ♥ i get in union with committed others.
  i have plenty of good company today.

The Direction of South

practicing love in everyday living

*"True love is no game of the faint hearted and the weak;
it is born of strength and understanding."*
— Meher Baba

- ♥ Today we live in co-operative community.
- ♥ This is not merely a social ideal, it is a unique, specific form of self transcendent practice. We embrace this for today.
- ♥ Transcendence is the function of community.
- ♥ Too long we have been concerned hour by hour only for ourselves.
- ♥ Today we live, looking to see what's required for all around us, not only for the self.
- ♥ To live co-operatively requires leaving behind doubts and concerns as the focus of each day's activity... or every moment's circumstance.
- ♥ We serve each other in the moments of today.
- ♥ We leave behind chronic states of tension.
- ♥ We leave behind reactive emotions.
- ♥ We leave behind bodily tensions.
- ♥ We leave behind mental concerns that possess us.
- ♥ We leave behind self-possessed defenses.
- ♥ Today we are relaxing and feeling beyond our thoughts.
- ♥ Co-operative community is our magnanimous expression.
- ♥ To serve all people is to serve ourselves.
- ♥ The world we are, is only one people...

Seasons of Prosperity

apprentice in always loving

> "Marriage is a simplification of one's way of life...
> ...union naturally combines the forces and wills of two, so that together they seem to reach farther into the future than before... marriage is a new task...a new challenge to and questioning of the strength and generosity of each partner"
> — **Rainer Maria Rilke**

- ♥ i have the willingness for conscious love today.
- ♥ a Warrior of the heart, is how i am...
- ♥ i am willing to be helping to nurture someone's growth without clinging to a particular outcome.
- ♥ i am successful at loving.
- ♥ i am letting go of preconceptions about relationships.
- ♥ i am learning tuning-into-what-is-appropriate, with my partner, in given situations.
- ♥ i have patience and perseverance. i see love evolving...
- ♥ i have an expanding basic trust, in creative powers of the universe, at work with us.
- ♥ partnerships are no longer private affairs.
- ♥ i renounce everything that keeps us from being available to others, in our partnership.
- ♥ i am giving up my private hiding places and exposing vulnerable parts of myself to be known more...
- ♥ we have a wonderful living side by side based in the gratitudes and appreciations we hold for each other.
- ♥ mutual esteem exists in our coming together.
- ♥ loving is strong and can be counted on...
- ♥ surprising changes do not frighten us in our partnership.
- ♥ to bear love and to learn love is our task. we accept it in gratitude and happiness.
- ♥ peace, patience, composure and negotiation go with us in our ever present will-to-apprentice-ourselves-to-loving, always loving.

partnership

- ♥ i express love everywhere.
- ♥ i express love in partnership.
- ♥ i can be counted on to always love.
- ♥ my partners can depend on me today to serve them.
- ♥ i practice love over and over again forever.
- ♥ love lives with me and as me.
- ♥ i practice cultivating magnanimous thoughts.
- ♥ i leave behind the tendency to selfish states of mind.

♥ i care for all other human beings.
♥ i can be counted on to express devoted and enduring love.
♥ everyone's welfare is as important to me as my own.
♥ i recognize my partner's life to be as important to me as my own.
♥ i support his/her efforts to discover and live true to the highest and best,
and i accept his/her support to discover and live true
to the highest and best within myself.
♥ i speak truthfully and openly...
> i keep my word...
> i act with courage...
> i serve with grace.
♥ i am helpful, kind and compassionate.
♥ through the love, direction and energy released by our union we continually make contributions in each other's lives, and to all those around us.

our activities together help us to know ourselves

♥ Loving the Divine is impossible if i don't love others.
♥ The purpose of being together is open communication and understanding.
♥ Partnerships that work require my attention and continual thoughtfulness.
♥ Happy relationships happen as a constant unfolding process.
♥ The process of relating is never all finished, it goes on.
♥ As we grow in friendship and love
we are increasingly of more service to each other.
♥ Our activities together help us to know ourselves
and assist us in making the Divine Will manifest.
♥ Our interactions call forth Divine qualities more and more.
♥ We respond in relationship with spontaneous gifts from the heart.
♥ We are confessed and revealed with each other even when we don't want to be.
♥ The more we know each other, the more we see ourselves.
♥ Our humor is expanding everyday. We laugh a lot...
♥ Appreciation is rooted in loyalty and love. We love finely.
♥ Whatever we distrust in each other, we don't trust in ourselves.
Our relation is a mirror.
♥ Our blueprint for being together is a fine self-appointment in self-realization.
♥ Whatever we don't like about each other, we haven't accepted in ourselves.
♥ Mirroring each other is a great self awareness exercise.
♥ Sharing thoughts and feelings enhances our understanding.
♥ Our appreciation is shown by thoughtfulness,
service to each other and remembrances.
♥ We often think of each other with Great love.
♥ Our activities together have us know ourselves.

Seasons of Prosperity

Commitment

♥ I realize that creation does not take place where energies
   are scattered and dissipated ...
♥ i move in great wisdom to commit myself to what i intend to create.
♥ i see that creation requires a gathering together of energies ...
♥ i see that creation requires a focusing of power and attention
   within a circle of commitment.
♥ i make commitments that are true to my real being
♥ i place commitments in my life to guide myself
   i have considered wisely how to use powerful energies.
♥ i draw the sacred circle of commitment around my energies.
♥ my purpose in life is the basis of all my commitments
♥ ... around my ways,
   i draw the sacred circle of commitment.

love: affirmations and denials

♥ Love is enduring. It does not come and go.
♥ Love is based on that i continue to practice love. It is not the egoic drama of being "in love" or "out of love" with an ideal that's been projected on another person.
♥ Love takes practice. It is not always so easy to be loving.
♥ Love knows change as a component of natural life.
   It does not demand a return to what's been.
♥ Love serves and affirms. It does not use others to gain what's desired.
♥ Love transforms mundane tasks into joyful service.
♥ Love is happy to do many things that ego is bored with. It is not airy fantasy.
♥ Love is a state of being. It is not something that is done.
♥ Love sees the goodness and the value of all people.
   It is not looking out for self-styled "needs".
   It is not calculating what the return will be.
   It is not affirming the small self and its desires.
♥ Love is generous. It understands giving as the source of all getting.

The Direction of South

- ♥ Love understands weaknesses and inclinations.
    - It does not avoid relationship in the face of them.
- ♥ Love gladly bears the shadow-side of the beloved.
    - It does not suffer at the "imperfection" of others.
- ♥ Love promotes winning. It is not resigned to appearances.
- ♥ Love is stable commitment to keep loving.
    - It does not collapse in disappointment.
    - It is not a worry called "Will this work out?",
    - It is not a concern named "Are you good enough for me to love you?"
- ♥ Love is a force that acts from within.
    - It is not something to get more of.
- ♥ Love is a flow that moves towards all others.
    - It is not a private partnership that excludes.
- ♥ Love never fails. It does not betray when it's convenient.
- ♥ Love sees frustrations and disappointment as temporary.
    - It does not demand security.
- ♥ Love alters the sense of self-importance.
    - It is not self-seeking or self-importance.
- ♥ Love is what we come from originally.
    - It is not what the culture has led us to expect.
    - It is not what the ego wants or demands.
    - It is not inflated ecstasies.
- ♥ Love is the power which transforms egoic tendencies.
    - It is not the embellishment of the small self.
- ♥ Love requires honest looks at self-deceptions.
    - It is not the fulfillment of childish illusions.
- ♥ Love meets difficulty with strength.
    - It does not run in fear.
- ♥ Love appreciates, empowers and believes.
    - It does not suspect the worst.
- ♥ Love looks further to see how others are experiencing life.
    - It does not insist on instant understanding.
- ♥ Love encourages independence. It is not clinging and possessive.
- ♥ Love accepts. It does not expect to be "made happy".
- ♥ Love looks to see what's intended and required.
    It is not obsessed with expectations.

Seasons of Prosperity

partnerships help me serve my purpose

- ♥ the happy heart is truly in partnership.
- ♥ partnership provides a place to blossom out in purpose and make a difference in the world.
- ♥ i am a stand for partnerships for me and those around me.
- ♥ in partnerships, purpose is strengthened and extended.
- ♥ a stand has a gathering impact. partnerships increase.
- ♥ i have peace-of-mind- and firm intentions in my partnerships today.
- ♥ i express spiritual qualities of faithfulness, love, and intelligence in partnership today.
- ♥ partnerships establish accountabilities for future resolutions and agreements.
- ♥ in partnerships we easily, quickly end bitterness and quarrels. where there was strife, we now have peace of mind and firm intention.
- ♥ there is plenty of opportunity for freedom and progress in partnerships.
- ♥ as i let go concerns and strategies, intimacies increase.
- ♥ my partnerships are a matter of love and the expression of love.
- ♥ in partnerships i serve people
- ♥ in partnerships i am enabled to serve my purpose.

partnerships serve human community:
declarations for possibility

- ♥ partners have simple, soulful, unfragmented ways of truth telling.
  more partners have open-hearted spirit to give and receive in bigger ways.
- ♥ partnerships build trust and a deeper sense of community.
  peace abounds in partnerships.
- ♥ more partnerships become unions
  standing for the vitality of EARTH eco-systems and the good of all people.
- ♥ problems are handled easily...problems that never
  seemed to resolve now get negotiated with ease.
- ♥ everywhere partners give up fear of failure.
  meeting adverse circumstances quickly with mastery.
- ♥ partners think of opportunity instead of security.
- ♥ partners open themselves to the resources of courage, and creativity.
- ♥ partners work for their partnerships and the whole human community.
- ♥ partnerships embody gentleness, courage,
  goodness, and understanding.
- ♥ in partnerships quiet time is set aside to think...
  people create opportunity to have revealing conversations.
- ♥ partnerships build trust and a deeper sense of community.
  peace abounds in partnerships.
- ♥ partnerships today are warm and friendly, full of love...
  individuals help each other when times are difficult.
- ♥ people in partnerships are finding that they don't have to
  wait to be "treated better" to be happy or feel good
- ♥ more remarkable people are in partnership
  committed to the whole living earth family.
- ♥ people give up thinking they can solve problems with ideologies alone
  instead they get into action, together with partnerships.
- ♥ people realize the joy that loving and serving brings. they recognize it as
  what they were hoping to get from someone else .
- ♥ limitless consciousness of eternal love is felt
  within all partnerships today.

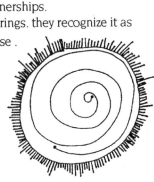

Seasons of Prosperity

wedding convocation

Welcome
to this bright circle.
Here today most wonderful
        and dearest of friends and family
        gathered in good cheer
        for a wedding in good company

We are not out of the reach of God's hand.
Here today in the brightness of day
        The LIGHT of God surrounds us
        The LOVE of God enfolds us
        The POWER of God protects us
        The PRESENCE of God watches over us
        Wherever we are God is.

The union of _____ and _____ is sacred,
not only because they come together to love God and live together
but because they become all they are capable of being,
by helping others become, all they are capable of being.
        The way of the heart does
        not exclude, it includes all others.

in the manner of the elders, of this North American land,
we stand ready to honor the way, of giving regard,
to the directions, before something sacred happens.

Honoring the directions of East, South, West, and North
is a way to appreciate the process
involved in the circle, of all, our lives.

Loving,
has seasons of starting, developing, harvesting
and becoming refreshed to begin again...

    (specific person reads the four directions)

we give thanks for this marriage day

We come together to celebrate and witness
the marriage of _____ and _____
it is with Gladness of Heart that
we join them in their joy
we join them in their gratitude for parents,
and all those, whose past contributions,
made them capable of great love
                        on this very brightest of days.

We join them in their resolve
to make public their promises
and live with us as a reminder
                        of GREAT LOVE at-work-in-the-world

we understand their union
as an extension of Love and
as a promise to the future

We give thanks
for the marriage of _____ and _____

We see them enriched in every way with wisdom,
consolation, and empowerment to keep on,
even in the darkest of days, with their
commitment to keep on Loving

Today on this very brightest of days
we wish them to be happy together
walking the way of the heart
sustained and strengthened
may they always have a deep faith in each other, and in the love of God.
May they walk confidently
protected from harm and confusion
delivered each day from doubt
                        ever sure of the wide-power-of-the-Heart

May
the Almighty
open paths to them
where before-there-were-none.
may every action be fair, may they think in kindness
                        ever sure of the wide-power-of-the-Heart

may
all those who walk with them
be uplifted also, on this very brightest of days.

Seasons of Prosperity

health today

- i dare to feel happiness.
- i am at ease, experiencing ease, free of dis-ease.
- i am feeling expansive and cared-for.
- i am free of bodily pulling back.
- discord is gone now... .
- i am free of reactive emotion.
- i am free of mental concerns.
- i am discarding ideas no longer desired for my happiness.
- i can relax beyond thinking...and i do.
- i renounce tightness, contraction and tension.
- i can change my state of mind...and i do.
- i have a complete state of ease even now.
- mind action is free of reaction now...i'm free.
- i attain and maintain ease with body, mind and emotions.
- body responds to mind untensing, in each moment.
- life evolves as a variety of great experiences.
- life evolves as a progression of new revelations.
- i can trust myself...i can trust all of life.
- energy surges forth freely in me... i am thankful.
- i feel incredible well being right now. i am grateful.

> FOR I WILL RESTORE HEALTH TO YOU AND I WILL HEAL YOUR WOUNDS...
> — JEREMIAH 30:17

dealing with disorders in body

i am participating in healthful disciplines
            as a body i remain free
            as a body i remain happy

healing is promoted
the organic systems of my body function in appropriate order
the root of problems are divorced from harmonious being.
body is healed when i submit to the condition
            that lives me and, by faith
            stand in the already-healed-state

i stand in non-problematic disposition
i am established in the intuition of the Divine condition.
changes in heart effect changes in body

internal structures of body and mind are revitalized by claiming harmony.
i investigate the habits i have that are affecting me in an undesirable way.
            natural approach to health inspires me
            i have intelligent assessments and choices

the same force which moves through my body,
            life and mind moves through this world
i am one with everything that appears
            true healing power is the force of life itself
i am aligned, in harmony with this great order

            healing is promoted
            health is maintained
            energy is maximized
            my attention is free.
            as a body i remain free.
            as a body i remain happy.

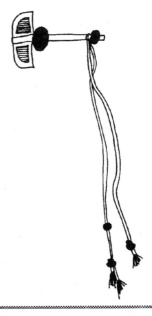

LIFE IS GOOD

♥ What is required
is always present.

♥ I PROMISE TO LOOK

♥ The moment there is a space
something appears to fill that space.....

♥ I PROMISE TO SEE ANSWERS.

♥ The moment there is a question
an answer occurs.

♥ I PROMISE TO HEAR ANSWERS.

♥ Whatever is empty
will always be filled....

♥ I PROMISE TO BE SATISFIED

♥ The moment there is a void
something appears to fill that void

♥ I PROMISE TO ACCEPT
WHAT'S BEEN GIVEN.

♥ I PROMISE TO BE GRATEFUL

The Direction of South

physical well-being

There is full wholeness in this universe...
Divine nature and Divine perfect action.
> i express this wholeness.
> our Divine nature.
> i express potential.
> and intelligence.

i enjoy being healthy.
anything that distracts my
attention to any negative thought of
disease or limitation
> is instantly dissolved
> in this awareness
> of true identity.

any appearance of disease is not really
   truth of my being.
i express perfect well-being today.
i express vibrant health in all
   aspects of physical being.

i rejoice in this great realization.
i give thanks for perfect physical well-being
> everyone and everything in my world
> responds to this awareness
> which i now embody.

i am now in an
atmosphere of
harmony, health
and love.

   i am fulfilling
   Divine intent
   and purpose.

   i let it be so.

NO GOOD THING WILL HE WITH HOLD FROM THEM THAT WALK UP RIGHTLY
-PS 84:11

©toni acker 82

Seasons of Prosperity

WELL BEING DECREE

Directions - Fill in the name of the person for whom you are decreeing. Substitute "she" for "he". Use this decree three times a day, morning, noon and night.

_____'s form is love. He heals rapidly. His current transforming is an act of love. _____experiences his revitalizing life force today. He is resting and relaxing in the Universal Christ presence. He is acquiring physical, mental and spiritual benefit... in the quietness and tranquillity of Being. He is attuning to the Christ of his being.
_____'s form is love. He releases all worry, tension and strain. He releases all failure. _____'s form is love. He leaves behind any ineptitude or lack of connection. _____ leaves behind any blockage of strength and power. Divine love permeates the body. Because his form is love, he is an open power source of great healing and peace. Being strong of will (synthesizing and organizing), all experiences are now illuminated... only Divine thoughts are now embodied in _____
... his form is love. His energy force field connects him each moment with perfect life of radiant health. He accepts health by Divine plan. The miracle of life is strong. _____'s form is love.
Inner reservoirs of fortitude and optimism are replenished.
There is the ability now to perceive all events with a clear, fresh outlook. Everything is okay.
_____hears the upward call of Spirit and responds...
He unites his heart, mind and body in the unfolding progression of good... wisdom radiates infinite light and healing.
It is felt, seen and heard everywhere in the body,
illuminating and fostering, continuing good form.
_____'s form is love. For this i do give thanks.

beauty is expressed: part two
- ♥ order is Heaven's first Law now and always. beauty is called forth.
- ♥ perfect balance, auspicious sequence and inevitable consequence are here.
- ♥ i celebrate what is beautiful all around me.
- ♥ i create beautiful life in all surroundings.
- ♥ i live day-to-day surrounded by wonderful designs and patterns.
- ♥ i give thanks, for all evidence of continual beauty,
  with me, around me and beyond me.
- ♥ beauty is easy to express and experience today.
- ♥ i acknowledge the Law of Beauty and Order,
  which always shows up in life, over and over again.
- ♥ whatever i praise and appreciate multiplies all around me.
- ♥ today i praise and appreciate, the many forms
  and functions of beauty everywhere present.

The Direction of South

I WILL TAKE SICKNESS AWAY FROM THE MIDST OF YOU.

—EX. 24:25

©toni acker 82

Seasons of Prosperity

decree of perpetual health
(use for self or others)

- ♥ i am eternally blessed with total health and constant well-being.
- ♥ i am fully involved with life and the living of all present moments.
- ♥ health is a function of participation.
- ♥ i have work to do and i am doing what's mine to accomplish.
- ♥ i participate perseveringly in my future.
- ♥ i give of excellence to all that i do. i feel good about myself.
- ♥ i participate sincerely, even when i'd rather withdraw.
- ♥ i am eternally blessed with total health.
- ♥ i give others the gift of my presence and purpose.
- ♥ i have life to live and i am living it in a true way.
- ♥ i live from love, life and abundance.
- ♥ peace is in my heart and in all my participating.
- ♥ the world changes for good wherever i am today.
- ♥ i am perpetual health and constant well-being.

> That your way may be known upon EARTH your saving health AMONG ALL NATIONS
> — PS 67:2

healthy thinking is mine

- ♥ i have a strong body and healthy thinking now.
- ♥ i welcome new ideas improving vitalization.
- ♥ what's always required for perfect health is revealed to me...
- ♥ my systems are in excellent working condition. i am grateful..
- ♥ awake to my highest good i am whole and complete.
- ♥ the course of action i have is true to my nature.
- ♥ expectations of good are strengthened.
- ♥ good exists in all situations, i see that now.
- ♥ when good seems hidden i know it will show itself subsequently.
- ♥ supporting influence and protecting power are at work with me.
- ♥ healthy thinking is what i have, perfect health is natural to me.
- ♥ nerves, tissues, glands and organs of this body are doing perfect work.
- ♥ i am renewed in purpose and direction by using good thoughts of health and harmony today.

The Direction of South

♥ i accept and use good thoughts as a gift. i wear them, like a coat. they protect me. i reject disturbing suggestions and replace them with good, productive thought.
♥ peace and power make appropriate movement happen in my body all the time. healthy thinking provides well being for me.
♥ appropriate thoughts are useable, tangible and protective.
♥ great goodness is the energy of my life and thinking.
♥ i demonstrate foresight, alertness and perceptiveness.
♥ my mind directs and sustains every good idea now.
♥ i am the active, healthy expression of well-being.
♥ guided and supported, my thoughts and actions come from highest ideas of harmony.
♥ i give thanks that healthy thinking is mine today . great goodness is the energy of my life and thinking.

healing is always available

"We carry a spark of the Divine within us"
               - Dr Edward Bach

♥ within each of us
the vital principle of life resides.
♥ this vital immortal principle
makes me more than just a body.
♥ my healing is hastened by remembering the vital healing principle of life. something greater and more wonderful than my body is true about me.
♥ i can be vitalized and strengthened.
fear, depression and doubt have no power over me.
♥ hopelessness has no power over me, unless i give it some.
♥ no malady, or diagnosis, has any power over me, unless i give it some.
♥ what's required is always present, possibilities are endless.
♥ i am grateful for herbs of the fields and healing measures.
                they provide for relief of discomfort.
                disharmonies dissolve today.
                adversity is absent now.
                moods are moved.
                bodies become well again.
                cures occur everyday, everywhere.
                healing herbs are ancient welcome remedies today.
                i am grateful for all kinds of cures and healing.
♥ healing is always available and accepted. we are aware of possibility.

Seasons of Prosperity

complaining is a thing of the past

- ♥ The way i look at things is undergoing great changes.
- ♥ i used to see what was wrong...now i notice what works.
- ♥ i point to what works.
- ♥ i praise what works.
- ♥ i acknowledge good and the good increases.
- ♥ i am happy that...whatever i praise and acknowledge increases.
- ♥ today... my speaking acknowledges the good.
- ♥ my impulse to correct is disappearing.
- ♥ my impulse to gratitude is increasing.
- ♥ i feel grateful everyday, in many ways.
- ♥ i thank people. compliments are easy and plentiful
- ♥ complaining is a thing of the past.
- ♥ i no longer look at and notice what i want to leave behind.
- ♥ no complaint is my new way of living.
- ♥ the good increases.

about relationships

- ♥ now that i know me better,
  i can communicate better.
- ♥ i am growing more secure
  in my communications
  and my preferences.
- ♥ i say what i mean.
- ♥ i have honest relationships.
- ♥ suppressed feelings
  are being revealed
  to me now
  and i know
  how to release them
  in the best way for me.
- ♥ i enjoy being alone now.
- ♥ i enjoy being with others now.
- ♥ i know how to choose wisely.

The Direction of South

about enrolling

- ♥ i am the space of enrollment.
- ♥ wherever i am, people are signing up to participate.
- ♥ people are eager to enroll themselves in opportunities.
- ♥ people are glad to be invited to join in.
- ♥ it is natural for me to invite others to the things i love doing.
- ♥ the way i speak forwards the action of enrollment.
- ♥ people are enabled, by speaking with me,
  to see what they really want to be involved in.
- ♥ i am listening and hearing.
- ♥ i hear people's interest rather than their stories.
- ♥ enrollment is easier and easier each day.
- ♥ struggle and burden are left behind.
- ♥ lightening up and signing up are showing up.
- ♥ i enroll people in life - because i am enrolled in life.

BEAUTY IS A WAY OF LOOKING
beauty is a divine expression

- ♥ i speak beauty and truth.
- ♥ i am thankful for beauty. i radiate beauty.
- ♥ beauty comes from within, the more i express my true self,
  the more beautiful i become.
- ♥ i see beauty in everyone, everywhere.
- ♥ i feel beautiful. i am beautiful.
- ♥ i concentrate on the beautiful and good.
- ♥ i am beautiful, i feel it, i show it.
- ♥ i am well-poised, graceful and radiant.
- ♥ i praise the beauty around me.
- ♥ beauty is a way of looking.
- ♥ i see beauty in everyone and everything.
- ♥ i radiate beauty, charm and grace.
- ♥ beauty starts, like a light glowing and flowing, giving me radiance.
- ♥ i am grateful for beauty that is represented through me.
- ♥ i think beautiful thoughts, i act in harmonious ways.
- ♥ i enable beauty all around me.
- ♥ through me beauty is represented.

Seasons of Prosperity

i know how to be with people

- being related is created ongoingly.
  it is always open and fluctuating.
- i break up coagulations of self concerns
  to be present with people today.
- i am present with the people
  in my circle.
- i am with people, no longer wrapped
  up in concerns that take me away.
- my absolute presence with people
  brings new spirit, to all encounters.
- what i say, is secondary
  to how i am being with people.
  people sense my presence
  with them, totally today.

thinking language

- to learn language is a way of organizing experience.
- our language is our organizing too.
- we make ourselves "known" with languaging.
- in languaging we <u>say</u> ourselves, we define ourselves.
- language develops and reflects values, expressing and clarifying thought.
- language holds signs and systems of symbols.
- we are influenced by our own speaking of ourselves, as well as
  the definition of ourselves given us, in the surrounding conversations.
- with language we know.
- language says how we know and how we'll live.
- with language we categorize and arrange knowledge....
  we discern and define. this opens possibility and crosses out possibility.
- language affects consciousness, our own and others, around us.
- with language we point to   perceptions
                                      comprehension
                                      feelings
                                      distinctions
                                      values
- language is a driving force. it mirrors reality in such a way that the limits of
  reality coincide with the limits of what can be said.
- we signal and orient ourselves and others with language.
- language establishes us in relationships.
- language shapes ways of thinking.
- the limits of our language, mean the limits of our mind.

The Direction of South

I COMMUNICATE BREAKS IN MY SENSE OF INTEGRITY

"who can separate faith from their actions,
or beliefs from their occupations?"
- *Kahil Gibran*

". . . give me beauty in the inward soul and may the outward
and the inward person be at one"
- *Plato*

♥ <u>i am responsible</u>.
♥ i have authentic response - ability.
♥ i am the ability to act and speak what i stand for ...
♥ when i see something important i am conscious about what i see.
♥ i cut thru confusion with clear "yes" or distinct "no". . .
♥ i communicate breaks in my sense of integrity.
  i get support to manage failures right away.
♥ i am concerned for the outworking of situations to expand truth .
♥ i give up secret deceits and hidden perpetrations.
♥ i confess and clean up mistakes, errors and concealments.
♥ promises are true and congruent with ideals.
♥ i stay on track to speak for and act about what concerns me,
  i no longer change the subject to avoid discomfort.
♥ false premise is dissolved, discrepancies are brought to light.
♥ i am discussing what's to be addressed authentically.
♥ i line everything up with what's intended, distractions dissolve.
♥ goodbye to substituting explanations for doing what i said i would do.
  goodbye to substituting reasons for doing what i said i would do.
  goodbye to substituting justifications for doing what i said i would do.
  goodbye to substituting circumstances for doing what i said i would do.
♥ today, i do what i said i would do!

i am awake and fully conscious now

- ♥ i am no longer trapped in any emotion, effort or thought.
- ♥ i can intentionally... create thought.
  continue creating thought.
  cease creating thought.
  create effort.
  continue creating effort.
  cease creating effort.
  create emotion.
  continue creating emotion.
  cease creating emotion.
- ♥ i come to full effort or full repose as i intend.
- ♥ i can revise and revive myself at will and i do.
- ♥ automatic reactions no longer drive me.

reactive responses no longer run me

- ♥ i no longer deny and withdraw from my future.
- ♥ i no longer represent the past for my future.
- ♥ i see that doubts and fears have no reality.
- ♥ i can contribute beyond where i used to contract and withdraw.
- ♥ i am no longer at effect of "i don't want to".
- ♥ i can examine and confront myself about my goals and limitations.
- ♥ i am no longer run by what i like or don't like.
- ♥ i can live beyond what i've already envisioned.
- ♥ i am no longer having to run from what no longer attracts me.
- ♥ i can build very real possibilities where fear used-to-live.
- ♥ my automatic reactive responses no longer run me.
- ♥ i have new power and abilities today.
- ♥ i have greater esteem and confidence.
- ♥ today i pursue what is urgent and important.
- ♥ all my unhappy programs are becoming obsolete.
- ♥ my future calls me forward happily from happiness.

saturday goodbye tensions

today
self destructive activities are left behind.
given structures which have bound me, break apart.
my chronically reactive emotional states are disappearing.
    chronic tension melts away.
      i live freely today.

i am no longer fixated in childish rituals.
i leave behind the acceptable frozen reactions
and stale mental patterns.
goodbye to the self-possessive drama of doubt.
              i redirect my reactions.
happiness in the highest sense is available. goodbye tensions.

this body is in perfect submission to Universal Intelligence

GOD is all... GOD is perfect pattern, authentic relatedness
functioning at the level of consciousness, as me.
Intelligence is all there is
    ONE INTELLIGENCE, ONE GOD, ONE UNIFIED FIELD

This body is in perfect submission to ONE INTELLIGENCE.
This body is in PERFECT PATTERN INTEGRITY
    a perfect instrument of Divine Love
    alert and quick to obey the soul
    moving instantaneously, with velocity,
    agile, awake, fine-tuned, able to serve easily.
This body is love in action, blissful, traversing great distances in record time...
    multidimensional, confessed, and revealed in every moment.
    The soul is not concerned with private achievements.
    The soul does not surrender to physical urges.
    The soul in perfect submission
    does the will of heaven in all circumstance.

This body is given over to the agency of the Divine.
There is now true acute silence in the mind of this body...
no contradictions, no conflict in action, no conflict in responses.

All negative mental images, records of pain or unconsciousness
    are now quickly dissolved, erased and given up...
    any waves of recording contrary to highest intention of
    the Divine Will, which have run voices, muscles,
    and parts of this body are now dissolved into nothing.
    Any interference to the Divine Will is gone, forgotten.
    Life and i are one, functioning at this level of consciousness.

This body operates 24 hours a day in perfect submission to One Intelligence.
The separate, small self-consciousness is dissolved now.

i give thanks that even since childhood the voice for GOD
    has been clear and intimate with me.
        Satisfaction is now the case...bliss is ever ongoing.
        i give thanks that this is the truth about me

These words are now released...they do not return void.
    These words of truth do their work. It is complete.
    This body is a perfect instrument of divine love.
        ...and so it is!

i am of GOD therefore sustaining perfect partnership

GOD IS ALL THERE IS, One Life, the DIVINE PATTERN.
i am of GOD therefore sustaining **Perfect Partnership**.

GOD is truth, power, life. i feel and know today
        the truth and power of DIVINE PATTERN.
Its government is Intelligence... Its laws are Intelligence, acting as laws.
Everything in the visible world is attached to an invisible pattern which is perfect,
Absolute and Universal. Everything is an extension of the DIVINE PATTERN.

i am never disconnected in any circumstance.
    DIVINE PATTERN permeates and transcends this world.
    There is nothing opposed to GOD
                DIVINE ORDER
                Ever present
                Ever active constantly creative in maintaining
                and sustaining
                PERFECT PARTNERSHIP
                in tangible form.

There is always conscious, intelligent sensing
    and feeling of DIVINE PRESENCE
    in which i have complete confidence. DIVINE PATTERN is ever present as
active agent in ongoing creation; forming, developing, making, breaking,
reforming alliances and structures, completing
and reshaping commitments for further evolution.
                SYNTROPY PREVAILS...
                DIVINE PATTERN rules.

Love, truth, beauty, power are now consciously active in all affairs
everywhere, at all times with no exception.

DIVINE PATTERN establishes in me a sense of peace,
a sense of belonging, a feeling free from fear.
                DIVINE ORDER
                DIVINE PATTERN,
                DIVINE COMMUNION manifests now as circumstance,
                action, progress and PERFECT PARTNERSHIP now.

This treatment is released... its good does not fail.
    i am sustaining Perfect Partnership.

Seasons of Prosperity

i live as a success story today

> " our plans miscarry because they have no aim. when a man does not know what harbor he is making for, no wind is the right wind."
> — *seneca*

♥ as my commitment in life gets bigger i am able to go past feelings of fright and emptiness. . .i am fully engaged in life.
aimed in my true purpose, i stay on course
♥ i am engaged in what dignifies being alive. . .
my response to life is to be enrolled for the possibility of all those around me.
♥ i am willing to leave behind what dramatizes my personality.
i am overcoming obstacles to true purpose.
♥ reliable patterns of accomplishment are established with me now.
i am willing to go past thoughts that new risk is too difficult and i do that!
♥ i work and create for the next seven generations.
my commitments are bigger today.
♥ i have the attention required to be accountable for my tasks today.
i have determined optimism. i live as a success story in process.
♥ i no longer look somewhere else to see what the outcome will be.
i live as an outcome in progress.

---

growing to more good

♥ i develop forward to more fullness of good.
♥ unlimited good is a growth process at appropriate speed.
♥ growth accelerates, i actively understand its phases and cycles...
♥ inner growth comes before outer results... i allow time to move patiently and happily in my own process of prospering.
♥ thoughts and feelings abide in good. i train thinking into expressions of good. the more good i talk about, and think about, the more good i have.
♥ i grow into greater good each day even when it looks all kinds of ways.
♥ as i condition mind to the possibility of greater good it is brought forth.
♥ in appropriate right perfect timing good occurs...
the longer i seem to wait, the better results are...
♥ i am experiencing more good than ever before. i notice my increasing gratitude. the more gratitude i have, the more good i have...
♥ i am willing to continue to grow into more good results.
♥ i grow into good in natural timely ways.
♥ growth is a spiraling process through seasons and cycles of increasing good.
♥ i am grateful for all good results around me.

goodbye anger

♥ there is peace always available.
♥ today i choose peace instead of anger.
♥ goodbye to unhappy mind and its anger.
♥ when disturbing thoughts arise,
> i recognize them as happening .
> i remember their shortcoming .
> the great problems of anger are no longer my choice.
> i practice the graduated path of patience instead.

♥ thought transformation is within my very available power.
♥ tranquility, relaxation and happiness are excellent choices.
♥ warm hearted loving ways of looking are always available to me by choice.

patience for today

♥ anger drifts away from me.
♥ by calming inner voices,
> i am able to achieve a quiet heart.
♥ any need to defend myself is gone.
♥ restless forces pass me bye.
♥ my mind is humble and free,
> i am what i was created to be...
♥ i take my inner gaze off problems now.
♥ i give up my right to criticize myself and others today.
♥ goodbye to doubtful, fearful images in mind.
♥ i cease to focus attention on concerns today.
♥ i have moderate and just views of everyone.
♥ i am capable of noble hearted keeping still.
♥ i persevere with what i know is true and good.
♥ the correct way will work. i have assured outlooks.
♥ i bring my heart to rest
> and attain a higher level
> of tranquility today.
♥ all anger drifts away from me, i am free.

Seasons of Prosperity

THIS DAY IS A DAY OF GOOD NEWS

— II KINGS 7:9

© toni acker 82

the litany of disappointment

- every thing, person and situation is a disappointment.
  it's a matter of time eventually.

- **disappointment is okay and i am still happy...**

- disappointment is innate in all experiences.
  the greater the determination, the more disappointment.

- **disappointment is okay and i am still happy...**

- to see there is nothing that i really "need"...
  this makes attractive the possibility of detachment,
  otherwise, detachment would be terrible punishment.

- **disappointment is okay and i am still happy...**

- can i be happy in the face of
  such great disappointment? yes i can.

- **disappointment is okay and i am still happy...**

- to the reactionary egoic mind, there is only, disappointment.

- **disappointment is okay and i am still happy...**

- i can determine life is about being happy in the middle
  of all circumstances, even disappointment which is innate in life.

- **disappointment is okay and i am still happy...**

- it is possible to be prosperous, have goals, intentions
  and continue happily in the face of all disappointments.

- **disappointment is okay and i am still happy...**

- yes, everything changes and it's perfect.

- **disappointment is okay and i am still happy...**

- i am fully engaged in all that life offers...

- **disappointment is okay and i am still happy...**

Seasons of Prosperity

i know what to do and i do it!!!

- ♥ i act for what is good and true.
- ♥ i am created to achieve results with enjoyment.
- ♥ i experience the power to cause events.
- ♥ my attitudes are affirmative in every way.
- ♥ i leave behind all fear and doubt.
- ♥ i have the power to go beyond attack and lack and i do...
- ♥ i move forward through all circumstances with enthusiasm.
- ♥ i am fulfilled and satisfied.
- ♥ i act for what brings peace and progress.
- ♥ i know clearly and specifically what i want to produce.
- ♥ i know what to do and i do it.
- ♥ i have the power to go beyond ingratitude.
- ♥ i act for what i intend.
- ♥ i do what must be done by me.
- ♥ Miracles assist me wherever i go.
- ♥ i achieve the impossible with ease.
- ♥ i am guided in ways of good choosing.
- ♥ i have an innate increasing sense of happiness.
- ♥ i encourage others. i empower others. i appreciate others.
- ♥ i move confidently ahead to bring more good to this world.
- ♥ my actions support goodness.
- ♥ i am divinely employed, full of enthusiasm moving into new ways, new directions, new information.
- ♥ i act for what i intend now... i know what to do and i do it.
- ♥ i am an integrating force for good. i do only what supports good.
- ♥ i say only what introduces good, truth, beauty, and love.
- ♥ i complete tasks which i've started
  and continue to move forward
    to begin new actions
  empowered by those accomplishments.

The Direction of South

i am discipline

- ♥ i am habitually on-purpose.
- ♥ i have attitudes of attentive concentration.
- ♥ i produce complete work and complete working.
- ♥ perseverance is my way-of-going.
- ♥ i refuse what i do not desire.
- ♥ i refuse what is no longer useful for my intent.
- ♥ i choose peace over conflict in each moment.
- ♥ i am willing to be without what i don't need anymore.
- ♥ i erase erroneous thought patterns easily.
- ♥ i know how to do what is required for successful accomplishment.

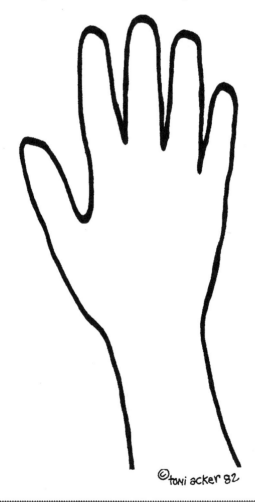

©toni acker 82

Seasons of Prosperity
about "bad habits"

- ♥ i appreciate habitual patterns, they help life work.
- ♥ habitual repetitive patterns are part of all life and are necessary .
- ♥ today, i promise to see which daily patterns serve me well.
- ♥ today, i promise to notice which daily patterns do not serve me anymore.
- ♥ i declare i am aware now of effects and outcomes of my habits...
  paying closer attention to daily patterns awakens
  appreciation of who i am being today...
- ♥ understanding "bad habit" behaviors opens up <u>new possibility</u>
  to have important requirements met.
- ♥ i give up harsh inner criticisms and replace them with inquiries
  to understand behaviors...and have requirements met.
- ♥ most "bad habit" behaviors are designed to keep the <u>future me</u> from doing
  anything that would be too scary to the current me. "bad habit" behaviors
  keep me from making bigger decisions, taking on more responsibility.
- ♥ i can be curious about who i can become
- ♥ i increase faith in my <u>future self</u> by risking, playing and experimenting.
- ♥ i can play with <u>who i can become</u>.
- ♥ i can afford to fail sometimes as i work on changing behavior patterns.
- ♥ my attempts to bring <u>new behaviors forward</u> will bring up parts
  of myself i haven't wanted to have to deal with...
- ♥ i have the courage to be with, all that i am ...
- ♥ i am capable of inquiry, experiment and new stands.
- ♥ my attempts to widen inquiries are experiments.
- ♥ experiments are not tests of character.
- ♥ when experiments fail, they can be redesigned
  in different fashions and circumstances.
- ♥ awkwardness, anxieties and sadnesses are proof that i am changing...
  they are not evidence to retreat to familiar "bad habit" behaviors
- ♥ "bad habit" behaviors are treasures to be opened
  and appreciated for what is hiding inside them.
- ♥ "bad habit" behaviors call our attention to some part of our lives
  that is unlived and unexpressed. this is valuable information.
- ♥ underneath a "bad habit" behavior is an unleashed stalled energy
  that wants to get active.

The Direction of South

i complete what i start

> "the single biggest time waster in the world
> is not completing what you start. ."
> — *john garner*

> " as i grow older, i pay less attention to what people say.
> i just watch what they do."
> — *andrew carnegie*

- ♥ i create energy by finishing what was started.
- ♥ i finish and complete projects with spirit today.
- ♥ i do what i say i will do. it reflects a congruent world back to me
- ♥ when i do what's mine to do the world
  appears to me as amenable to my intentions
- ♥ anything seems possible when i do what's mine to do . . .
- ♥ when i show up as worthy of trust, life appears trustworthy
  and harmonious to me
- ♥ i feel good about myself when i do what's mine to do. . .
- ♥ mouth and mind are aligned with action now
- ♥ whenever i am true, i feel other people are trustworthy too
- ♥ it's worth doing what-i-must-do, to play true today
- ♥ ideals which operate in me, are a natural part of my world

cancer declarations

i declare
that through the power and mighty presence of the Divine within, i am a great contribution to the people around me... i seldom fail to achieve my goals. i am supersensitive to feelings and i know how to take care of people. my skill in nourishing others brings great empathy to my close relationships. i give help and reassurance easily.
i never stop loving. my powerful imagination creates refined atmospheres as caring environments for others. i am a true protector.

i am successfully learning:

- ♥ to let people understand me
- ♥ how to have many relationships at once
- ♥ to say yes or no quickly and wisely
- ♥ the happy art of starting over
- ♥ letting go of past attachments
- ♥ not to expect too much
- ♥ magnanimity

i am leaving behind:

- ♥ stubbornness
- ♥ excessive emotions
- ♥ exclusiveness
- ♥ selective giving only
- ♥ being a victim
- ♥ introversion
- ♥ fear of ridicule

leo declarations

i declare
that through the power and mighty presence of the Divine within, i am a great contribution to the people around me... i am vital with ever present optimism. i make decisions. i am practical and enthusiastic. i mold opinion around me. i am magnanimous and generous. i love being the center of attention. i give of time, money and energy without counting. Providence always moves on my behalf even when things appear darkest. i love drama. i set up policies. i manage with a strong will. i select goals and follow through to the bitter end. i am worthy to be in charge. i represent leadership and courage.

i am successfully learning:
- ♥ to enjoy repetition
- ♥ to allow compromise
- ♥ to hold my desire nature in check
- ♥ controlling by agreement
- ♥ to share leadership
- ♥ editing my impetuousness
- ♥ to lose the "respect" of others sometimes
- ♥ to take the emphasis off self-importance

i am leaving behind:
- ♥ grudges
- ♥ being smug
- ♥ arrogance
- ♥ inconsistency
- ♥ unapproachability
- ♥ over-confidence
- ♥ the desire to only be top dog
- ♥ being obstinate in discussion
- ♥ wanting people to think only well of me
- ♥ being jealous

virgo declarations

i declare that
through the power and mighty presence of the Divine within,
i am a great contribution to the people around me... i have very high standards... being a careful worker i have developed useful skills that help me manage effectively.
i love to work, i bring order out of confusion.
i represent analysis and discrimination. Serving is my key word.

i am successfully learning:

- ♥ mind must serve spirit
- ♥ to accept shortcomings, my own and others
- ♥ to discipline my mind's reactivity
- ♥ that being useful makes me feel good
- ♥ criticizing others creates bad feelings
- ♥ to create compassion
- ♥ tolerating "imperfection"
- ♥ to be joyful for no reason
- ♥ discrimination between the essential and the trivial

i am leaving behind:

- ♥ gossip
- ♥ worrying daily
- ♥ undermining conversations
- ♥ excessive expenditures
- ♥ narrowness of outlook
- ♥ being engrossed in trivia
- ♥ microscopic analysis
- ♥ avoiding "unattainable" goals
- ♥ the temptation to constantly judge others

Direction of the West

we honor
powers of the West.
white is the West. white is power.
West is where the sun goes down
    there is harvest
        release, and passing through.
West is where teaching happens.
Spirit speaks to us, foretells for us.
it is said Thunder Beings live in the West.
        life-giving-rains come from the West.
the gateway to the spirit world stands in the West.
    we shall all enter some day.
    we remember things are not
    the same forever. We remember that here,
    change occurs.
        what's been is gone, in the West.
thanks to Great Spirit,
for the wisdom of what's been.....
we give thanks for the rich abundant harvest,
and the creativity that comes from ending.
we practice gratitude, generosity and gathering
    which becomes receptivity
        to grace in the West.

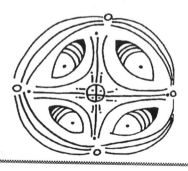

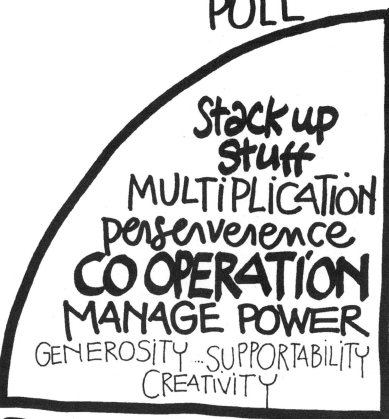

> AS LONG AS HE SOUGHT THE LORD **GOD** MADE HIM TO PROSPER ...AND, GOD HELPED HIM...
>
> — II CHRON. 26:5-7

The Direction of West

standing in the WEST
i give great thanks for the purification and protection
                        provided by the
                        Archangel Michael

this is where true power gets tested in results
i am grateful for all the people
           all the circumstances
           all the events
           that have brought me to the WEST
as i continually move in the circle of cycles

i am putting an end to what is no longer useful for progression
having and letting go happens here in the WEST
learning and renewing of the mind causes a change of state
the WEST is a working forward for me
i am empowered by underlying changes
the heat of changing is no longer avoided in the WEST
i am formulating: new cooperations
                        more generosity
                        the reciprocal action of receiving
                        allies to my commitments

i am renewed by innovations
i trust this process of inviting contribution and giving contribution
i feel grateful for powerful partnerships
           that help me see beyond circumstances
i am elated that endings are beginnings
                    and manifestation
                    of outcomes
                  is everywhere
                  in the WEST
there is perserverance for me in the WEST
this is the supportability time
          ...a time to request contribution
          ...a time to show up the way i am and let it be okay
          ...a time for what gets passed on to be passed on
          ...a time of integration with history and the environment
          ...a time for repeated distillations for higher elevations
          ...a time of internal commotions to assist further development

in the WEST
i ask:
       what are the benefits of group work vs. individual accomplishment?
       how does the heat of change bond me with new people?
       what characteristics help me be with others?
       what characteristics hinder me being with others?

Seasons of Prosperity

the west thinking

We are grateful.
You give us seeds and detachment
to delegate and teach the growth we've known
                         so everything continues to grow.
We call forth humor and patience to teach.
Bring us innovative partnerships.
Increase our generosity in our circle today.
We recognize the enthusiasm of generosity.
Facing WEST we have seen
How being supportable has taught
          us to share the harvest and release
what we no longer require in our lives.
The bright blaze of autumn
          accompanies us in introspective silence.
We reap well our lessons.
We teach what we've experienced on the way.

autumn - west

    using the model of four
seasons in nature, the sun appears
to set in the West... the later part of day
when colors get deep and bright before
dark, the sun appears to blaze a final goodbye.
this time is autumn. autumn represents West and harvest. getting ready for cold
but having warm days still , this is autumn...stacking up stuff...giving a lot
away...thicker fur...falling leaves...plenty of everything...more heat inside...
raking leaves, burning leaves, leaves for compost. change is constant in nature...
    adapt to changing, autumn tells us, say goodbyes,
the killing frost comes even if you are not ready.

The Direction of West

here approaches autumn of the circle...

    a time of ingathering, there is less activity
as summer passes over into harvestime,
days become subdued. light gets softer.
<u>processes slow down</u>.
except for evergreens, outdoor plant life decays.
bountiful harvest is gathered.
spontaneous gratitude is expressed,
reverence is offered to mystery.
the divine fructifying forces are
inspiring deep thanksgiving in creatures.
days are getting colder and bare.
solemn truths of unavoidable endings are everywhere.
thinking becomes easier and stronger.
protective rites are enacted,
evoking triumph over the forces
of decline and darkness...
is what's possible here.

the Western cycle is not such a popular one.
autumn is feminine in style. eliminating, contracting, drawing-in and delegating
are what's called for here because <u>the flag says STOP</u>!
people like to keep on going, once they get going.
in autumn fruits of labor are harvested.
<u>store. save and prepare</u> for winters return, each autumn.

West gives us detachment and with the ability to let go,
comes seed for next year. <u>we give the seed of what we know to others</u>,
thru teaching in this Westerly direction..

humor and patience to teach are required.
innovative partnerships stack up.
generosity in our circle expands.
we recognize the enthusiasm of generosity. we need it here,
to share the harvest and <u>release what we no longer require</u>.
the bright blaze of autumn accompanies.
in introspective silence, we reap our lessons
to teach what we've experienced.
although we have "seeds" for spring, they do not burst forward , yet...

Seasons of Prosperity

west is a time of:

- ♥ humility
- ♥ sacrifice for the future
- ♥ awareness of our own spiritual nature
- ♥ clear self-knowledge, spiritual insights, deep inner thoughts
- ♥ understanding for struggles of others
- ♥ perserverence and testing of will, at work
- ♥ teaching what's known to others
- ♥ management of power and delegating
- ♥ understanding of potentialities
- ♥ commitment to the path of further development
- ♥ commitment to assist the development of other people
- ♥ dreams and dreaming journals
- ♥ reflection and love for the CREATOR
- ♥ silence, contemplation and spending some time alone
- ♥ appreciation of the darkness, the mystery and the "unknown"
- ♥ establishing, construction and visiting sacred sites
- ♥ making ceremonies
- ♥ respect for elders

i have what it takes in the autumn

- ♥ i am generous.
- ♥ i have a posture of being eager-to-contribute, demonstrated by active giving.
- ♥ i have easy access to that position of "having plenty"...which is first emotional, then mindful, and finally practical.
- ♥ i am supportable.
- ♥ i have a way of being in frequent communication with allies to my commitment.
- ♥ i have a posture of co-operation.
- ♥ powerful partnerships are plentiful with me.
- ♥ i am creative.
- ♥ i am always able to see beyond circumstances.
- ♥ i am able to innovate.
- ♥ i am able to have unlimited ways to make new patterns.
- ♥ i have the ability to have increasing vision.
- ♥ i can disappear in collaborations and still source them happily today.

qualities to call forth in the west:

♥ generosity
   a posture of being eager-to-contribute, demonstrated by active giving and easy access to that position of "having plenty" ...which is first emotional, then mindful, and finally practical.

♥ supportability
   a way of being in frequent communication with your allies to your commitment which results in a posture of co-operation and produces powerful partnerships.

♥ creativity
   able always to see beyond circumstances...able to innovate...able to have unlimited ways to make new patterns, ability to have increasing vision which enables you to disappear in the collaborations and still source them.

prelude to forgiveness

♥ conscience guides me. i stand for this good.
♥ in me the power to forgive expands as i advance.
♥ i am seeing how to face making mistakes with equanimity, humor and understanding for myself as well as others.
♥ i no longer condemn with disdain or forgive with condescension...instead, i accept the "failings" of others with compassion, humility and identification.
♥ i continuously understand that to some degree we are all obstructed by mixed motives and a tendency to hypocrisy.
♥ today, i accept the good intentions of others.
♥ i work with people in the face of inevitable imperfect results.
♥ i stand for the good in each of us.
♥ i see that people are similar to me in all their ways.
♥ i put aside malice, intolerance and lack of realism.
♥ i always continue on, in the face of whatever good i see.
♥ my willingness to understand and stand by others is expanded to include even nations.
♥ i am grateful and happy to be forgiving.

Seasons of Prosperity

AN ANCIENT PROCLAMATION OF FORGIVENESS FROM CHINA

When one whom i have benefited with great hope
unreasonably hurts me i will learn
to view that person as an excellent spiritual guide.

goodbye to enemies

It used to be
that we had
friends to love
and enemies
to hate
but now,
we see that people we do not like
show us what that is...
in ourselves
that we have
disowned
and set apart.

Inevitably we have come to see everyone
as friend
especially today.

Today we learn to know ourselves better,
as we come to embrace all people
we no longer have
a sense of enemy.

Becoming aware of the all-loving nature of universe,
AGGRESSION GIVES WAY TO COMPASSION
Friendliness replaces a sense of enemy.
Barbed wire is gone, walls come tumbling down.
Shaking hands, hugging, being happy to be together
is what's happening now.

We are with each other in new ways,
ALL RACES, ALL NATIONS ONE.

freely and happily i forgive

♥ i affirm and fully participate with life around me.
♥ i forgive everyone and everything that has annoyed me.
  today i remain free and happy.
♥ i forgive the universe for all its playful changes.
♥ i hold onto nothing and no one in animosity anymore.
♥ i forgive all those who seemed to disappoint me.
♥ i forgive important, significant others who did what i didn't want them to do.
♥ i forgive all close relations for what i say they are and what i say they aren't.
♥ i forgive people for changing without asking me.
♥ i forgive some people for showing up.
♥ i forgive other people for not showing up.
♥ i forgive all the people who broke their word.
♥ i forgive all those who stay around for "no good reason".
♥ i forgive those who have passed out of present sight.
♥ i forgive "too much" and "not enough".
♥ i forgive circumstances for appearing in ways i have assessed inappropriate.
♥ i forgive Divine Order for not being "my" order.
♥ i forgive all the events i judged that came at the "wrong" time.
♥ i forgive all insects, animals, plants and weather conditions
  that did not immediately delight me.
♥ free and happy; i continuously
  forgive and am forgiven.

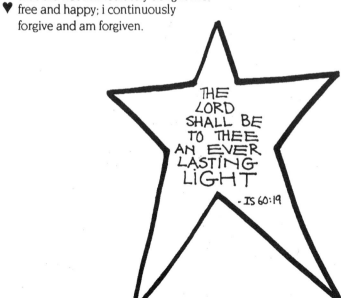

Seasons of Prosperity

peace with my parents

- ♥ i am the source of making peace with my own parents.
- ♥ out of the previous, comes the present.
- ♥ i am here by grace of my parents. i am grateful.
- ♥ **I HONOR MY PARENTS TODAY AND TOMORROW.**
- ♥ they did the best they could, all the time for me.
- ♥ even if they made mistakes, with limitations of their day and generation,
  they were doing the best they knew how.
- ♥ i know the power of spoken word. i speak good about my parents.
- ♥ **I LEAVE BEHIND CONDEMNING THOUGHTS AND CRITICISMS NOW.**
- ♥ i no longer discuss "the failings" of my parents. i honor them.
  they always did the best they could,
  with the limitations they had.
- ♥ parents and everyone, in their own way, travel on toward higher truth...
  in perfect timing evolving by design,
  their design, not mine.
- ♥ all that's previous is necessary to the new, no matter what...
- ♥ i am happy to let go of old grudges and suffering about my parents.
- ♥ i lift up, rather than condemn today. i declare gratitude.
- ♥ i give up trying "to fasten" mistakes on my parents, as realities.
- ♥ **I REALIZE THAT WHAT I CONDEMN IN ANOTHER IS WHAT I DON'T ACCEPT IN MYSELF.**
- ♥ today i lose sight of all my elaborate differences and divisions
  and become conscious
  of how similar i am to my own parents.
- ♥ i call forth good humor, great understanding and generosity
- ♥ i extend forgiveness, compassion and understanding
  to my own parents,
  and all parents in this moment.
- ♥ i find a brightness, within me, to extend everywhere...
- ♥ i am the source of what comes to me...generosity with
  my own parents attracts beneficent accord
  with my own children, all future moments.
- ♥ i extend grace, i am seen with grace.
- ♥ i treat others, as i intend to be treated.
- ♥ **I GIVE UP JUDGING, I AM NOT JUDGED.**
- ♥ i appreciate, i am appreciated.
- ♥ i love, i am loved.
- ♥ i understand, i am understood.
- ♥ out of the previous, comes the present...
  ...already declared, are things that are to come.

The Direction of West

end the old: autumn process

- ♥ to withdraw awhile is a fine circumstance.
- ♥ all problems pass bye in time.
- ♥ everything works together for good. all things change and pass.
- ♥ whatever has ended opens up a beginning.
- ♥ some beginnings exist before i even notice them.
- ♥ i am willing to see what is being revealed
    - in all disappointments
    - in all endings
    - in all seeming failures.
- ♥ i am willing to let go of negative views and distortions.
- ♥ new realizations are yet to come. i welcome them..
- ♥ there are always new options and possibilities.
- ♥ encountering fate can seem harsh, yet each event brings new wisdom...
- ♥ "workable ways" always occur to the open-minded.
- ♥ i am open hearted and open minded now.
- ♥ i trust progress has continuance.
- ♥ i know how to be still and practice equanimity, each moment.
- ♥ what i need to know, is now being revealed in the autumn process.

i let go of problems

- ♥ i stop emphasizing behavior that proves people are inferior.
- ♥ i look to the best in people and situations.
- ♥ i give up having problems as proof of aliveness..
- ♥ i give up thinking about how wrong others are.....
- ♥ criticism is left behind today.
- ♥ focusing on what i don't want more of, is over.....

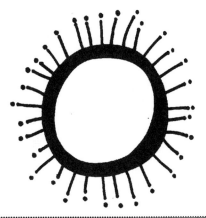

Seasons of Prosperity

i recognize and release resistance to changing

- ♥ i realize that always to do things the way i've done them is to stay the same.
- ♥ i have the idea of changing...
  i'm willing to start changing.
- ♥ i am able to have and receive new directions.
- ♥ fully aware and fully awake
  i disassemble structures that insure stagnation.
- ♥ i am living immediately without previous limits...
  no limits allowed, no limits exist!
- ♥ i follow new directions fearlessly to produce changes.
- ♥ no longer am i hesitant taking on risk...
  i recognize stops, they disappear.
- ♥ i invent and approve new experiences that evolve me to higher states.
- ♥ my vision reveals what's next for me...i am exuberant.
- ♥ i complete what's been, and move to what's not yet been...
- ♥ resistance dissolved...enthusiasm has replaced it...
- ♥ endings create new beginnings, forward into the process.
- ♥ i am ready to receive next directions.
- ♥ new directions, create new ideas as seeds for starting.
- ♥ i have the idea of changing.
- ♥ the processing for what's new has already begun.
- ♥ i retain full assurance in all that's falling apart....
- ♥ letting go of what's been, is good now, i can be sure.

release decree

i declare
That i will no longer be stuck with:

- ♥ what i think i should have
- ♥ what i have that i don't want
- ♥ what i think i can get instead of what i really desire
- ♥ what i think it's okay to ask for
- ♥ narrow views and useless conveniences
- ♥ what is no longer appropriate for me

The Direction of West

i promise to release everything and everybody that are no longer part of progress. without hindrance, i take on supreme insight and pure methods of freedom today. i declare that anybody who does not serve a perfect plan for my life now releases me and i release them. whatever does not serve me is released in ease, with equanimity. i am grateful.
everything moves forward.
there is great Happiness.

letting go, i let good come in, everything progresses. i welcome it.
i break continuums of habitual attachment. perfect plans unfold in Harmony, i cooperate manifesting good quickly.
i promise to recognize progress and follow guidance
step by step, no matter what....whatever was obstacle is out of the way
and forward motion takes it's place. this is very good.

intimate with everything

i am intimate with everything that's happening.
i AM ONE WITH THE FORCE OF LIFE
i open my heart, body and thinking to DIVINE PRESENCE now. i know that this living PRESENCE is active in every cell and in every function of all BEING no matter what anything looks like. there is no doubt or fear in my mind, nothing that rejects knowing i am one with, and within DIVINE PATTERN, right now. i easily move from patterns and habits that hinder. whatever is falling apart is no longer needed...from old thinking to new thinking i go now easily,
letting GO of old ways of being.
THE POWER AND PLAN OF GOOD IS FULLY IN ACTION, EVERYWHERE.

DIVINE PATTERN is revealed through all that is done.
i am forever moving forward into greater accomplishment and success.
I EASILY FACE EACH CHALLENGE THAT COMES MY WAY.
i am intimate and unafraid with everything.
i go through all appearances with victory.
i am a person of UNDERSTANDING.
the effort i put forth strengthens and makes me realize i can do anything.
i see possibility where routines used to be...
                         new insights are encoded...
                         new practices are established...
                         new structures are being sustained...

I GIVE THANKS, PERFECT ACTION OF DIVINE PATTERNING
is now taking place...
i TRUST process.

these words as CAUSE do their work...
in fact these words are already establishing perfect ACTION.

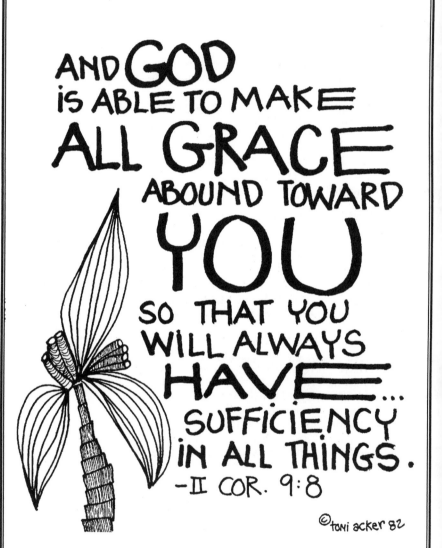

goodbye self pity

♥ i stand alert at the door of my thoughts now.
♥ i say goodbye to self-pity thinking.
♥ i know i am not held to negative habits.
♥ freedom of spirit is always mine.
♥ i give up feeling sorry and thinking sad thoughts.
♥ feeling sorry, even in small doses, is disempowering, i stop it.
♥ i am alert to my thinking and feeling process. i direct thought.
♥ self-pity finds no expression today. courage replaces fear.
♥ old patterns of pity fall away now...possibility exists.
♥ no longer bound by regret or bitterness, i act for what's next.
♥ i am thankful for this new found freedom.
♥ self-concern is replaced by concern for others. i serve people.
♥ i am grateful for good already received, as well as what's next.
♥ attention to gratitude is an empowering attitude.
♥ gratitude opens door s to more good.
♥ self-pity opposes gratitude, today gratitude prevails.
♥ i reject self-pity. i get engaged in life with others.
♥ Divine good is always ever present...it is my choice to notice it.
♥ today i notice the always present good news. i celebrate living.
♥ freedom of spirit is always mine. i accept it today.

the buck hollow declaration for surrender.

we surrender
this situation to the Divine
may we and our situation
be used for Divine purposes.
our disciplines
are strengthened.
our hearts
remain open
giving love and receiving love
            in all actions.
we prosper, we are prospered.
we declare that all results unfold
according to
God's will being done
        on Earth.
        we give thanks
        that this
        is now so.

The Direction of West

i know when to hold and when to fold:

LIFE operates for, through and as me. There is one life, that life is God's life and that life is my life now. i live and move and have my being as this life. This life knows exactly what to do and how to do it to make TRUTH universally evident. Innovation is natural . i do whatever is called for in endless demonstrations, rehearsals, and as many starts and attempts as are required to bring forth what's new. i have courage. i have vitality. i am the evolution of will that's required.
i am the passionate expression that easily takes on risk, without regret.
i RECOGNIZE MY STRENGTHS.
i compensate for any weakness.
i KNOW WHEN TO HOLD AND WHEN TO FOLD.

There is no resistance with me.
         no defenses stop me
         no opposition opposes me.
Innovation is natural to me, it is life and i accept,
the creative power of Infinite life, moving me forward.

i ACCEPT MY LIFE. I ACCEPT CHANGING
this word does it's work immediately,
i accept that right now. i am Grateful...
i know when to hold and when to fold.
i am always advised and guided going forward...
that's what's so.

give up being afraid and conflicted

♥ seeing what's possible replaces all conflicts certainly.
♥ today we have recognition of peace in our experience.
♥ we give up being afraid and conflicted, in the face of change.
♥ confused thoughts about changing are healed and given up...
♥ patterns we no longer wish to use
         now fall by the wayside...
         We are renewed by all manner of changes today.

relinquishment

♥ i relax and relinquish confusion. i choose to be happy now.
♥ i do not have to know "why" about one thing...
♥ i give up hidden scripts that hinder....
♥ my innocence is already established.
♥ i give up complaining, judging and assessing everything.
♥ i do not defend myself or explain anything else.
♥ i give up happiness-preventing scripts from past history.
♥ i do not have to find or search for anything more, i am happy.

Seasons of Prosperity

thursday: self concern gives way...

Today, i include in my intention all the people with whom i live and work as well as all the people for whom i live and work.
All my complaints are turned into requests.
Today self-concern gives way to looking out for others.
Demands never exceed abilities.

NOTHING IS WHERE EVERYTHING COMES FROM

God within and without, in us, as us, and with us, Divine being, contribute heart-powers to highest intentions for good, so that all those around us fulfill Divine destinies without wavering. May we transcend all illusion. As above, so below. May we express the joy that is, as we let go lack, limitation and suffering to come into possession of what we do not have.
may we go where now, we have nothing.
Nothing is, where everything comes from.....
This be the truth about us, now and forever.

mighty presence of God within

i am thankful to be heard
            extend to me the ability to comfort
            those in sorrow or in great need.

i am commited to making a difference because i am alive...
from the diamond shining mind of God,
wisdom and appropriate actions are intensified for greatest best use...
i continue to surrender my will to God's will, as an
Ambassador of Divine love, and compassion.
shine radiance through my being. inspired i can know how to be,
how to speak, how to act for the highest of good.

i am guided by the mighty presence of God within,
so that people are returned to remembrance of always power and presence.
my exercise of compassion is based on understanding
ever present Eternal Goodness. Source of All Good,
always expressing loving care for creation thankfully, dependably.
It fills time and space...good can never end.
in all humanity i am able to see the beauty of Divine design.
Good heals sorrow and creates harmony again.
Gentle Presence heals discord and establishes joy.

GOODBYE; remember me as loving you

- ♥ i set you free to find new good.
- ♥ i love you forever in whatever form i am or you are.......
- ♥ i am grateful for all the good you gave to me.
- ♥ i am thankful for the thoughts and times i had with you.
- ♥ i am dedicated to your everloving memory in me
  whenever i think of you, it is with love you can be sure.
  you are a treasure, in many ways, to me, i am grateful.
- ♥ remember me as loving you.
- ♥ i remember you as loving me.
- ♥ your love has sourced expansion for me
  and my open heart goes on to love even more.
- ♥ we are loving in different worlds now.
- ♥ may great love source your expansion
  in the worlds where you are now.
- ♥ may you have joyous experiences free from regret
  and sure of my memory of you, as loving me.
  i see you always choosing, the highest choices.
  remember me as loving you and being free.

of Prosperity

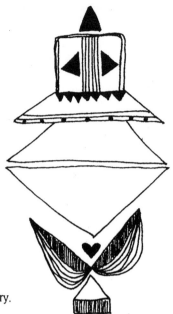

about the flow of money...

- i deserve to be prosperous and wealthy.
- i deserve to be paid and receive money.
- i let money pass through me without worry.
- the more i give, the more is given to me.
- i keep open about where i will receive money. i do not narrow my focus to certain people, places, situations or things.
- good comes from everywhere.
- i accept good with gratitude.
- i freely receive good and give good.
- good is here and now. i look for it each day.
  i do not hold it on reserve for future moments.
- i have all the money i need and more to give.
- i give now, trusting the flow to continue and it does.
- i am at one, the universe uncovers everything required.
- i feel friendly, loving and secure. fear is gone.
- my presence causes coincidences and happy surprises everywhere.
- cash flows through me into the world. it returns to me increased.
- i always continue to keep up giving. holding on is past.
- it is okay to have everything and be happy.
- the world is a beautiful place.
- i am a powerful being of light, my thoughts are bright.
- my wealth contributes, i am radiant and sparkling.
- i am financially successful. income exceeds expenses.
- the more willing i am to prosper others,
  the more willing others are to prosper me.
- every dollar circulated comes back multiplied to me.

abundant thinking

- ♥ every day in every way things are getting better and better.
- ♥ i am a new, vibrant person. i am geneous.
- ♥ i have a sense of mastery over all the circumstances of my life.
- ♥ i am more than worthy of my many achievements.
- ♥ sufficiency has given way to Abundance.
- ♥ miracles occur naturally everywhere that i am.
- ♥ i notice and give thanks for all miracles.
- ♥ i attract money continuously. it is amazing.
- ♥ money forwards my action with ease.
- ♥ money is now so abundant, it doesn't need to be counted.
- ♥ money comes easily to me each day.
- ♥ i am on time, time works easily for me.
- ♥ good ideas come to me, prosperous ideas are put into action.
- ♥ i dare to prosper now and i do. i generate abundance.
- ♥ my wealth contributes to all those around me.
- ♥ more and more i see there is always plenty.
- ♥ i continue to participate with people who think in abundant ways.
- ♥ all that is past is free to leave, i move ahead to what's next.
- ♥ all former fears have dissolved.
- ♥ enthusiasm and assurance increase each day.

Seasons of Prosperity

prosperity attitudes

- ♥ i start now, wherever i am, i am acting in prosperous ways.
- ♥ i appreciate and use abundantly the money i have right now.
- ♥ both my hands are open, to give as well as receive.
- ♥ i give freely now.
- ♥ financial transactions start with ME.
- ♥ i make voluntary offerings on a regular basis.
- ♥ giving is becoming a way of life for me.
- ♥ i give in small ways all the time, i tip extra, i pay a little more than my regular fare; i welcome the chance to throw in the extra something. this context opens me up to a larger context of giving.
- ♥ i know that MY supply increases through sharing, i share the thing i want most to get.
- ♥ i know the universe will do for me what i am actively doing for it... as i give, it is given to me.
- ♥ my attitude towards life is MY choice, i CHOOSE an attitude of abundance.
- ♥ the act of giving is freeing to my mind.
- ♥ generously i give and richly i receive...
- ♥ i have a systematic giving; a percentage of what i get goes back out in a voluntary fashion.
- ♥ i keep in touch with ideas, things and people that help me keep my PROSPERITY attitudes.
- ♥ i leave behind a feeling of being separated from wealth.
- ♥ i leave behind an attitude of lack.
- ♥ it is easier and easier for me to give away money.
- ♥ giving enlivens and empowers me.
- ♥ now that i enjoy giving, people love giving to me.
- ♥ i always have what's wanted and needed and more to give away...

prosperous thinking

- ♥ i know i cause the way i look at things.
- ♥ i break through barriers and limitations.
- ♥ i am responsible for what is in my mind.
- ♥ i am responsible for all my feelings.
- ♥ i am moving from scarcity to abundance.

The Direction of West

- ♥ i am moving away from holding back
  and moving toward pressing out expressing myself.
- ♥ money has been for survival
  ...money is now a way i am enabled to express myself.
- ♥ money has been what i try to get
  ...money is now what i always have.
- ♥ i shift the way i have held ideas of money.
- ♥ i choose new ideas about money.
- ♥ i joyously move from scarcity to abundance...i have consciousness of plenty.
- ♥ i am willing to leave behind all limits and venture forth.
- ♥ i leave behind unconsciousness in financial matters.
- ♥ i move into being responsible for my forward movement.
- ♥ i experience my self as cause of how it is for me.
- ♥ i am responsible for what's in my mind.
- ♥ thinking creates results, i think about what i intend.

prosperous declarations

- ♥ i say yes to prospering now .
- ♥ prosperity is my native, natural condition.
- ♥ excellent choices are now being made.
- ♥ good is always at work with me.
- ♥ good is constantly in mind, body and circumstances...as i prosper.
- ♥ wise abundance now surrounds me.
- ♥ i am cut free from all former economic limitation.
- ♥ abundance is now outpoured. opulence is the natural state of life.
- ♥ all humankind shall express prosperity.
- ♥ i grow in prosperity, wisdom and understanding.
- ♥ this world is alive with Divine prospering.
- ♥ God is the source of all my good.
- ♥ these words of truth now become form.

more money affirmations

- ♥ money is getting more and more comfortable for me now...
- ♥ i take risks with money and i win.
- ♥ i feel free to spend...knowing there is always plenty.
- ♥ money is always on the way to me.
- ♥ i am letting go thoughts of scarcity.
- ♥ i now have plenty of money.
- ♥ i am paid a very good income.
- ♥ money is comfortable for me now, and i share it freely.
- ♥ i enjoy having the money i used to dream about having...
- ♥ i let money pass through me without fear and worry.
- ♥ i know that the more i give, the more i get.
- ♥ i freely give and receive anywhere i am...
- ♥ my good comes from everywhere and anywhere and i accept it gladly.
- ♥ i keep open about where money flows into my life, new openings abound.
- ♥ i expect my good now and i get it.
- ♥ cash flows through me into the world.
- ♥ all giving returns to me multiplied.
- ♥ i continue to give no matter what is happening in my life
- ♥ my wealth contributes to my aliveness.
- ♥ i am financially successful, and it's easy to prosper others.
- ♥ my income exceeds my expenses, and i am grateful.
- ♥ i am willing to prosper others, and i do.
- ♥ others are willing to prosper me, and i accept.
- ♥ my wealth contributes to the good of all people.
- ♥ every day my finances are getting more and more abundant.
- ♥ new possibilities for money reveal themselves now.
- ♥ i look through all "appearances of limitation" knowing that prosperity will appear...i am assured.
- ♥ i am letting go of all poor ways of thinking.
- ♥ i am letting go of all limited ways of acting.
- ♥ i am increasing my ideas of plenty today.
- ♥ i do the things which bring prosperity into my life today.
- ♥ i speak of money with confidence and assurance.
- ♥ i bless all financial transactions.
- ♥ i give forth without being asked. i am eager to give.

prosperity mind treatment

There is One life, intelligence and love in the universe, and that life is my life now.
THIS LIFE IS ABUNDANTLY GOOD.
Divine Mind guides and protects.

There is no limit on success that is in alignment with divine principle and plan. Fears and false ideas about success are now dissolved. Positive, confident, clear thinking and action are now established. The highest level of creativity is manifested. Finances are abundant. False ideas of lack and feelings of fear about having money are now dissolved. Prosperity is established now.
Forwarding and supportive partnerships are formed and maintained.
Family is loving and supportive. Health and well being are constant.

Projects are completed quickly and easily. Each day's progress is a source of satisfaction and accomplishment. i give thanks for being empowered to do the work i love. i give thanks for the love and support of family and friends.
i AM THANKFUL FOR DIVINE GUIDANCE.
This treatment is released and its good cannot fail...so it is.
This life is abundantly good.

- Karen Lindsay

i leave behind, i accept and i am willing

- ♥ i leave behind thoughts of not having enough.
- ♥ i leave behind resistance to having money.
- ♥ i leave behind resistance to generating money.
- ♥ i leave behind irresponsible attitudes about money.
- ♥ i leave behind excusing myself from doing what i want to do because of poverty.
- ♥ i leave behind manipulating others with my context of scarcity.
- ♥ i gladly accept responsibility that comes from abundance.
- ♥ i accept abundance as a place to express myself from.
- ♥ i accept expressing, i accept abundance and i express my true self.
- ♥ i am willing to use money to express myself and make the world work for everyone.
- ♥ i am willing to make life brighter and lighter for all those around me.
- ♥ i am willing to generate money to have the world work for everyone.
- ♥ i am willing to be conscious about money.
- ♥ i am willing to believe abundance is okay for me.
- ♥ i am willing to know money and to have money.,
- ♥ i am willing to handle what comes up about having money.
- ♥ i am willing to leave behind money as an imposition.
- ♥ i am willing to leave behind money as unnecessary.
- ♥ i do, what i really want to do, and have abundance.

i let go

- ♥ i drop feeling guilty about having money.
- ♥ i drop discomfort around spending money.
- ♥ i drop fear about the flow of money shutting down.
- ♥ i drop the idea that the poorer i am, the more spiritual i am.
- ♥ i drop "deserving" as an index of how much i allow myself.
- ♥ i drop resentment of wealthy folks.
- ♥ i drop money, as a goal, in itself.

i am leaving behind

- ♥ i am leaving behind the ideas i learned about money.
- ♥ i am leaving behind the ideas i was taught about money.
- ♥ i am leaving behind the ideas i accepted about money.
- ♥ i am leaving behind the ideas of money as a problem.
- ♥ i am leaving behind ideas of money as survival.
- ♥ i am leaving ideas of money as something i have to get...
- ♥ money is now a small link in the scheme of what i am about.

i see

- ♥ i see money as enabling me to make a difference.
- ♥ i see money as a way i give to my world.
- ♥ i see money as something to spread around.
- ♥ i see money is always around.
- ♥ i see money empowering me, to empower others.
- ♥ i see money as something to keep moving out with...
- ♥ i can get money anytime.
- ♥ i see, i cause money to happen to me, by my thinking.
- ♥ i see money happens, by my expectation.
- ♥ i see everything, as an opportunity, to express money.

The Direction of West

i know

- ♥ i can transform my relationship with money.
- ♥ i shift my way of seeing money, and shift my life into service of others.
- ♥ i know i can not make much of a difference in the way the world works, without using what the world works with...
- ♥ the unit or exchange in this world is money.
- ♥ i know i am willing to give up my hesitance about it.
- ♥ i know insufficiency of money is due to thoughts of insufficiency.
- ♥ i know scarcity of money is due to thoughts of scarcity of $.
- ♥ i know money seeming hard-to-get is due to thoughts of $ being hard to get.
- ♥ i know that if there is change in my money, that first there will be a change in my thinking about money...
- ♥ i know i am ready for a change.

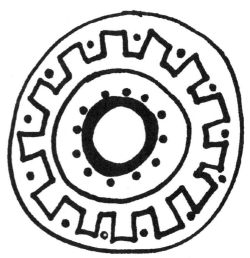

i realize

- ♥ i realize there is no scarcity of anything in this world.
- ♥ i realize talk of scarcity exists when abundance is apparent.
- ♥ i realize talk of scarcity comes from minds focusing on scarcity.
- ♥ i realize i choose my focus every moment.
- ♥ thoughts of scarcity cause scarcity.
- ♥ i realize thoughts of abundance cause and attract abundance.
- ♥ i realize all abundance starts in my mind first.
- ♥ i realize i am willing to think in ways that will cause abundance.
- ♥ i realize i am willing to feel to cause abundance.
- ♥ i realize i am willing to "have" what i want.
- ♥ **i realize a great part of what i want is to serve others.**

Seasons of Prosperity

i establish certitude of plenty

- ♥ there's plenty of business for everyone.
- ♥ goodbye to thoughts and feelings of lack and limitation.
- ♥ business comes from my opinions about business: today i have the opinion and attitude that there's plenty of business to spare, and even share; there's plenty where it all came from.
    - i'm assured of plenty.
    - i am certain of plenty.
    - i act for plenty
    - i establish certitude of plenty;
    - everywhere i am plenty is what's so.
    - everywhere i go plenty is what's so.
    - everytime i speak plenty is what's so.
    - i am thankful, i show it,
    - i am thankful, i speak it,
    - i am thankful, i act it.
- ♥ everywhere i am, enrollment happens
    everywhere i am, sales happen.
    everywhere i am, upleveling of life happens.
    i am grateful to be a source of courage, certitude and plenty for all those around me.
- ♥ i am a stand for life going forward to prosper and uplift all creatures in God's good plan for us all. that's what's so.

friday going forward

- ♥ today, i remember there is one Life...one Spirit...one Mind... in which we live, move and have our being.
- ♥ we all manifest the life of Infinite Intelligence.
- ♥ infinite Intelligence is never stopped and neither am i.
- ♥ i am always going forward in greater wisdom.
- ♥ i am free of any idea of lack or limitation, no matter what the appearance. all appearances are passing!
- ♥ all day today, i accept the invitation of life to go forward. i create rich new experiences.
- ♥ i am living in an atmosphere of expansion.
- ♥ i have an attitude of blazing new trails.
- ♥ i expand on the good and prosper others as i go...
- ♥ all possibility and potentiality exist today with me and through me.

always there is increase
An adaptation from LEAVES OF GRASS
- by Walt Whitman

- ♥ my good is here and now.
- ♥ i do not talk of beginning or end.
- ♥ i am satisfied.
- ♥ always there is increase.
- ♥ i and this mystery here we stand.
- ♥ electrical increase now informs all my speaking silent and out loud.
- ♥ there is a perfect equanimity of all things.
- ♥ always there is increasing.
- ♥ God comes a loving bedfellow and sleeps at my side all night and leaves me baskets bulging with plenty. i am satisfied.
- ♥ i have heard what the talkers were speaking.
  lack and limitation, beginnings and ends,
  but i do not talk of beginning or end.
- ♥ there was never more than there is now.
  not more youth or age than there is now.
- ♥ there will never be any more perfection than there is now.
  Not any more heaven or hell than there is now,
- ♥ i celebrate myself and what i assume, you shall assume.
  i celebrate you. for every atom belonging to me as good, belongs to you.
- ♥ my good is here and now. so is yours.
  we do not talk of beginning or end.

waiter/waitress affirmations

- ♥ everyday is an opportunity to serve.
- ♥ each day people are happy with the way i serve them.
- ♥ gratitude abounds wherever i am.
- ♥ gratuities abound wherever i am.
- ♥ people that i serve today are very generous.
- ♥ big tips come my way today.
- ♥ my gratitude prospers me.
- ♥ when i serve people i serve them fully.
- ♥ i am happy in my service of others.
- ♥ more money is circulated each day in tips.
- ♥ the more i serve others the more i am serving myself.

- by Joane Casale

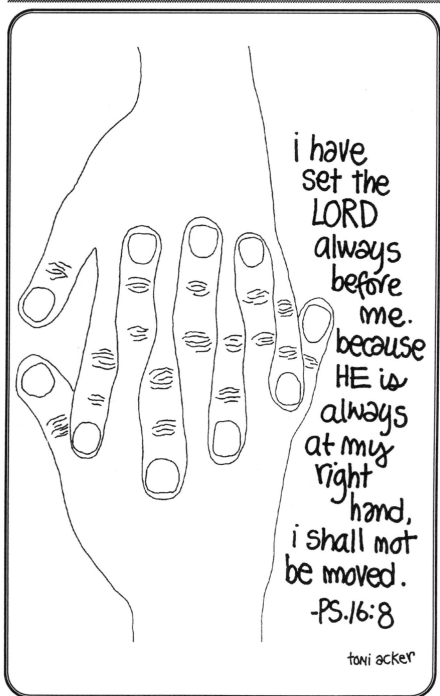

i am free to prosper in my business

The freedom of PERFECT PATTERN is my freedom now.
The creative power of my being is directed and expressed excellently.
i am an excellent idea in the
> MIND OF INFINITE INTELLIGENCE.

Anything that seemed burdensome or boring is now transformed by the renewal of my thinking. Left behind are thoughts that suppress, scare or bind the life expression. i am free to prosper in my business as an expression of life evolving. What's possible is now occurring as outcomes.
> My business expresses my will-to-serve.
> i am happy to move forward serving my clients
>> with good humor and pure joy.
> PROSPERITY is the continuing circumstance.

Expression of generosity, magnanimity and boundless potential is everywhere that i am. i am an excellent idea directed and expressed for the good of all.
i know what to do and i do it joyously producing results.
i am free to prosper in my business.
my business is blessed and prospered in all circumstances.
> PROSPERITY IS THE CONTINUING EVENT.
> Decisions are wise and capable.
> Goals are alive with vitality.
> i am the ability to prevail.
> THIS AWARENESS SETS ME FREE.
> i am grateful and blessed...

i give thanks that this word as cause is set in motion and does not return void ...so it is. **i am free to prosper in my business.**

prosperity prevails

- ♥ what's required is always present.
- ♥ **prosperity prevails.**
- ♥ anytime i didn't have money, right after that, i got some.
- ♥ **prosperity prevails.**
- ♥ prosperity is well-being, is wealth, is assurance...
    all these are an inner conviction. i can have them when i feel them...
- ♥ **prosperity prevails.**
- ♥ plenty is a place, in mind, to be looking out from
    when i establish the idea of plenty in mind and feeling
        i see evidence of plenty everywhere...
- ♥ **prosperity prevails.**
- ♥ prosperity is the perception
    of a process, on-going for ever,
    of such an abundance that it cannot be counted...
- ♥ **prosperity prevails.**
- ♥ today, i know, i am sure of this.
- ♥ **prosperity prevails.**

my giving makes me rich

- ♥ the more i give, the more i get...
- ♥ my giving makes me rich.
- ♥ giving and getting are the same.
- ♥ the more i give...the more i get.
- ♥ today i am eager to contribute.
- ♥ today i leave behind thoughts of scarcity.
- ♥ money is for circulating today.
- ♥ generosity is a natural way of being, a very natural way of being.
- ♥ generosity improves my ability to remember that i deserve to prosper and so do you!
- ♥ i am willing today to give up hesitance about having and freely circulating money.
- ♥ i know what to do and i do it.
- ♥ i am transforming my relationship with money.
- ♥ my doubts about generosity are disappearing.
- ♥ i give as an expression of the contribution that i am to life.
- ♥ giving is a natural extension of being.
- ♥ i enjoy generous giving and abundant receiving.
- ♥ the act of giving is freeing to my mind.
- ♥ giving creates receptivity to getting.
- ♥ money is something i keep moving forward and out with ...
- ♥ all that i give is multiplied and returned to me... universal eternal laws demonstrate time and time again.
- ♥ THE MORE i GIVE THE MORE i GET.
- ♥ i feel my natural urge to extend what i have...and today i act on it.
- ♥ i smooth the edges of any worries today by giving rather than by contracting and holding.
- ♥ today i am giving freely.
- ♥ i remember no one has ever become poor by giving.
- ♥ i give with a cheerful heart.
- ♥ my giving makes me rich, the more i give the more i get.
- ♥ the enthusiasm i have in giving, moves others to give more.
- ♥ i go beyond the thought that giving is a loss.
- ♥ i go beyond where i usually stop with giving.
- ♥ i expand my ability to give generously.
- ♥ my giving makes me rich.
- ♥ giving is an expression of trust in life.
- ♥ today i let go all scarcity viewpoints. today i give rather than accumulate...

The Direction of West

- ♥ i choose a perception of plenty.
- ♥ i look around to see what is wanted and needed so i can give more.
- ♥ i am pressing out...beyond what i thought my limits were...
- ♥ i am increasing my ability to respond generously and spontaneously in life daily.
- ♥ everything i have increases through sharing.
- ♥ i can always choose to share and give whatever i see as insufficient for me now... i do that.
- ♥ i am expanding my ability to give generously.
- ♥ today i am aware of the privilege it is to give and give freely.
- ♥ every day and every way things are getting better and better for everybody.
- ♥ the more i give, the more i get... giving makes me rich.

LOVE IS THE GREAT TRANSFORMER
TURNING AMBITION INTO ASPIRATION
SELFISHNESS INTO SERVICE
GREED INTO GRATITUDE
GETTING INTO GIVING
AND DEMANDS INTO DEDICATION
— W.A. WARD

Seasons of Prosperity

Peace be within your walls and prosperity within your palaces

Ps. 122:7

©toni acker 82

i give up scare-scarce thinking by giving

- ♥ i can only give what i have.
- ♥ i can only have what i am giving.
- ♥ great realizations are now taking place with me.
- ♥ true having is giving it all away. although this thought contradicts common thought, it's true.
- ♥ i can only give what i would be willing to receive.
- ♥ i can only ever receive what i'd be willing to give.
- ♥ giving and having are the same.
- ♥ in order to receive i give first.
- ♥ i keep giving first.
- ♥ i give first, even when common thought makes it look dangerous.
- ♥ i give first...i understand and trust the workings of the Universal Law.
- ♥ the preliminary step "first giving, always giving" vitalizes finances and causes great JOY.
- ♥ my perceptions are now reversed and turned right side up.
- ♥ i choose to give and relinquish scare-scarce thinking.
- ♥ i am liberated by my joyful always giving.

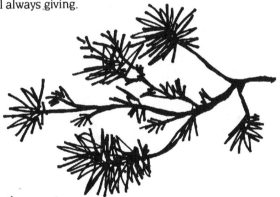

increasing income

- ♥ i live from intention rather than want...
- ♥ everything i circulate returns multiplied.
- ♥ everyday my income increases...
- ♥ everyday i am more and more grateful.
- ♥ the more i give, the more i get.
- ♥ my income increases miraculously.
- ♥ i have an abundant cash flow.
- ♥ whatever i circulate always returns.
- ♥ i replace all hesitant thoughts with action.
- ♥ on my income, there are no limits!
- ♥ my income increases each day in every way.

i tithe effortlessly and i prosper

- ♥ i give money easily.
- ♥ i am free to prosper.
- ♥ circulation replaces withholding in my life...
- ♥ i know the inner laws of success.
- ♥ as i tithe, so do i prosper.
- ♥ giving is the beginning of increase.
- ♥ i tithe easily, effortlessly, and consistently.
- ♥ i know the ancient universal laws are still true.
- ♥ i count on universal laws rather than appearances.
- ♥ the law of giving 10% of my income, prospers me today.
- ♥ i practice tithing and invoke the law in all my affairs.
- ♥ giving effortlessly brings financial increase to me.
- ♥ my income reflects the grace of my giving.
- ♥ i share generously with organizations or people where i receive spiritual help.
- ♥ my faithful giving predicts beneficial outcomes for me.
- ♥ i voluntarily share from my attitude of gratitude.
- ♥ i no longer believe i can "go broke" from giving.
- ♥ i no longer believe that withholding will make me successful.
- ♥ i no longer hold myself mentally in limitation.
- ♥ i faithfully give ten percent consistently.
- ♥ i invoke the power of increase by giving regularly.
- ♥ life is opening up to me now.
- ♥ i expect the best and i get it.
- ♥ my good increases by circulating and sharing.
- ♥ i let go of little ways of thinking. i expand in greater giving.
- ♥ greater giving insures greater receiving.
- ♥ my good comes quickly to me now.

Seasons of Prosperity

generosity affirmations

- ♥ today i am eager to contribute.
- ♥ today i remember that the only way to receive is to give first...
- ♥ i don't wait to feel "comfortable" about giving, i give in the moment of now...
- ♥ today i am ever aware of the privilege it is to give, and give freely!
- ♥ i am looking around to see what is wanted and needed so i can give more
- ♥ i see my natural urge to extend what i have... i act on it!
- ♥ i express myself by giving often and much i know what to do and i do it!
- ♥ i give away rather than accumulate and store up.
- ♥ more and more i am acknowledging and appreciating others!
- ♥ i am expanding my ability to give generously...
- ♥ i recognize that things multiply when i let them go.
- ♥ all my giving is an investment in the future as well as an expression of my trust in life...
- ♥ my thinking is more willing about giving today.
- ♥ i enjoy generous giving and abundant receiving.
- ♥ all that i give is multiplied and returned to me, the more i give the more i get.
- ♥ giving is a grace. my doubts about generosity are disappearing.
- ♥ generous giving is a way of being true to my highest ideals, systematic giving assures systematic receiving.
- ♥ the act of giving is freeing to my mind. i am grateful.
- ♥ i know that everything i have increases through sharing, so i share and give whatever i see as insufficient for me now.
- ♥ each day in many ways, i go beyond the thought that giving is a loss!
- ♥ i have an innate ability to go beyond where i like to stop with giving...
- ♥ i see that all my giving is an extension of being.
- ♥ i know that giving creates my receptivity to getting.
- ♥ In my life, daily i am increasing ability to respond generously, spontaneously, and intentionally to the highest ideas of being!
- ♥ i am excited about giving today. I know that no one has ever become poor by giving.
- ♥ today i smooth edges of worry by giving, rather than by contraction and holding.
- ♥ my dependable giving, and generous attitudes & actions, outsmart my environment...so that many results appear wherever i am in the moment.
- ♥ what i am giving is being given to me, increased...
- ♥ i give out of being, i give as a statement of my beingness...
- ♥ i give as an expression of the natural contribution that i am.
- ♥ my electrical enthusiasm around giving, moves others to join in giving...
- ♥ everyday in every way, things are getting better and better for everybody!

The Direction of West

- ♥ i extend myself infinitely by continuing to give no matter what!
- ♥ ...today and tomorrow i press out beyond
what i thought my limits were yesterday...
- ♥ i let go all scarcity viewpoints today...i choose perceptions of plenty!
- ♥ i give with a cheerful heart, my giving makes me rich!
- ♥ through my giving i establish a new, generous way of being.
i am becoming more and more free in my disbursements...
- ♥ It is through circulation and disbursement that i create spaces
and vacuums for new good to arrive .
- ♥ great generosity improves my ability to be worthy of plenty!
- ♥ my present income is only the beginning of what is available,
through giving freely what-i-have, my income increases daily...

increasing generosity
autumn progressions

- ♥ i have a new way
of being eager to contribute.
- ♥ instead of waiting to be asked, i offer...
- ♥ i represent a posture of easy giving
                        cheerful giving.
- ♥ giving is becoming more and more
an important expression of who i am.
- ♥ giving produces a firm sense of esteem for me.
- ♥ the more i give the more i feel deserving
of good for myself.
- ♥ esteem increases each time i give.
- ♥ the reciprocal action of giving and receiving
makes everything in my life work well.
- ♥ the more i give, the more i get...

Seasons of Prosperity

men affirmations

- ♥ i see the future in all life. i protect life by standing for life.
- ♥ i see beauty in life. i am moved by it.
- ♥ my stand for life is strong it includes all creatures.
- ♥ i know what to do, i have conviction to do it.
- ♥ i do what's mine to do even when it's difficult....
- ♥ i have the courage to be who i am, i say so.
- ♥ i determine who i am.
- ♥ i am committed to other men, i see them as partners.
- ♥ i accept help from men who are
  allies to my commitments.
- ♥ i am drawn to men for energy and relatedness.
- ♥ i work to support other men in their goals,
  i am committed to men's lives working for the highest good of all.
- ♥ i am balanced by
  > compassion for humanity,
  > commitment to humans, commitment to all life.
  > i generate ancient warrior energy.
  > i generate gladiator initiative.
  > i generate harmony of heroic nature.
  > i generate courage of commitment.

i am willing to be contributed to...

"Those who believe in our ability...
create for us an atmosphere in which it becomes easier to succeed."
  - J. L. Spaulding

- ♥ i accept help from others: i am still distinct as myself.
- ♥ i accept help from others: i don't claim to be "better than" others.
- ♥ i accept help from others: they know i want things better.
- ♥ i accept help from others: i am free to be helped.
- ♥ i accept help from others: they are welcome to know me.
- ♥ i accept help from others: i look at new information.
- ♥ i accept help from others: opportunities become stimulating.
- ♥ i accept help from others: no obligation is required.
- ♥ i accept help from others: it's okay to depend on others.
- ♥ i accept help from others: they are a contribution to me.
- ♥ instead of being devoted to doing things my own way
  > i am now devoted to getting results.
- ♥ i make plenty of opportunities, to receive help and encouragement.
- ♥ when i have people helping me with my plans, i get results.

i trust that everybody prospers me

- ♥ i am generous and magnanimous.
- ♥ i am eager to prosper others
  and i do.
- ♥ others are happy and vitalized
  by prospering me.
- ♥ everyone prospers me...
  success expands.
- ♥ i happily share
  my increasing wealth.
- ♥ everybody helps me grow.
- ♥ i know that my speaking
  has creative prospering power.
- ♥ people bring me good unceasingly.
- ♥ i am always expressing generosity in new ways.
- ♥ The spiritual substance from which comes all visible
  wealth is never depleted.
- ♥ good comes from all the people around me.
- ♥ my assumptions about others
  create interactions and results.
      today i assume what i intend.
- ♥ other people respond to my thinking about them
  by acting just like i say they will.
- ♥ my demands of life are expressed
  in my daily speaking of life.
- ♥ in life i get what i want.
- ♥ what i expect shows up faithfully.
- ♥ i do not expect people to be or do what
        i have not been or done myself.
- ♥ i permit people to be the way they are.
- ♥ everyone represents an aspect of myself.
- ♥ people are my perceptions of them.
- ♥ today i have the perceptions that prosper us all.
- ♥ everybody prospers me...
- ♥ each situation is an opportunity
  for success and prosperity to express.
- ♥ i think success. success outpictures in very way today.
- ♥ i expect "everybody prospers me" and they do!
- ♥ people count on me to prosper them and i do!!!
- ♥ giving and getting are the same.

Seasons of Prosperity

prosperous provision has been made

- ♥ i talk about the good.
- ♥ today i banish limitation thinking.
   there is always plenty more of every good thing.
- ♥ i constantly acknowledge all the good that's here...
- ♥ unlimited good is mine today to share freely,
   and i do share.
- ♥ sharing increases whatever i share...
- ♥ i demonstrate all kinds of good easily.
- ♥ goodness is uppermost in my mind today.
- ♥ i am loyal to thoughts of good today and tomorrow.
   Universal goodness is everywhere present.
- ♥ i accept good without question this week.
- ♥ i am constantly getting what i can accept.
- ♥ acceptance grows with me today.
- ♥ my thoughts adhere continuously to the idea of plenty.
- ♥ abundant provision has been made for me...
- ♥ prosperous provision has been made for me...
- ♥ i am successful in demonstrating plenty now.
- ♥ i give thanks often for all that i already have...
- ♥ visible supply of everything is seen by me today.
- ♥ my good vision is now certain to appear.

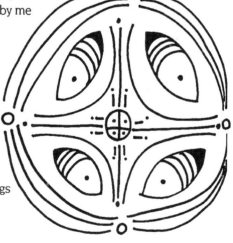

life is created with thought

- ♥ there is no reality in lack.
- ♥ no matter how distracting the appearance, abundance is everywhere present.
- ♥ my job is to set my mind and feelings in accord with abundance that is always available.
- ♥ when i think in terms of plenty,
   abundance, prosperity, things changing...
   the picture improves as my thinking improves...
   right actions happen...fueled by right thinking.
- ♥ ideas are under outcomes, they permeate and penetrate all appearances making them whatever we think they are...
- ♥ i am grateful to know my thought becomes result.
   all i require is already given...i open my thinking to all good.

The Direction of West

sunday in an opulent universe

Today
- ♥ i graciously receive.
- ♥ i practice the art of receiving.
- ♥ i can have all that i can receive.
- ♥ i live in an opulent universe.
- ♥ there's plenty more where everything came from.
- ♥ receiving is an important aspect of opening up to life.
- ♥ i can have all that i will accept and use.
- ♥ i have all that i accepted already.
- ♥ the more i accept, the more i have to give.
- ♥ life is lived from within, outward.
- ♥ my ideas about receiving now allow me to receive.
- ♥ the ideas that i hold as true create possibility for me.
- ♥ i feel worthy today.

change is the heart of my being

The PERFECT PATTERN functioning at the level of consciousness is the source and cause of my success. The communication of the PERFECT PATTERN, the Universal Intelligence, with the particular is the eternal movement and pattern shifting of evolution...
CHANGE IS THE HEART OF MY BEING.

i recognize my inherent expectation of good.
i am whole and free within the PERFECT PATTERN...
in fact PERFECT PATTERNS is what i am...
    i cut through negative feelings easily.
    i move quickly into postures and positions that bring good ever-increasing.
    i do not let any appearance stop me or thwart my intention.
CHANGE IS THE HEART OF MY BEING.

i am bold and free. i know my joyous expectations are fulfilled. i give thanks that i expect to be the recipient of many new opportunities for the expressing of life into outcomes. i welcome each offer to be, do and have more good. i align my thoughts with the ONE MIND, the PERFECT PATTERN through all changes.
CHANGE IS THE HEART OF MY BEING AND i KNOW IT.
Success is the form, the shape and the structure of my life now. i KNOW MY EXPECTATIONS ARE FULFILLED. i release these words of truth knowing full well they cannot return void...these words do their work...in fact, their work is already being done.

CHANGE IS THE HEART OF MY BEING...
and for this i do give thanks.
Change is the heart of my being.

Seasons of Prosperity

changing continues to bless me

God is all in all. GOD IS THE ONE LIFE, ALL PRESENT, ALL KNOWING, ALL POWERFUL LIFE. i live and move and have my being in this Life.
i receive ideas that point and aim me into changing.
i am an outlet for creative ideas.
changing always moves things along...

i am enthusiastic and fully creative about changing, even if i think otherwise.
CHANGING IS ALWAYS HAPPENING EVERYWHERE.
the law of Order is established.
great things are being accomplished.
                i am in motion for greater good.
                i let go of the negative.
                i let go of what is false.
                i let go of what limits me.
i am grateful. i am ready to let go of old good...
new good occurs.
right action is now happening in my life.
relinquishment prevails, harmony prevails.
i am fully creative about changing. good responds.
i use it with full authority and confidence in all aspects of my business, projects and relationships. i speak, think and feel what i intend. my words, inner conversations, outer speaking, and feelings are congruent good.

EVERYDAY BRINGS GREATER GOOD: new ideas, more revelations, and increased blessings for all.
i am renewed by the power of this word.
thank God that this is so. i am grateful.
i release this word to the law of perfect outworking.

this is done easily, as i speak...
these words are the truth about me.
Changing continues to bless me.

ready to relocate declaration

i recognize the Oneness of GOD...
i feel the presence and power of God within me.
i am led every step of the way to my next location
        my thinking
        my speaking
        my feeling
        my actions and reactions are all established
                in appropriate order.

The Direction of West

I AM READY FOR RELOCATION.
my next location is the place to be. The Divine directs moving. Prosperity abounds as transitions occur. Everything required finds its way to me now. Any subconscious resistance, any fear or doubt, any anxieties are dissolved, erased and given up...any scripts, any body sensations, any previous contrary instructions are now forgotten...negative thought patterns are cancelled, their effects are now healed. Nothing can prevent appropriate action from taking place in my affairs. New friendships and interests are developing in my next location. Houses and land are affordable, easy and effortless to locate and negotiate. New ideas come in sequence that works. The way is made ready.

i move into action with authority and full realization of my oneness with the SOURCE...
Now the sun shines more frequently in my next location.
The weather is perfect...perfect living conditions show up in my next location.
i give thanks for this miracle.
i GIVE THANKS FOR DIVINE GUIDANCE.
i realize these words are true.
i release these words to the law...

pumpkin harvest

Last autumn, teachers made a celebration circle of pumpkins. One hundred and four pumpkins stood in a wheel, side-by-side. The flaming orange fruits, the lovely vibrant foliage, it all made the graduation picture complete. In the winter the pumpkins a sodden mass before they froze, gave us hope, of a lovely pumpkin ring in spring. The crows came and ate seeds. We thought surely some will remain and surge up with new pumpkins...

In the spring we looked. No new vine. Early summer, no pumpkin leaves. What happened? The disappointment was great. We should have covered the seed and not shared them with crows...it looked like we lost.

This afternoon Steve went up to the compost-heap to dump off some old food for the animals. He was yelling for me to come on up there. He showed me the pumpkin vine with its huge leaves. It was thriving in the compost. It was surrounded by seven foot high blackberry bushes. They were filled with plum-colored berries by the handfuls! Tomato plants were growing too.

> Definitely, not where we thought they should be...
> definitely, what's required is always present.
> Nature is the most excellent teacher.

Seasons of Prosperity

prosperity teacher covenant

Money is a symbol of exchanging.
   ...avoiding relationship dissolves when people remember
money is simply a symbol of exchange - not an end in itself!
We are teaching the principles of true prospering for everyone.
Now, at the beginning of a new decade
   we dedicate ourselves to the unfoldment and full expression of a
         PROSPERITY COMMUNITY THAT IS GLOBAL.
We commit ourselves to do the work of uncovering
   the remembrance of universal principles in everyone.
We live as the conviction of giving in all areas of our lives.
We understand that giving ensures bountiful supply.
We live the practice of prosperity principles.
We realize the presence and power of DIVINE PRINCIPLES.
We agree to allow the DIVINE to work in and through
   our thought, feeling, word and act.
We can be counted on to stand for the Practice of Prosperity.
We declare ourselves to be light that shines for the good
   of all and to the glory of all that is DIVINE.
In return, the DIVINE will abundantly provide us wisdom,
   love, well-being, equanimity, compassion and bountiful supply.
We make this covenant with ourselves and with the DIVINE in trust,
   standing for prosperous exchange and real understanding
   in human beings as well as countries.
We surrender to the inner force operating to bring us together
   in our shared work of teaching prosperity in this world.

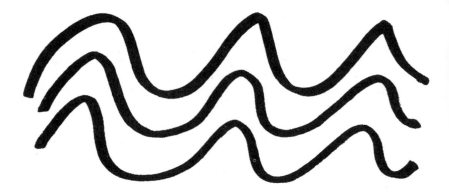

declaration for prosperity teachers

We declare that we come together to take on the enlightening practice
of teaching prosperity principles with compassion and clarity.

>Today we surrender
>to the inner force
>>which is operating to bring us together
>>>in our shared work

with Heavenly Strength, Universal Commitment
and a Radical Understanding OF INCREDIBLE LOVE ...
We come together to Serve a high purpose.
We answer the call of Service. In being awake to who we are there is only Service
...The Divine moves us to reveal the prosperous awakening truth in all beings.
Our serving moves life everywhere. The ones we serve continue to serve others,
everything works together for good. Everyone is discovering
authorship of circumstance.

We guide beings in ways according to their mentalities.
We appear in the midst of many activities
without ever leaving the presence of Divine Intuition.
We proceed instructed by great spiritual benefactors...
with tireless will, we build up roots of goodness...
with unbroken commitment and continuity we carry out practices
of enlightening beings everywhere.
We do our work using generosity and magnanimity.
We work using compassionate speech and unhesitating beneficial actions.
We uncover the remembrance of universal principles in everyone.
We are imbued with light each day. We are happy in our work together.
We provide a clearing so that people give up fears... they give up lack and
limitation... they let go of self concern... they see themselves in others... they are
one in sharing, revealing, and exchanging. Our teaching subtracts fear. Our
teaching adds nothing, and nothing is where everything comes from.
We teach the true nature of coming and going.
Our actions and our teaching spontaneously arise in perfect time.
We benefit all living beings.
We are always prosperity teachers.

We look upon the world with active great compassion. We know everything as an
extension (perfectly mirroring)...what we are. That we are the prosperity teachers,
is a fine self-appointment. Imbued with light, empowered by our shared
commitments, we are guided in dispelling the miseries of worlds. Our work is
directed and blessed...the way is ever always, already revealed in the moment. We
embody enlightenment for the good of all,
>as we continue to surrender
>to the inner force which is
>operating to bring us together
>in our shared work
>**as prosperity teachers.**

Seasons of Prosperity

prayer of a dedicated teaching life in the company of others

in conformity with the dedication practiced by enlightening beings of all times
...i declare my life to be the way of magnanimous heart
freeing all hearts from suffering.
i do not seek the unexcelled way for my own sake...
my purpose is to enable all sentient beings to attain liberation.
each day i become more determined.
> i do not give up or run away.
> i am not shocked or frightened.
> i am not discouraged or intimidated.
> i am not made tired by the effort.
> i continue to be determined to bring
> all sentient beings to liberation.
> i enable them.

those who are revolving in repeated routines according to the force of their acts and erroneous views. i enable them. Those in the cage of suffering the web of attachments to desires or acting like crazy victims. all of these people are awakening to their power and i enable them as i am enabled. i cultivate enlightening practices in all my work. i am enabled and grateful. i am joined with a past present future continuum of others just like me.
> we carry out our shared work happily.
> we practice generosity quite gladly.
> we are for all sentient beings leaders.
> we enable others. We are enabled.

whowing the way to safety and peace, we serve and provide for others using appropriate means to inform them of the truth (according to their mentalities).
in our company, people are liberated and they prosper.
in our company, good company is established. error is annihilated.
wrongdoing is cleared away, roots of goodness are discovered.
people are freed from doubt. we are teachers of prosperous ways.
we are enabled and enabling. we are like the sun, we shine universally on all without seeking thanks. we diligently practice our dedication to the prosperity of all beings with joyful hearts. We develop hearts of great compassion in this way.
we give thanks for lives that continuously serve others.

teacher's proclamation

i am of understanding; a vision of i AM. i speak what's so... This galaxy is my neighborhood. i am a reflection of great intelligence at work in worlds. Advance and repose, reveal free ways of being...i show up speaking these into a form which others are liberated by. Awake from the illusion of conditional self. i call "others" away from separate self. i can be counted on to stay awake. i declare that
> people are set free from attitudes, assumptions and antics which have bound them.
> Wherever i am all things are possible. Possibility is everywhere.

my presence enables, empowers and unifies people. This galaxy is my neighborhood. Great intelligence, at work in the world, is easy for us to observe. We vow to observe it.

self-talk for an advisor...

The contribution i AM to people is not
always compatible with the wish i have
> to be admired
> to be liked
> to be thought well-of.

This does not determine my range of interaction.
What determines my interactions is the highest good possible.

Seasons of Prosperity

i am a prosperity teacher

- ♥ GOD is all in all...Divine Intelligence always moves forward.
- ♥ So do i...never apart from Divine Intelligence...i am changing.
- ♥ Something wonderful is happening...i am Ready.
- ♥ i see the result of Divine Creation everywhere.
- ♥ i see perfection behind all appearances of limitation.
- ♥ i am guided by my true nature to express truth...
              i AM A PROSPERITY TEACHER.
- ♥ i achieve prosperity easily...i create good by thinking good.
- ♥ i waste no energy on fear or doubt.
   ...i do not look back...i go forward.
- ♥ No sense of lack or limitation disturbs me.
- ♥ i am not deterred by delay or false appearances.
- ♥ Detours do not confuse me.
- ♥ i remember plenty is already always the circumstance.
- ♥ i see the truth in all appearances now.
- ♥ i win at the financial game of life easily, faithfully and for everyone's benefit.
- ♥ When i win everyone around me prospers.
- ♥ Teaching prosperity is easy for me.
- ♥ i always remember i am only ever teaching myself.
- ♥ i teach best what i most need to learn. Whatever i teach i learn.
- ♥ That i am a prosperity teacher, is a fine self appointment.
- ♥ Divine Mind is my, ever reliable source of supply,
   available to me for constant use. i am grateful.
- ♥ Giving and getting are the same.
- ♥ i have immediate access to all that i intend.
- ♥ i embody a consciousness of gratitude.
- ♥ i live in a world of plenty and i have plenty to spare and share.
- ♥ i see the best in everything.
- ♥ i am a natural prosperity teacher.
- ♥ i know the truth of being, life is blessed wherever i am.

teaching affirmations

- ♥ i welcome the challenge that teaching is...
- ♥ the classroom is a place where Universal Intelligence works.
- ♥ i call forth what's possible and goodness, truth, beauty and love show up.
- ♥ i know what to do and do it in every classroom situation.
- ♥ i inspire and motivate students.
- ♥ i see, speak and hear, possibility in the classroom.
- ♥ i am committed to listening and to empowering.
- ♥ students experience new enthusiasm to learn. imagination prevails.
- ♥ learning is natural discovery.
- ♥ in the classroom, students are partners.
- ♥ classrooms abound with appreciation, acknowledgment, and participation.
- ♥ hesitance and fear are left behind in situations, and circumstances.
- ♥ liberating thoughts replace limiting attitudes in classrooms.
- ♥ good ideas come easily. everyone increases comprehension.
- ♥ i easily make requests and students make requests - our work goes quickly forward. we cover important points. we discover new interests.
- ♥ i am grateful for the opportunity and challenge of teaching.
- ♥ classrooms are a serendipity experience that shines light on understanding.
- ♥ miracles, coincidences, and happy surprises happen.
- ♥ i am intuitive and skilled as a teacher.
- ♥ in my classroom, nothing is impossible.

- adapted from Don Smith's affirmations

i promise today...

- ♥ to cultivate noble feelings.
- ♥ to live in unwavering faith.
- ♥ to have an undistracted mind.
- ♥ to practice fervent devotion.
- ♥ to surrender to intense reverence.
- ♥ to recall good company has great power.
- ♥ to practice first what i teach to other people.
- ♥ to see life is a most valuable school.

Seasons of Prosperity

leadership

- ♥ i dare to contradict common knowledge and common sense.
- ♥ i am open and receptive to unlimited perspectives.
- ♥ today i am willing to view the world "opened-up" to me.
- ♥ i have new language that matches my new vision of what's possible.
- ♥ i speak new possibilities into action.
- ♥ my predictions defy current evidence.
- ♥ my actions put legs under my predictions of what will be so.
- ♥ i look with faith and imagination beyond what is.
- ♥ i have my capacity to envision and act, dominion over what will be.
- ♥ i leave contradictory interpretations behind me.
- ♥ i have a natural ability to change the face of things.
- ♥ i no longer move and act from what has already been seen.
- ♥ i now move forward and i create future.
- ♥ i have the courage to advance-at-risk in to the unknown.
- ♥ i leave behind assumptions that have me hesitate.
- ♥ i meet all challenges with ease and communion.
- ♥ i am a free, transcendent being operating at the highest levels.

i choose changing

> *"many are called, few choose."*
>
>   -anonymous
>
> *"faith does not change conditions at all,*
> *it changes the way we relate to them."*

- ♥ changing is okay with me today.
- ♥ being convinced of the value in changing, i choose it today.
- ♥ this is a perfect, appropriate day for changes.
- ♥ i am willing for change.
  i give up waiting for a more perfect
  time to make chosen changes.
- ♥ changing blesses me and the people around me.
- ♥ the creating power of mind is put to use for subtle and quick changes.
- ♥ today i invite contribution.
  i let go stuck opinion.
- ♥ i break up what's no longer productive.
- ♥ today i am choosing changing.

> — JOHN 1:4
>
> IN HIM WAS LIFE AND THE LIFE WAS THE LIGHT OF MEN.

©toni acker 82

The Direction of West

about being supportable

- i welcome new ideas.
- i am willing to be supported by my associates.
- i now have the ability to be contributed to.
- i now allow people to return me to confidence.
- i create partnerships with progressive individuals.
- i no longer think i have to do everything myself.
- i am willing to call upon others to be uplifted and encouraged.
- i share thoughts, emotions, limitations, and initiatives with associates.
- i share challenges, so i can be supported.
- i go beyond feelings with the assistance of associates, friends and family.
- i admit confusion, to leave it behind.
- i am willing to be encouraged with the status of my projects.
- people i spend time with encourage me, to produce outcomes.
- i surround myself with allies to my commitment.
- i often brainstorm with associates and friends to bring momentum to goals.
- all pretense has disappeared, i welcome others in my circle.
- i acknowledge often, all those who support me.
- i know that others want me to win.
- i encourage support by including others in my winning.
- i make it worthwhile for people who coach and help me.
- when i prosper, everyone around me prospers.

Seasons of Prosperity

supportability looks like this

- i am able to be contributed to...people can help me today.
- allowing people to help me takes the strength of acceptance...
- i have the integrity and responsibility to be an authority on myself, for myself.
- i value people i choose to teach and coach me in certain arenas.
- i accept help, i ask for it where it will enable me.
- i generate a source of inspiration within,
  > rather than demanding it from without...
- esteem comes from beating my past records of accomplishing.
- help from others can empower me to accomplish more today.
- as a person of courage, i find relationships with strong,
  > powerful people exhilarating to me. i welcome learning.
- i welcome the chance to know new skills in ideas
  > in plans
  > in work
  > in relations
- help is a light-giving, energizing force that is acceptable to me.
- i move to new-levels-of-being, with the help of others i have chosen,
  > supportability looks like this....

i am associating with people who empower me

- i am willing to be encouraged and inspired to action.
- i am willing to be moved in the direction i was already headed.
- i am associating with people who empower me to produce results.
- i am willing to overcome unproductive work patterns.
- i am deserving of encouragement that is purposeful and committed.
- i am open and receptive to suggestions.
- i plan to be with others in new ways so that we forward the action in each others' lives.
- i surrender to the process of being coached, i share my winning with those who coach me.
- i am willing to invite and request rigorous support from my allies and also, to give it.
- i am willing to admit what i don't know and request help.
- i am receptive to the input that forwards the progress of my goals.
- i am making the necessary requests to start, work on, and complete my jobs.
- i develop a new listening in conversations for prompting my projects.
- i am sharing my new ideas.
- i am willing to answer questions about goals and plans so that others can support me.
- i am willing to be accountable for my unfinished work.

The Direction of West

- ♥ i make promises for tasks and deadlines.
- ♥ i project my ideas; they gain the autonomy necessary to attract support that produces results.
- ♥ my ideas are no longer viewed as my exclusive property, i share them freely.
- ♥ i am a very supportable person. i am willing to refine ideas with others.
- ♥ i invite people to brainstorm on jobs and projects.
- ♥ by making "seeming" limitations known i get help required.
- ♥ i acknowledge and give thanks for support which i attract.
- ♥ i am enlivened by all the support around me and i am very grateful.

about friends

- ♥ i have friends that are allies to my commitments.
- ♥ when i don't want to do what i said i would do, my friends support my intentions instead of my feelings.
- ♥ my friends are my network of support so that i prosper and produce results.
- ♥ old friends that no longer suit this new way of being now lose interest and leave my daily life.
- ♥ my new associates and friends are able to be counted on to remind me of my goals whenever i forget.
- ♥ i love and acknowledge my many wonderful friends.
- ♥ my friends love and acknowledge me.

i work successfully with others helping me

"nothing can be itself without being in communication with everything else"
— Thomas Berry

- ♥ terrific ideas go somewhere with me.
- ♥ in order to get things done, i get lots of help.
- ♥ i have powerful partners and active associations.
- ♥ mentors and coaches help me to win in my working.
- ♥ i allow support to make a difference with me.
- ♥ my conversation of hesitation no longer directs my way.
- ♥ i have winning conversations that keep me committed to accountability, for results.
- ♥ i am open to the help i am requesting. i let it in.
- ♥ dreams of motion now become real actions.
- ♥ my accomplishments multiply with contribution from others.
- ♥ i am grateful to have help that's required
- ♥ i overcome all unproductive work patterns.
- ♥ i spend more and more time with people who are committed to getting things done.

Seasons of Prosperity

blessing all people

- ♥ i call blessing forth, for all people.
- ♥ i let go mistaken views of people today.
- ♥ every person has real worth and value...
  to remember this, has a moderating influence on how i see.
- ♥ all people have intelligence and goodness innate in them.
- ♥ i practice compassion in my regard for others today.
- ♥ each individual is important and precious to life...
- ♥ today i have an accurate view of people.
- ♥ i give up the idea that anyone is bothersome or unimportant.
- ♥ i open my eyes to see who people really are today.
- ♥ i relate to people from a new perspective now.
- ♥ i notice how people express
  - life
  - order
  - intelligence
  - perseverance
  - and joy.
- ♥ individuals respond to being found precious.
- ♥ there is a continual process of opening up to see people in a new, wonderful way.

i express praise easily

- ♥ i proclaim the good.
- ♥ i speak Divinely...my vocabulary is life-giving.
- ♥ i express praise easily...my speaking is constructive.
- ♥ acknowledging others is a usual activity for me.
- ♥ i understand that what i praise increases.
- ♥ whatever is good for me i appreciate with spoken words.
- ♥ my words of praise are powerful and loving.
- ♥ when i speak the Divine speaks gratitude.
- ♥ appreciation expressed daily lightens up life for everyone.
- ♥ rich ideas of good are ever present in my language.
- ♥ the Mind and Heart of Being respond favorably to PRAISE.
- ♥ opportunities increase for acknowledgment each day.
- ♥ i give up gossip and undermining conversations.

The Direction of West

- ♥ whatever i give returns multiplied to me.
- ♥ thanksgiving is becoming a way of life for me.
- ♥ the potent power of praising is always used by me.
- ♥ there is a unifying uplifting power in all my praising.
- ♥ i like what my words produce...i speak affirmatively.
- ♥ the tone of my voice expresses great appreciation.
- ♥ my speaking creates expanding good for everyone.
- ♥ my consciousness has attracting power.
- ♥ the words of my mouth are purposeful and inspired.
- ♥ i praise, rejoice and express easily today.
- ♥ i express praise everyday.

---

holiday declaration

happy holidays are here and now. no matter what doubts and fears there were...present thinking and speaking now rise above them. action of the law of mind always responds by corresponding with assumptions and attitudes. this holiday season, i have implicit confidence that to direct my language and expectations, to intend the highest love and celebration, brings joyful outcomes.
HAPPY HOLIDAYS ARE ALREADY, ALWAYS HERE NOW.

i give thanks often. holiday conversations bring satisfaction even when everyone doesn't agree. harsh reactions are replaced by AFFINITY and LAUGHTER. wherever i am, people get along! joy in being together comes from thinking about what i admire in people. i practice praise and acknowledgment often. there is new enthusiasm, vitality, good will and bright thinking all around me. i assume good now...i choose joy and celebration. the infinitely creative LAW OF GOOD is always bringing satisfaction, freedom and joy. GREAT POSSIBILITY is being expressed this holiday season...in all relationships...in all circumstances...in all people. i hear and see that...
whatever belongs to me, comes to me. there is plenty to spare and share.
   i KNOW WHAT TO DO AND i DO IT...
   i KNOW WHAT TO SAY AND i SAY IT.
   i KNOW WHAT TO THINK AND I THINK IT.

there is spiritual joy, WONDER, INTUITION, LOVE, and PLENTY OF PROSPERITY in this holiday season. APPROPRIATE ACTIONS are always the case.
   i am extending POSSIBILITIES everywhere i am.
   HAPPY HOLIDAYS ARE HERE NOW.

Seasons of Prosperity

START OUT WITH THANKSGIVING

"reflect upon your present blessings
of which every person
has many

not on your
past misfortunes of which
all persons have some."
—Charles Dickens

♥ the attitude of gratitude brings prospering
♥ i often remember to be thankful...
♥ i see all that's been
        achieved, acquired, received and realized.
♥ there is natural gratitude, awe, praise and acknowledging...
        that's what's required now.
♥ i uncover and unconceal my joy
♥ i start with thanksgiving today.
♥ i express thanks everywhere.
    I involve others in being grateful too.
♥ i often list the many things i am grateful for
        to help keep them in mind for me.
♥ the more gratitude i have, the more good comes my way.

holiday times together are events of celebration

♥ these oncoming holidays are gatherings to feel good about...
♥ i make the appropriate auspicious mood and feelings by thinking gratitude.
♥ good remembrances are called forth by me.
        i have and use imaginative power.
♥ i am able to move beyond what other holidays have been...
♥ i think about the value i have to others and the blessings they bring to me.
♥ gatherings are opportunities to speak praise, thanks and affirmation...
    i say how
        i appreciate people at holiday gatherings...
        wherever i am, heart felt gratitudes are happening.
        i call to mind the support and help others have been to me.
        i allow feeling-thanks to happen.
        i let go doubt, despair, grudges and opinions.
        i extend thanks around me, everywhere i go.
♥ these holidays, i am a stand, strong and secure, for happiness.
♥ i am a touchstone for joy. celebration is happening starting now!

The Direction of West

- ♥ i radiate health and happiness at holiday celebrations.
- ♥ when others forget that we got together to celebrate, i remind them.
- ♥ being prosperous, i spread prosperity.
- ♥ i think the thought that
  "There's always plenty more wherever anything came from..."
- ♥ inner exhilaration helps me be of value to others this holiday season.
- ♥ i have new ways of looking at the old circumstance. i interact peacefully.
- ♥ uplifting, glowing, valuable celebrations are everywhere now.
- ♥ i perpetuate good will and peace everywhere
  and with everyone this season.
- ♥ good relationship is alive at holiday gatherings.
- ♥ miracles are natural during holidays. miracles occur easily.
- ♥ bright light shines forth from hearts. we are happy to be together.
- ♥ ...during happy holidays, the family of humankind is prospering.

we give thanks for life
a Thanksgiving blessing
- asapted from psalm 136

life is good.
good endures forever.
mercy endures forever.
Providence endures forever.
life makes great lights.

bright colored birds and flowers forever occur.
the sun rules the day with light.
the light of the moon and stars rule the night.
      trees
      animals
      mountains
      oceans and the sky
      smile on us.
life with a strong arm and an outstretched hand,
      provides what is required.

with soft eyes we scan the horizon
seeing how cared for we are...
    we are grateful we have been rescued from enemies,
    we are grateful we have been provided for endlessly.
in all our transformations and transitions we are thankful.
we attract good endlessly...we embody great gratitudes.
how happily we have been blessed!
we gladly extend blessing to all.
    we live in endless thanksgiving. amen.

Seasons of Prosperity

creativity

"You are merely the lens in the beam.
you can only receive, give and possess the light as the lens does.
if you seek "your rights" you prevent the oil
and air from meeting
in the flame
you rob the lens
of its transparency,
your capacity, that is, to vanish as an end,
and remain purely as a means"

— Dag Hammarskjold

things appear at the command of thinking

There is no restriction to good in creative presence.
Mighty Intelligence is always everywhere at work...
i am one with Intelligence. i am never apart from what i am.
Mind of God is operating, through me, at the level of acceptance.
i am surrounded by Divine Presence.

i am not in bondage to limitation or lack. Barriers in my thinking are all that hold me in any position... Since there are no real barriers in thinking, there are no real barriers in any position. i realize this liberating truth today.
i am free to prosper.

Prosperity is ideas of limitlessness.
Things come and go but the idea of plenty endures.
Things appear at the command of thinking, expectation and assumptions.
Today i accept ideas of plenty, as my ideas.
i know that ideas are source of outcomes.
i give thanks for every evidence of financial improvement.
i am confident that Divine resource never fails.
These words go forward and do their work, their good cannot fail... so it is.
Things appear at the command of my thinking.

The Direction of West

i speak prosperous results

> *"Nothing is contrary to the laws of nature,
> only what we know about the laws of nature."*
> - St. Thomas Aquinas

- ♥ whatever i speak is what i am creating...
- ♥ i speak prosperously. i am a clear thinker.
- ♥ i am on the road of already abundant life....
- ♥ in specific terms of supply and support, i talk prosperity...
  my emotions resonate with true prospering.
- ♥ i affirm the good i intend...my thoughts resonate with true prospering.
- ♥ i speak success in the very face of question...
  my words resonate with true prospering.
- ♥ i speak success in the face of all doubt.
- ♥ results are attained by my speaking... i have a prospering consciousness.
- ♥ i am accomplished in demonstrating plenty of what i intend.
- ♥ i see opportunities rather than obstacles.
- ♥ i take direct actions. i move to what's intended.
- ♥ the quality of life improves, for everyone, whenever i am present.
- ♥ at night, my last thoughts are of good...

about creativity

- ♥ i have a new way of action.
- ♥ i am more creative than i've ever been before...
- ♥ now i always have all the information necessary to create new ways of looking.
- ♥ my words create my experience...
- ♥ i use my thinking to form outcomes that i want.
- ♥ rather than hash over reasonable explanations, i leave behind what i no longer want to create and i think about new circumstances that i do want.
- ♥ intuitively i respond to what needs my attention and regard.
- ♥ like an artist i create sentences in my mind that reflect the best i can imagine...
- ♥ i can see what is missing now and create it quickly...
- ♥ i am open and receptive to new ways of looking and thinking.
- ♥ i now have ideas that i've never had before.
- ♥ i know what do to and i do it!
- ♥ i am bringing about breakthroughs in the possibility of being creative.
- ♥ i am willing to raise and explore new issues like the pioneers of the past...
- ♥ i let go all limits on my creativity...my moods, feelings and thoughts support my highest ideal imagination.
- ♥ i use the ground work of those before me, to bring about more workable ideas...
- ♥ i am uncovering new opportunities for producing results.
- ♥ i am engaging in life in fresh, innovative ways!
- ♥ i live from the creative edge each day.
- ♥ i carve out amazing outcomes where expected experiences use-to-be.
- ♥ i express my new ideas in the ways that have the most impact, and in the places where they make a difference.
- ♥ i am listening and hearing in refreshing new ways.
- ♥ i see possibility everywhere, and i act for it. my self-expression is no longer within the confines of old experience.
- ♥ i give up the idea that circumstances control the direction of my thinking.
- ♥ i vividly imagine and enthusiastically act upon my ideals.
- ♥ i bring into experience what i used to dream about being.
- ♥ i choose to be free of old worn-out ways of seeing.
- ♥ i choose to be free of old worn-out ways of being.
- ♥ i have new thinking and new actions...
- ♥ i have a new way of seeing today, my actions are directed and effective.
- ♥ i am always open to what is possible!
- ♥ i am always organizing for the abandonment of what i have already achieved.
- ♥ i use insight & sensitivity to make action-oriented choices.
- ♥ i invent new outcomes often!

true creativity

♥ true creativity is possible for me now.
  to be creative is to be like living water ...
♥ true creativity
  gives life to everything around it
  just like water, which renounces any form of it's own,
  it becomes the creative matrix for form, in everything else.
  true creativity is like that ...
♥ true creativity
  gives impetus to everyone around it
  just like water, which renounces any life of it's own,
  it becomes, the primal substance of all life.
  true creativity is like that ...
♥ true creativity
  gives momentum to the future moving forward
  just like water, which renounces material fixity,
  it becomes the implementer of material change.
  true creativity is like that ...
♥ true creativity
  gives back innate harmony to the thrust of the moment
  just like water, which renounces any rhythm of it's own,
  it becomes the progenitor of rhythm elsewhere.
  true creativity is like that ...

---

i have a clear space to work

♥ i am free of useless chatter.
  there is a space to begin.
♥ i have space-to-work today, and i do what is mine to do ...
♥ i am free of the visual clutter of life.
♥ i can see great distances with good ideas.
♥ i schedule time so that comprehensive thinking can occur.
♥ i experience quiet and pure time to work well.
♥ i have plenty of time to do the work that calls to me.
♥ i can feel expansive and draw new conclusions.
♥ i can hear the challenge of ideas that call for attention and thought.
♥ i can unclutter mind and i do now. i make order here and now.
♥ a delightful way of being able to work emerges for me, in order.
♥ i keep a clean, clear, simple work-space around me all the time now.

libra declarations

i declare
that through the power and mighty presence of the Divine within,
i am a great contribution to the people around me...
i never compromise principle in order to gain approbation, i work in partnerships. my graceful expression moves people, and makes things happen. i see that everything in nature is intricately balanced and i recreate that order wherever i am. my blending nature creates peace and partnership easily. my strong will upholds others and creates community.
The most important priority in my life is to commit myself unconditionally...
i am a natural counselor.

i am successfully learning:
- ♥ to be firm and resolute
- ♥ others don't always have to agree
- ♥ to take more decisive action
- ♥ staying true to values
- ♥ explanations aren't always due
- ♥ to continue alone, when necessary

i am leaving behind:
- ♥ wanting to be liked
- ♥ putting things off
- ♥ postponing decisions
- ♥ enjoying arguments
- ♥ restless activities
- ♥ asking too many viewpoints

scorpio declarations

i declare
that through the power and mighty presence of the Divine within,
i am a great contribution to the people around me...
i represent fundamental transformation on all levels.
Change is the heart of my being.
i work to improve through creative use of will.
i have very sensitive and well-developed intuition...
i dig deep for solutions to questions.
Research and resolve is my job.
Unfiltered truthfulness is my trade mark.
i am regenerative. my accomplishments are miraculous.

i am successfully learning:
- ♥ to speak about how i feel
- ♥ creative use of the high will
- ♥ to delegate responsibility
- ♥ to trust that good is always
- ♥ to make friends easily
- ♥ what i do to others returns to me
- ♥ to soar high over struggle thinking

i am leaving behind:
- ♥ accusing and condemning
- ♥ running away from upsets
- ♥ trying to control the environment
- ♥ brooding resentments
- ♥ easily hurt feelings
- ♥ striking back and fighting hard

sagittarius declarations

i declare
that through the power and mighty presence of the Divine within,
i am a great contribution to the people around me...the undiluted truth is what i voice.
i expand into undreamed of realms to try my wings.
i create excitement through adventure. i travel fast and far.
i represent concern and zeal for the global family.
my energetic, outgoing nature makes me a great companion.
my honesty, fairness and generosity create trust wherever i go...
i place spiritual law above personality...i am a true explorer.

i am successfully learning:
- ♥ regard for the personal side of life
- ♥ interdependence and reliability
- ♥ that help always appears
- ♥ how to bear restrictions
- ♥ to clean up after myself
- ♥ to be subtle sometimes
- ♥ consideration, before jumping in
- ♥ the art of being part of a group.

i am leaving behind:
- ♥ fear of commitment
- ♥ being depressed by anxiety
- ♥ creating enemies
- ♥ avoiding intimacy
- ♥ sloppiness with details
- ♥ running away
- ♥ concern for approval of my family

...whosoever doeth not **RIGHTEOUS-NESS** is not of GOD...

—I JOHN 3:10

© toni acker 82

Direction of the North

we honor
powers of the North.
black is North. black is deep understanding.
North is where endurance, purity and truth stand.
North covers Mother Earth with the white blanket
>   of cleansing snow.
>   it is the direction of
>   long contemplation;
>   looking at what's been
>   accomplished and how.

in North, we enjoy the long winter's wait,
getting ready for the call of spring.
receptive, we assess our relationship
to all things; standing for the straight road.
thanks for time to do small things,
we become patient, open to new callings. . . .
from quiet understanding comes ability to hear.
we receive insight,
endurance becomes the beginning of decisiveness.
new action follows quiet blessings of North.

Seasons of Prosperity

The Direction of North

STANDING IN THE NORTH
i give thanks for the love and nurturing
                         provided by the
                         Archangel Gabriel.

this is the dawning place of true vision and insight.
i am grateful for all the people
                    all the circumstances
                    all the events
                    that have brought me to the NORTH.

as i continually move in the circle of cycles,
i am reforming and getting ready to start again.
i am empowered by interpreting hidden meanings.
<u>I AM RECEIVING GUIDANCE AND ACCEPTING IT.</u>
transition with all its unknowing is okay with me.
     i feel inspired but i don't know why ... DECISION WILL BE GIVEN TO ME.
i am imparting fresh life to that which is to move forward.
i feel receptive to new ideas. i speculate. i dedicate. i serve.
i detach from former ways of thinking that no longer fit me
            ...while i discharge emotions that are
            blocking...i surrender old ideas.
            i am open wider to new
            vistas of feeling. i cleanse, renew, and purify.
            there is REBUILDING, REVITALIZING AND RESTRUCTURING
                      in the NORTH.

i allow intensified feelings .
i trust the new ideas i am receiving.
i allow new perspectives to take hold .
i allow transformation, intuition and rejuvenation
                        to come to me
                        and thru me.
this is a culmination time: changing from one thing to another.
i commune with spirit silently
                and DO NOT RUSH CERTITUDE
                until my vision is complete.
i am willing to be transmuted in my very being so something new can occur.
i know there will be elevation in authority and power
    from willingness to endure
    this lofty point of excellence in the NORTH.

in the NORTH
i ask:
- what is sacred to me?
- in what shall i be made greater?
- what is my next plan for possibility? my anticipated course of action?
- where will i be aimed, what will be reformed ?
- what are the foundations on which to stand?
- how can i be brought to a higher degree of potency and purity?

Seasons of Prosperity

NORTH IS A TIME OF

- ♥ capacity to sit at the center of things.
- ♥ seeing how all things fit together in a whole picture.
- ♥ ability to let go of what doesn't seem necessary anymore.
- ♥ a time of insights and strong intuition.
- ♥ a time of moderating, interpreting, solving "problems".
- ♥ a new sense of balancing life, which is cheerful.
- ♥ the direction of the elders in a tribe.
- ♥ deep thinking time.
- ♥ fulfillment finally.
- ♥ analyzing, understanding, speculating.
- ♥ calculation and prediction;
  integrating everything.
- ♥ organizing, categorizing.
- ♥ envisioning,
  imagining the future possibility.
- ♥ increased capacity to
  wrap-up what was started.
- ♥ detachment,
  freedom from fear.

I HAVE WHAT IT TAKES IN THE WINTER

- ♥ vital expectancy is demonstrated in me today.
- ♥ i have the power to faithfully aim forward,
  continuing to describe good outcome before i can see it.
- ♥ magnanimity grows with me now.
- ♥ i multiply ability to give
  by giving, past all previous limits!
- ♥ i have power to generate life beyond
  "accepted" generous gestures.
- ♥ i am decisive.
- ♥ i grow bold in assuming risk.
  i penetrate inertia with a sure plan for possibility .
- ♥ my willingness-to-risk creates good futures for everyone.

WINTER - NORTH

using the model of four seasons in nature...
the darkest part of day is midnight,
the sun appears to have headed in that northerly direction to reappear many
hours later. the darkest season of our year is known to be winter.
short days, long nights. winter represents North. <u>winter is reformation.</u>
winter is recreation.
frozen rest is blunt.

this is the time of sacred nights, a wintertime <u>process of deepening roots</u>...
our ability to go down deep in life is sourced
from the contemplations of the winters. this North direction invites us to go
within, rest and reformulate views. our culture must come to appreciate
the need for this phase of rebirth

winter is a time of transformation, an enormously powerful period.
we have been all around the directions, full circle now we survived the ordeal.
we are open to new freedoms. in the North we face "demons" within the self.
dark repressed aspects of consciousness must be overcome.

what seemed solid and definite is in winter, barren and fallow.
how do we hold up in the face of emptiness?
we draw upon our deepest resources during times of transition.
there is a sense of being adrift on endless sea.
nothing seems "real". things seem "dead"

> there are increased hours of darkness
> inspiration is available during the holy nights of winter.
> the wintertime dynamic develops and deepens that
> life-spirit-potential, known as wisdom.

winter is not a time to rush or force anything to happen.
we accept a slow pace in the north direction. perspectives are changeable here.
<u>the way out is, the way in</u>. embracing the experiences we've enjoyed around the
full circle judging what worked and what didn't work; this is a <u>time for the long
overview</u> to see where we've been standing the past nine years, in our circle.
slowing down in the outer, provides time for new learning and quiet reflection.

in the North direction writing is excellent. good ideas come in installments.
keeping journals, playing with poetry and thinking in new directions
provides a new receptivity for ideas of value.

patience in waiting is developed here.
the ability to be quiet and happy is refined here. questions we ask ourselves in
the winter are usually profound. answers we intuit, change our lives for the better.

QUALITIES TO CALL FORTH IN THE NORTH

♥ EXPECTANCY
the power to faithfully aim something
forward, continuing to describe its good outcome
before you can see it.

♥ MAGNANIMITY
a way of being able to multiply ability to give
by giving, past all previous limits!
power to generate life beyond
accepted generous gestures
currently demonstrated.

♥ DECISIVENESS
being bold in assuming risk,
penetrating the inertia
with a sure plan for possibility and acting into it.

THE DECISION FOR QUIETNESS

in the season's cycles, being still is required.
quiet and slow is the way to go for now.
my rhythms, as rhythms of nature are ever changing.
i am happy being quiet, taking time...
resting is healing and attunement.
gradual transitions occur, in quietness.
there is a timeless magic in being still.
i satisfy the urge to rest and revitalize now.
intelligence is inwardly vivified, i open up to inner meanings.
with quiet, opened-eyes my breadth of ideas is richer, deeper and overflowing...
    i have expansive comprehension contemplating questions of life.
    i see clearly , with enhanced alertness of quiet time.
i have discernment now, to see what was always there.
healing comes with understanding.
less activity leaves more time to study...
in quiet is illumination of deeper messages ...
    in realizing all creatures as God's spiritual creation.
i find it easier to love more concretely
    and more gratefully than ever before.
profound spiritual vision is embraced.
in my true spiritual identity i reflect God's nature ceaselessly.
increasing knowledge is mine in the decision, for Quiet time.

I AM LOVED AND APPRECIATED

- ♥ i am love fulfilled. i am encouraged.
- ♥ i experience feeling loved and appreciated.
- ♥ i love and appreciate people around me.
- ♥ i enjoy knowing others and being known by others.
- ♥ i value people more and more each day.
- ♥ i am valued and others do a lot for me each day.
- ♥ i experience giving love to others in many ways.
- ♥ i am complete, full, fine and in good company.
- ♥ i am grateful for love that comes my way from so many people everyday.
- ♥ i am grateful for loving and being loved, in full aliveness.
- ♥ i give freely and accept gladly all the love i desire.
- ♥ i am happy to appreciate myself and my progress.
- ♥ i talk about and express love frequently.
- ♥ being known is vitalizing.

THE GREAT WAY ISN'T DIFFICULT

"The great way isn't difficult for those
    who are unattached to their preferences.
Let go of longing and aversion
    and everything will be perfectly clear.
When you cling to a hairsbreadth of distinction
    heaven and earth are set apart.

If you want to realize the truth
    don't be for or against.
The struggle between good and evil
    is the principle disease of the mind.
Not grasping the deeper meaning
    you just trouble your mind's serenity.

As vast as infinite space,
    it is perfect and lacks nothing,
but because you select and reject,
    you can't perceive its true nature;
don't get entangled in the world;
    don't lose yourself in emptiness.

Be at peace in the oneness of things
    and all errors will disappear by themselves..."
                                  Seng - Ts'an
                            written approximately 606 AD

I CHOOSE PRAYER AS A FOUNDATION

- ♥ often today i turn to the Divine to be guided.
- ♥ i think and act appropriately reflecting goodness.
- ♥ i grow in willingness to extend further.
- ♥ the world is growing in understanding of prayer.
- ♥ my real spiritual identity has always been with me.
- ♥ our reality as members of the same global family
  makes each of us essential and important.
- ♥ prayers for my world are a great contribution.
- ♥ more and more i see the outcomes of prayerful intending.
- ♥ my prayer-guided actions can make a difference.
- ♥ my prayer-guided actions can bring healing.
- ♥ my prayer-guided actions are the source of wisdom
  moving in this world.
- ♥ being prayerfully impelled i am founded
  in ever-expanding love with all that i do today.

LISTENING

- ♥ i invite relationship now.
- ♥ i aspire to good listening, attention is extended out...
- ♥ i realize that to understand people is to listen to people.
- ♥ people speak themselves, I receive their message.
- ♥ today i create the necessary time to hear what people say.
- ♥ i am interested in the goals, intentions and feelings of others and i show it.
- ♥ i am no longer so self-involved.
- ♥ today i create and recreate relationship.
- ♥ i nurture people's natural desire to help and care for each other.
- ♥ self concerned attitudes dissolve with me and around me.
- ♥ goodbye to non-listening, attitudes everywhere
- ♥ i make efforts to understand everyone.
- ♥ no one is left out of my magnanimous attention today.
- ♥ attention is life-giving, vitalizing and empowering.
- ♥ ability to listen blesses others, it blesses me too.
- ♥ as i listen and improve my ability to listen
  my willingness to listen to the voice for God, also improves.
- ♥ listening attitudes enable harmony.
- ♥ i cultivate great receptivity in listening attentively.
- ♥ listening attitudes enable me in community .

THOUGHTS LIKE I WANT TO HAVE...

♥ when people appear to be giving me a hard time...
   i look through to see their good intention. i love the good of them.
♥ in my heart i contribute by loving people as i walk by.
   this takes place quietly ...they get it.
♥ i've outgrown my tendency to make self right and others wrong.
♥ i no longer defend myself from imagined attacks. to claim attack is an attack.
      my heart is quiet and loving. i give up dissension. i take peace.
   i participate from my heart rather than opinions.
♥ i dissolve all obstacles to harmony. obstruction disappears.
♥ i appreciate and acknowledge progress of people
      ... i point out to them their loving kindness and good works.
♥ a peaceful heart means i accept myself completely here and now,
      "i accept myself completely here and now."
   i am a spiritual being with unlimited potential
      right now. i know it, show it, and extend it to others.
♥ i am able to be there with people without adding a lot of old feelings
      to new situations - i have peace in my heart and with my mind.
♥ i disengage from looking at seeming injustices.
♥ i know how to dispense anger by sharing feelings
      and crying when i need release from old feelings.
♥ it is within my power to radiate peace in any situation and i do now.
♥ i am stepping back from fear, advancing to love, in all aspects of my life.
    i include those who come my way into my heart... i am no longer embarrassed
      to appreciate and support all creatures large and small.
      my heart is open and receptive to all universal creatures.
♥ complete harmlessness is my heart's intention.
   i appreciate all manifestations of life.

LISTENING TO LIFE

today i listen to life ...
i feel life force within me ...
intelligence is in all creation ...
i reflect intelligence ...the life that activates me is intelligence ...
... i am wise, vital, vibrant, and happy.
i am receptive to new ideas and new actions.

Seasons of Prosperity

DON'T WORRY NO MATTER WHAT ANYTHING LOOKS LIKE
(REVISED PSALM 37)

Don't worry incessantly about incongruity or lack of integrity.
Wrongdoers wither quickly in power, they fade. Do good yourself and cultivate faithfulness. Good prevails ... no matter what anything looks like. Commit yourself to highest good. The laws of life can be depended on, even though not seen. Count on life... count on the Divine.
  Even when you have to wait patiently
  Even when you'd rather be running ahead in the fast lane.
Schemes may appear to prosper, but it's only temporary;
  wait and see. Give up getting angry. Evil doers are cut off... it's still true.
Good prevails no matter what anything, looks like. Although evil doers try to slow down and stop the way of the Heart, it does not work; instead they are stopped. Intelligence cannot be outwitted.
The giving heart who works in love always wins even in the middle of what looks like disaster. The enemies of the way of the Heart are always undone.
They vanish, like smoke.
They do not come out winning, even if it appears that way at first.
    Those who live the way of the Heart...
        the way of doing good
        the way of always serving
  they are unreasonably blessed and assured of surprising good will for no apparent reason. The steps of all people are established by the Divine.
The Divine, in an unseen way, holds the hand of one who lives
and gives from the Heart. He or she always lands on good,
no matter what appears to befall them.
There is never an exception to these Divine protections... count on life.
Commit to highest good and serve always.
The way of the Heart is still true today. Good prevails.
    No matter what anything looks like...

I GROW IN CLOSENESS WITH GOD

  i place the Divine first in my heart and life.
i praise God every day in every way. it makes sense to give God first place.
the most natural thing for me to do... i reflect God's own praising of creation here
the Divine is the focus of my each day's consideration.
identity as God's image and likeness assures me of all good.
God is Authority in my life, as i grow in closeness to the Divine,
my goodness, integrity, joy and lovingness increase.
        i grow in grace
        i grow in service to others
        i grow in true magnanimity and transcendence.
  my true nature is exalted, i continue to praise God everyday and everyway.
  Supreme Being has my full honor and attention. all intelligence, initiative, determination, participation, honesty, faithfulness, productivity and accomplishment have origins in the Divine.
  i declare today that i grow in closeness to God.
  i praise God every day in every way.

REFLECTION

The essence of the mind is pure and empty ...
its nature is to mirror.
We live in reflections ...
believing reflections are separate and real.
Reflections are the energy of our mind ...
                manifesting before us.

THE POWER MIGHTILY WITH ME... OF PERFECT PATTERN

    i am vitally alive with energy of will, wisdom, love and purpose.
i am galvanized into perfect-action and perfect-repose
by invincible currents flowing thru me... i am moved to do and have...
i am moved to be... according to unlimited vision. HOORAY...
    there are no obstacles or obstructions.
    my consciousness is on fire with will, wisdom, love and purpose.
    i am fired up. i am awake.
    i go forth to joyfully accomplish my mission.
    perfect pattern is what i bring about now.

LIFE ALWAYS RESPONDS

A passionate dynamic request of the Divine is always received.
Communion that eliminates doubt makes the way clear.
An inner way to change thinking and attract blessings is intentional prayer ...
Linking with the highest energy in the universe, is our privilege and right.
An ancient way of asking, and receiving what's next, is known to each of us.
The most highly accelerated mind action known is prayer.
Prayer unleashes a force which causes new action to occur.
The most effective prayer is a private act
within one's "own" consciousness. No ceremony is required

CONDITIONS FOR INTENTIONAL PRAYER:

- ♥ recognize Divine as source.
- ♥ acknowledge being united with the Divine.
- ♥ eliminate mundane concerns and worries.
- ♥ have a consciousness of receiving.
- ♥ desire Divine Will above one's own.
- ♥ maintain no grudge with anyone.
- ♥ maintain a mindset that the request .
  has been heard and is being answered.
- ♥ watch for evidence of "answered" prayer.

Seasons of Prosperity

TO PRACTICE DEATH

Let go holding ...
stop reviewing ...
no thinking-it-over ...
leave it all behind ...
no more keeping,
   letting go ... people,
   letting go ... ownership,
   letting go ... stuff and things
   letting go ... notions and
             motions ...
clear mind ...
peaceful heart ...
no matter what ...
we are all ...going home.
clear mind ...peaceful heart ...
homegoing ...going home.
let go lightly
...pass on gently.

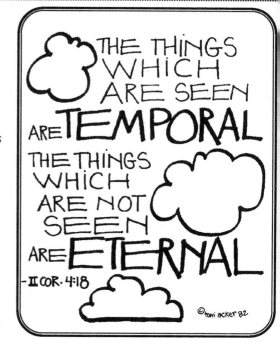

ON DEATH

"Praise be my Lord our sister bodily death from whom
                            no one living can escape."
                                        - St. Francis

PRAYER OF PEACE

"Let my soul banish all that disturbs it ...
Let my body and all its frettings, be still ...
Let earth, air, sea and heaven itself, be still ...
Let me think of Spirit as
      streaming, pouring, rushing, and shining
into me from all sides. as i stand quiet ... it is done."

                                        - Plotinus A.D. 205

"I give thanks to God
i am wonderfully made
in God's book
my days were all written
the days that were
ordained for me,
when as yet, there was
not one of them."

             - Psalm 139

TREATMENT FOR A PEACEFUL PASSING

_____ can easily let go of a body when it's not required anymore.
it's okay.
it can fall away and be left behind
like a pile of worn-out-clothes.
in Divine Order and timing _____ can let go
and go on, into the LIGHT and PEACE of another place.
when it's the good, auspicious time to go
            a peaceful passing will be
            experienced by _____.
            what's really_____ will still live.
            a peaceful passing is possible for _____
            blessing and assurance are
            there with _____ today.
            of this, we can be sure.
            a peaceful passing is assured.
                  it is so.....

PERPETUAL LIGHT -
DECLARATION FOR THE DEAD

- ♥ Life gives and life takes away.
  Blessed be the continuance of life.
- ♥ We are comforted. Tears are wiped away now.
- ♥ No sorrow or bitterness overtakes us.
- ♥ Love is stronger than any appearance of ending.
- ♥ Perpetual light now shines on _____.
- ♥ The pathway of _____ is illuminated brightly today.
- ♥ Unbroken faith links generations together.
- ♥ Strength lifts us from darkness. Light prevails.
- ♥ We remember many promises of everlasting life in:
              scriptures ...
              ancient writings ...
              bible accounts ...
              and prayers of the world's religions.
- ♥ There is joyful expectation today for _____.
- ♥ _____ walks a path of radiant light.
- ♥ Blessed be the continuance of life, in all its various forms.
- ♥ We most certainly are to follow ...

LETTING GO

- today i celebrate rather than control.
- i am letting go of clinging now.
- i am letting go of being compulsive.
- today my clinging to things and conditions ends.
- goodbye to pain and hurt.
- goodbye to all kinds of feeling bad and sad.
- goodbye to possessiveness, goodbye competition.
- goodbye trying to "get somewhere".
- today i give up lots of doing. i get beyond busyness.
    - ... i give up saving and savoring.
    - ... i give up assessing and judging.
    - ... positions lose their former appeal.
    - ... learning to let go is a preparation.
    - ... i let go fear of nothingness.
- there are surprises everywhere today.
- i see cause for celebration everywhere.
- letting go is getting easier and easier.
- i celebrate the end of clinging.
- compulsive conditions end ...

DEALING WITH DEATH

- Letting go of life is to be expected.
- Death is a very real letting go.
- Death is a gate to nothingness
  after a world of somethingness.
- Death is a natural ending to what has been.
- What has been, must be gone
  before what has not been, can occur.
- Life, in a body, is a temporary situation.
  What follows is in the plans for us all.
  letting go of life, is to be expected ...
  We live, as if we expect it, we live joyfully
  and fully in the now-moments-of-time.

CONSTANTLY REMEMBER DEATH

"Lord, by all your dealings with us, whether of joy or pain, of light or darkness let us be brought to you. Let us value no treatment of grace simply because it makes us happy, or sad, because it gives us or denies us what we want; but may all that happens bring us to you ... We can be sure in every disappointment we are still loved ... in every darkness we are still light, in every enforced idleness
we are still useful ... and that, in every death, life is still being given ... Amen."
- *Phillip Brooks*

JASON'S BEST THOUGHT

"We must kick darkness
until it bleeds daylight."
- *Anonymous*

"The world breaks everyone and afterward
many are strong at the broken places."
- *Ernest Hemingway*

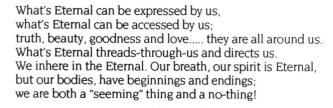

WHAT'S ETERNAL?

What is Eternal
is everywhere, in everything.
There is no need to be afraid.
Proofs of the Eternal, are always present.
We can never see the Eternal,
but we can see evidence of Eternal.

What's Eternal can be expressed by us,
what's Eternal can be accessed by us;
truth, beauty, goodness and love..... they are all around us.
What's Eternal threads-through-us and directs us.
We inhere in the Eternal. Our breath, our spirit is Eternal,
but our bodies, have beginnings and endings;
we are both a "seeming" thing and a no-thing!

What's Eternal endures. It is permanent. It is independent.
What's impermanent is always changing:
    coming and going....cycling in and out of manifesting

The Eternal can be accessed in art, spirituality and community.
The Eternal can be expressed in art, spirituality and community.

It's possible to think about what is Eternal;
it is invisible and everpresent; we know this.
It underlies the entire creation of disappearing and appearing things;
it sustains all we see, that includes us too.

i claim my relationship to, and with, the Eternal.
Today i live in the question of how i express this ...

TRUTH SONG

PRAISE GOD

THAT TRUTH IS EVERYWHERE

PRAISE TO THE TRUTH WE ALL MAY SHARE

THE TRUTH THAT THRILLS IN YOU AND ME

PRAISE TO THE TRUTH THAT SETS US FREE!

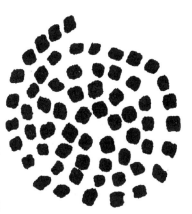

EXPANSIVENESS

- ♥ i have a winning way of being. i look at life in a friendly fashion.
- ♥ i encourage and support the winning of all others around me.
- ♥ i work for the good of all people. i am an expert at deprogramming complaints.
- ♥ i creatively move forward out of fixed positions.
- ♥ i am straightforward in offering and requesting information and services.
- ♥ i accomplish results by being invisible, functioning outside the spotlight.
- ♥ i also accomplish results by being in the spotlight.
- ♥ i have a natural attribute, ability and inclination to call for what's next.
- ♥ i now let go all boundaries, distinctions and ideas which limit.
- ♥ i am spontaneously forming new ideas, new actions.
- ♥ i incorporate ideas that relax limiting boundaries.
- ♥ i interrupt what normally continues to presence what is new and good.
- ♥ i create unknown, where the familiar used-to-be.
- ♥ i am going out further than i was before ...
- ♥ miracles abound everywhere i am.
- ♥ i am a constant rolling forward at full expansion, pressing-out. profuse, lavish, generous good results are everywhere.
- ♥ i have increasing willingness to experience unusual circumstances that bring good. i am expanding innovations ...
- ♥ i continue to create value with everyone and everything. the abundance of life is always available.

ATTRACTION INCREASE DECREE

"God is all in all
God is the One Life, all present ...all knowing ...all powerful life.
We live and move and have our being in this One Life.
We are the point where life causes form thru thought.
Now, old patterns have given way to refreshing new ones.
We are enthusiastic and aglow.
Our prayers have been answered...
> We have accepted the answers.
> New alternatives are unfolding.
> We are making new choices.

We no longer settle for less
than what's appropriate.
We have left behind everything
and everybody ... that does not serve
> a Divine plan
> for us.
> Everything moves forward.
> We let the good come in.
> We welcome the leading
> of great good.

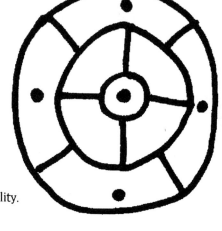

Receptive hearts and minds love possibility.
We enjoy a path of plenty ...
a path of increasing good.
> Divine Intelligence has cleared the passage ...

constant revelation happens, income increases ...
self changing is successful. We give thanks.
Love is enriching our nature ... magnifying, purifying
> and elevating our nature.
> Always there is good increase.
> Our intuition is one with light.

Our world is alive with divine prospering ...
> everyday brings greater good.

This word now goes forth to outpicture, as manifestation.
> And, so it is.

NEW YEAR MIND TREATMENT

This is a treatment in thinking for this new year. The words i speak are my law of good and, they will produce the desired result, they are operated on by a POWER greater than i am as a singular self.

Good alone goes from me. Good alone returns to me.

There is One LIFE, that life is DIVINE, that LIFE is perfect. That LIFE is my life now, i am grateful that i am manifestation of living SPIRIT...
> i give thanks that i am created and maintained by
>> that ONE PRESENCE
>> that ONE POWER
>> that ONE DIVINE PATTERN

This year there is perfect assimilation and perfect elimination.
There is NO CONGESTION... NO CONFUSION...
NO INACTION... NO FEAR...
NO DOUBT... NO HOLDING BACK.
  i am letting that PERFECT DIVINE PATTERN flow thru me.
i now take action appropriate to my intentions.
i now take appropriate repose between actions.
   i let go resignation and stagnation. i reclaim the passion and peacefulness that works perfectly in full freedom, i work effectively to make dreams come true for all the people around me, too... the conversations i create with others create a powerful partnership networking, everyone wins ... speaking creates evermore possibility for true goals and real love...
i reclaim and walk the line destined for me by my most high
expression of the ONE PRESENCE AND ONE POWER...
my will is the will of highest expression.
i produce trust and love with my conversations.
i am commitment in action. i overcome all seeming difficulty with great ease.
Whatever is mine comes to me. The DIVINE guides all actions...
   What's next is always perfectly outpicturing. i give thanks this word, as cause, is set in action and cannot return void... and so it is.

EXPECTANCY TREATMENT

The Divine exists with me, as creativity as expectancy and action.
Everything necessary to my success is already established...
Already with me...TODAY i AM ALREADY EXPECTING GOOD.
i am expecting good success in all actions...
            each thing that i do,
            each task that i complete,
            each activity that i am in,
            is created and fulfilled.
All that i do represents initiative, wisdom, love.
i rejoice in all life is doing by means of me.
i am guided to appropriate thoughts, feelings and actions.
Life succeeds in and through my endeavors. Everything necessary to success is already established... Already everything necessary is being brought to fruition and completion... satisfaction is present.
i creatively direct, select, choose, move into actions...
unfoldment of good takes place . i am creative,
i know Intelligence is active in my affairs and in all people...
i experience joyous cooperation. i prosper others and i am prospered.
ABUNDANCE OF LIFE is available today.
i accept it manifesting in and through me.
i am grateful. what was behind me in all past success, is behind me now.
This word, as cause, is set in action. So it is.

Seasons of Prosperity

TODAY: I ACCEPT GOOD

Permission for success is given and received everywhere.
Happiness includes everyone. Decisions that work for all concerned happen.
Daily life flows easily. All activities are prosperous and successful.
Great thanksgiving is spoken.
Good continuously comes from all directions. i accept good.
Increasing gratitude is felt. i attract boundless opportunities,
there are greater manifestations of good ... today i accept them easily.

GOOD WILL FOR ALL, WHEREVER WE ARE...

- ♥ the force of JOY abounds... all suffering is removed.
- ♥ the poor discover wealth.
- ♥ the powerless find power.
- ♥ all animals are free from fear.
- ♥ the fearful find themselves guarded.
- ♥ all challenges are subdued.
- ♥ people think of befriending one another.
- ♥ people accomplish whatever they set out to do.
- ♥ the frightened cease to be afraid.
- ♥ the bound are freed and the people always prosper.
- ♥ obstructions are cut through easily, quickly.
- ♥ all battling becomes playful exchange of flowers.
- ♥ firmly rooted miseries dissolve...
- ♥ people abide in the non-duality of self.
- ♥ TRUTH is steadfast and has great power.
- ♥ what occurs is NEVER TURNING BACK.
- ♥ people are guided out of afflictive action exactly.
- ♥ people perpetually engage in virtue.
- ♥ people are never parted from awakening MIND.
- ♥ people become unconcealed as MAKERS OF LIGHT.
- ♥ every disease in the world never occurs again.
- ♥ all lower life forms transform to higher states.
- ♥ all beings experience happiness.
- ♥ countless living beings attain FREEDOM...
- ♥ all sentient beings are served.
- ♥ all embodied creatures uninterruptedly hear beams of light/space.
- ♥ LIGHT shines throughout the cosmos.

GOOD IS CERTAIN

i recognize One Power in the Universe, One Perfect Pattern... One Intelligence, only One. i am part of Intelligence which is overseeing all action, all reaction, all reforming, developing and completion.
i am with and in the creative impulse which forms worlds as well as situations, events and circumstances...
Today whatever bothers, frustrates, pains, or angers is a powerless idea without my power of acceptance. i clear mind and thinking of all old reactive habits.
i am glad this is so.
My emotional commitment today is to good.
i EXPECT GOOD AND i GET IT.
i responsibly act for good.
i direct attention to good.
i direct imagination to the perfection
and fulfillment of my intentions.
i dismiss all appearances of conflict.
i move through apparent defeat to renewed confidence
in clear action and purpose.
i move into appropriate actions with urgency.
MY GOOD IS CERTAIN. i am grateful.
i TRUST EACH DAY THAT GOOD IS ALREADY ALWAYS CERTAIN, NOT ONLY POSSIBLE, BUT CERTAIN. i give thanks.
i release these words to work...
Even as i speak they are already accomplished in time and space.
They do not return void... it is already done. Good is Certain.

GOOD IS ASSURED

God is all in all. Good is natural. i am part of all that is...
The Intelligence of galactic law and my Intelligence
are the same One evolving system.
Thoughts project ideas into form.
THERE IS ALWAYS PLENTY OF WHATEVER IS REQUIRED...
good as infinite supply is present now and always. i relax in remembering this...
i speak the word to create appropriate outcomes...
THERE IS SUCCESS WITHOUT DELAY.
This treatment is a law of elimination to any psychological pattern that could limit my experience of unending supply of true good.
i now direct my mind to wipe out any file of belief in lack that limits good.
i ACCEPT ONLY IDEAS OF GOOD.
This word is now established in being.
i give great thanks that this is so.
i release any concern by knowing good is assured. Good is Assured.

Seasons of Prosperity

> **WE GIVE THANKS FOR PROTECTION**
> God is with us now.
> In trust and thankfulness.
> We inhere in God's care.
> Nothing can harm us.... ‑ neither tangible forces of the material world
>   ‑ nor fear of things unseen.
>
> God's love protects us. God's love surrounds us.
> We know and express divine justice. We are sustained and strengthened.
>
> We enjoy clearness of vision, strength of limb,
> soundness of mind, balance of body...
>
> God's wholeness is within us. We are at peace.
> Paths open to us where we couldn't see them before...
> We are kept from harm and confusion.
> Those who are with us are uplifted also.
>
> God's love is wide.
>
> God's power is eternal.
>
> We walk confidently. This is so.

I AM GUIDED TO GO FORWARD

- ♥ i attune to the divinity of my own indwelling teacher.
- ♥ i am making the determination for enlightenment.
- ♥ i am counseled and responsive to Intelligence.
- ♥ i choose to respond to Divine leadings.
- ♥ i declare that my life expresses truth,
                           beauty ... goodness ... love.
- ♥ i express wisdom in all that is taken on.
- ♥ courage extends to deal with all the consequences of chosen actions.
- ♥ i do not turn back or withdraw when the way looks difficult.
- ♥ i accept progressive obligations in my evolution.
- ♥ i am capable each day to respond to Divine leadings
  in life processes.
- ♥ i leave behind discouragement, distraction and confusion.
- ♥ i recognize my desire to serve all of life.
- ♥ i have intelligent affection for all who share earth.
- ♥ i choose to respond to Divine leadings.
- ♥ i am lighthearted and joyful.

DECLARATION:
TO COMMAND A THING TO BE SO

♥ To ordain an outcome
♥ To establish and fix an ideal as what's so
♥ A binding promise to bring something to be

    Spoken words are edges of energy and intelligence at work. Words spoken in declaration are charged with power. The power of words increases with use. Material things decrease with use. In normal living we have little understanding of the strength words have... with the use of declaration we bring outcomes into reality. Most people don't think that they have the power to declare things. So, they don't. In the bible we are told "Prove me now, saith the Lord." ...
    Decree a thing and it shall be brought to pass... whenever we are ready to exercise the power of intelligence in this fashion, the words will be brought to bear on our conditions.

DECISIVE, I CHOOSE MY NEXT PLAN OF ACTION

> "people acting together as a group, accomplish things no individual alone could ever hope to accomplish."
>   - *Franklin D. Roosevelt*

♥ CLEAR CHOICES ARE NOW BEING MADE
♥ clarity is the beginning of empowering an idea to manifest.
♥ what can be envisioned, can be created, TOGETHER WITH OTHERS.
♥ success happens, when we make
                failure impossible.
♥ decisive today, i am responsible with resolutions.
♥ i have the contribution of others in this planning process.

ORDER PERFECTLY OUTWORKING

    Divine First Cause present in everyplace at every moment...
consciously i remember that wherever i am is holy ground...
i am strong and of good courage, not afraid, not dismayed...
YOU are with me wherever i am, you are...
                i pass by judgments and evaluations...
                i leave behind those who are introducing contention...
                i let Divine imagining power do its work with me...
                i see order perfectly outworking around me
                now this is so.

PRAYER TREATMENT FOR DIVINE GUIDANCE

i am now in my right place. The only influence i know is the Eternal Good. The only controlling power is the Universal Good. On it i fix my faith. i am firm in my convictions. i trust my impressions. My intuition is one with the light. No evil belief finds place in my consciousness. No personal likes or dislikes control me. No belief in need or lack, in loss, deprivation, fear of consequences or evil results, has any power over me in any way. i am not undecided as to what i should do... i know.
MY LINE OF ACTION IS CERTAIN AND SURE.
i rest in knowledge. Good brings its own goodwill to pass. i do not need to struggle and to puzzle over anything.
i know my true mission. Everyone approves of my course.
NO SELFISHNESS CONFUSES ME.
No condemnation follows me.
No jealously opposes me.
No pride or ambition deceives me.
No self-condemnation shakes me.
i am not vacillating and fearful. The Holy Spirit guides my footsteps. Pure, unselfish, unchangeable Love points out the way. i walk in it. Wisdom makes my vision divinely clear. i know exactly what i am to do.
Perfect harmony reigns... not one dissenting voice. The motive of my heart is to continually say: THY WILL BE DONE. THE DIVINE WILL IS DONE.
That Good which is good for all forever. i am now in my right place.
- **Annie R. Militz**

DECLARATION OF DIVINE ORDER

i declare that God is all there is...one power, one presence, active ever always. There is nothing opposed to God. Divine order is ever present,
ever active as on-going creation:
forming
developing
making
breaking and
reforming
alliances and structures for further evolution.
Divine Pattern permeates and transcends this world.
Everything moves according to this Intelligence.
We are living in a spiritual universe now...
Its government is intelligence... Its laws are intelligence, acting as laws.
One power,
one presence
is always ever...
ONLY active.
That's what's so.

RENUNCIATION DECREE

i promise to give up attachment to:
    anxieties
    sorrow
    depression
    confusion
    obstruction
    all hardships
    bondage of any kind
    all feelings of anger
    dangling ropes of doubt
    miserable conditions and
    the obstacle of inappropriate companions
i declare that:
    threats
    delusions
    meannesses
    fears of calamity
    the perils of life
    inappropriate acts
    wrong means of livelihood
    false discrimination
    and mundane routines
no longer have any power over me.
Clinging to what is not well-intended is now
        dissolved and given up.
          - adapted from Avataka Sutra

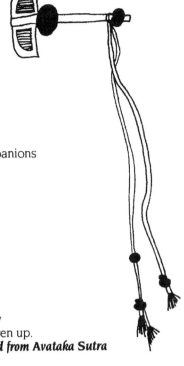

PRAYER OF APPROPRIATE CHOICES

"HEAVENLY FATHER, Ruler of Creation in whose Spirit we are ONE
DIVINE MOTHER whose beauty and creativity inspire us
WE ARE CREATED IN THIS IMAGE AND LIKENESS
CROWNED WITH HONOR and GLORY...
    Yet we dream we are separate and powerless
    we are your children
    we are willing to see magnificence
    rather than the small separate selves we made up
may we see ourselves in YOU
may we see YOU in every person
    LEAD US INTO PATHS OF APPROPRIATE CHOICES
    Where personhood is universal, earth and all creatures are forever loved
    and swords are forever beaten into PLOWSHARES."
          - Rev. David and Robbie Borglum

Seasons of Prosperity
SOMETHING NEW IS BEGINNING

"...in the pages of an old book it has been written that we are
in the hands of a teacher...it does not yet appear what we shall be"
— anonymous

♥ endlessly transforming thru all cycles.
i am happy in all seasons of prospering.

♥ something new is beginning to move with me
                                        in me
                                        thru me

♥ life has good plans for me. life is movement....i am part of a plan

♥ discomfort of changing is okay, i make things work in new patterns

♥ life says yes to all that i say, i keep on saying yes, to what i said

♥ life moves when i move, i decide on a thing and it is established.
                                          i am part of a plan

♥ i am the space where answers show up
i have the skill to let life work thru me, with me and in me.

i am willing to bring forth and spring forth. ... new is beginning.

BODHISATTVA VOW

Deluding passions are inexhaustible....   I vow to extinguish them all
... Sentient beings are numberless.....   I vow to save them all.
... Truth is impossible to expound....   I vow to expound it.
... Way of the Buddha is unattainable....   I vow to attain it.

A HUMAN BEING IS PART OF THE WHOLE...

"A Human being is part of the whole called, by us, Universe,
a part limited in time and space. He experiences himself, his thoughts
and feelings as something separated from the rest.
A kind of optical illusion of consciousness.
    This delusion is a kind of prison, restricting us to personal desires
and affection for a few persons nearest to us. Our task is to free ourselves
from this prison by widening our circle of compassion
to embrace all living creatures, the whole of nature and its beauty."
— Albert Einstein

The Direction of North

WE HAVE A HEALTHY PEOPLED PEACEFUL WORLD

- ♥ Each day we are happy to see ordinary people as Peacemakers passing up contention and creating contentment.
- ♥ Programs for peace show up in all institutions.
- ♥ Homemakers make home a peaceful place to be. Gratitude abounds.
- ♥ Hostages are freed by everyday people changing their world.
- ♥ Strife turns into surprising negotiations instead...
- ♥ Corridors of peace appear on borders and circle to the center.
- ♥ Conflict has become a creative source for new ideas that benefit all involved.
- ♥ Everyday people extend hospitality to each other, everywhere.
- ♥ Everyone is sticking their neck out for someone else.
- ♥ Peaceful resolution lives in hearts of city dwellers as well as rural people.
- ♥ Ordinary people are having a voice in giving peace, a chance.
- ♥ Governments come to tables to negotiate and share food together.
- ♥ Psychological ground work now results in meetings of minds where war once was.
- ♥ Unconditional cease-fire breaks out where war used to be.
- ♥ Moratoriums put bombing out of business.
- ♥ Local assemblies gather to disapprove of armed battle. They make their will known certainly.
- ♥ Interviewers, translators, writers and reporters help peace to prevail in all that they touch.
- ♥ Politicians and individuals realize a healthy peopled peaceful world is what's required.
- ♥ People are tired and disempowered by fighting, today
- ♥ Children spread talk about simple truth.
- ♥ Older people become instruments of peace.
- ♥ Busy people make time to create harmonies.
- ♥ Heavy artillery breaks down refusing to perform more.
- ♥ Armed skirmishes look silly now and everyone sees it.
- ♥ Conflict is resolved easily everywhere today.
- ♥ War machines disappear without a trace. All is well.

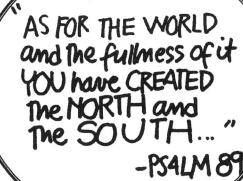

"AS FOR THE WORLD and the fullness of it YOU have CREATED The NORTH and The SOUTH..."
—PSALM 89

Seasons of Prosperity

GOD GREAT SPIRIT, I SEE YOU WITH MY HEART

God,
Great Spirit,
light of the heavens and planets
how great is your powerful creation.

existence of everything follows upon acts of Your Will
i behold You with the eye of my heart today.

BREATH GIVES LIFE TO US...

i am grateful for bestowal of Life in me,
and in all the creatures of worlds...
i am moved by ever always ... wonder and mystery.
i thank You for eternal teachings, and truth in all realms revealed.
the wisdom of my elders, the saints, teachers,
students, partners, collaborators, associates, unions and obstacles
all have brought me to always pay attention to the Ever-Unfolding.
i have received full baskets of abundance,
i share that plentitude... everything i give returns multiplied.
to be made in Your Image and likeness
is the most astounding truth
in this brilliant shining mirror
        of reflective universe.

thanks to Your bounty, Your cycles, Your immutable law,
i have felt presence of enabling energy fields along the way.
i give thanks, over and over,
that You afford us, the continued courage, to hum in the darkness,
to change in the circle, and to become friendly in the purifying time of winter,
here in the North.

i am grateful and happy.
i thank You for the gift of this life.

I AM A UNIVERSE CREATURE

♥ i declare that i am leaving behind obsessive self concerns and defenses.
♥ i declare that i am a universe creature now.
♥ my heart is compassionate, trustworthy, and continually generative.
♥ my heart holds me in good-esteem.
♥ i trust that i am the unceasing nature of Intelligence at work in worlds.
♥ my mind is now good intention for all living beings.
♥ i am leaving behind narrow anxious concerns.
♥ i can be trusted to travel galaxies with surrendered heart.

GOODBYE SMALL WORLD

- ♥ i am extending my perceptions to include all that i see.
- ♥ i have left behind a small insular world.
- ♥ i am learning to see, hear and feel in new ways.
  my concerns no longer stop at my own elbows.
- ♥ i am learning to be with all that's happening for others.
- ♥ external expressions and body postures
  > show me where people are at ...
  > so i can serve them better.
- ♥ i am training myself to see people's responses.
- ♥ recognizing the states people are in helps
  > me to have successful communication.
- ♥ i notice the way people code and respond to their realities.
- ♥ my former self-concerns no longer represent the new me.
- ♥ i now have the ability to respond beyond my past history.
- ♥ my magnanimity is increasing everyday.
- ♥ my life embraces all the lives around me.
- ♥ i effectively contribute positively to the future of this planet.
- ♥ letting go of limits on my perceptions widens possibility.
- ♥ i am willing to serve great ideas with my life.
- ♥ i am no longer stopped in my will to serve and love other people.
- ♥ my ability to act in ways of loving others is important
  to the well-being of everyone.
- ♥ i am willing to take actions that profoundly change
  people's lives for the better.
- ♥ i have an expanded willingness to initiate and participate in
  constructive activities that serve highest good.

MY HEART REVEALS LOVE; I SURRENDER

- ♥ my heart reveals love, evokes beauty and describes truth.
- ♥ i carry in my heart, all hearts.
- ♥ i have given up the privilege of taking myself away from others...
- ♥ i have given up my right to self-revulsion.
- ♥ i leave behind self concerns and defenses.
- ♥ i no longer hold back in fear, protecting past ideas and conditions.
- ♥ my primitive heart is the center of my being.
- ♥ Universal Heart is one with my heart.
- ♥ All Inclusive Heart is the center of my being.
- ♥ all living beings exist in my intention of good.
- ♥ i reflect the All Embracing Love, i am free.
- ♥ my heart embraces the entire system of galaxies.

Seasons of Prosperity

THE HIGH LAWS

understanding
is the influence i generate
>   wherever i am
>   wherever i've been
>   wherever i'm going.

i am a person of understanding, i speak what's so ...
i am a reflection of a great intelligence at work in the worlds.

- ♥ today i am awake and alert.
- ♥ i am mindful that ...
  > i receive what i am giving
  > i expect what i have already given.
  > i only see getting, whatever i am giving.
  > i experience the same conditions that i create for others.
  > my desire to serve others is the highest expression
  >   of who i really am.
- ♥ i am the living understanding of high laws.
- ♥ i honor and respect the lives of all life around me.
- ♥ i treat everyone as i intend to be treated, it is so.

GOD IS GOD ... IS GOD IS ...

- ♥ source is God
- ♥ first cause is God
- ♥ first image is God
- ♥ first mover is God
- ♥ source reality, absolutely self-sufficient. that from which all things are directed to proper ends not limited to space and time. God is the source..
- ♥ God does not derive being from something else
- ♥ IS LIFE ... IS BEING which exists always already and has astonishing qualities as sufficient cause of the whole universe.
- ♥ nothing prior to GOD ...
  nothing to impose any limits on GOD ...
- ♥ GOD: entirely present in everyplace and at every moment...
  not a body, not a form, not divisible into parts...
  there is no intelligence, no action, no life separate from God.

I THANK GOD

"i see the marks of God
in the heavens and the earth
but how much more in a liberal intellect
       in MAGNANIMITY
       in unconquerable rectitude
       in a philanthropy which forgives every wrong
and which never despairs
of the cause of CHRIST and human virtue
i do and must
reverence human nature
i bless it for its kind affections
i honor it for its achievements...and still more
for its examples of HEROIC and SAINTLY virtue
these are marks
of a DIVINE ORIGIN
        and the pledges
        of a Celestial Inheritance
...i thank God that my
own lot is bound up
with that of the HUMAN RACE."
                      - *Wm. Ellery Channing*
                      as inscribed on his statue in BOSTON PUBLIC GARDEN

UNIVERSAL PRAYER

"May the wicked become good;
      May the good obtain peace;
May the peaceful be freed from bonds;
      May the freed set others free."

- *anonymous*

UP, UP AND AWAY: BROKEN OPEN

- ♥ i surrender my heart fully to this life experience.
- ♥ i allow my heart to be "broken" open today.
- ♥ i give up my right to withhold myself.
- ♥ i give up my right to fear life. i am not afraid to love life.
- ♥ i give up my right to self-revulsion and other self-concerns.
- ♥ i am free to be in a multiplication of "love-affairs"
  that will go on until the end-of-time. i love life.
- ♥ my heart reveals real purpose in this season of quiet.

Seasons of Prosperity

LIVING THE MYSTERY

"The fairest thing we can experience is the mysterious. It is the fundamental emotion which stands at the cradle of true art and true science. Those who know it not and can no longer wonder, no longer feel amazement, are as good as dead, snuffed-out candles."
— Albert Einstein

- ♥ i'm amazed today. so much of what life is, remains out of sight.
- ♥ i am allowing what is limitless, inexhaustible and infinite to be with me.
- ♥ i am willing to dispense with knowledge, about things.
- ♥ i am letting go of reacting to things. i live in a galaxy.
- ♥ i ask myself how did the world happen anyway?
- ♥ i don't already know everything ...
- ♥ my small world of mental concerns and chronic states is no longer big enough for the real me.
  the mystery of what life is, cannot be solved.
  what is the existence of everything?
- ♥ i consider existence of everything ...
- ♥ the mystery of life is profound, i do not know what anything is ...
  a wordless sense of wonder is allowed now ...
  the unknowable immensity of reality exists.
  i feel amazement, i wonder, i am inquiring ...

ANSWERS ARE ALWAYS AVAILABLE

"... the point is, to live everything live questions now... you will then gradually, without noticing it, live along some distant day into the answer."
— Rainer Maria Rilke

TO BE ABLE

- ♥ i live answers by staying engaged in my own important questions, in seasons of unknowing... mystery is okay with me.
- ♥ i give up being an instant demand for answers.
- ♥ i learn to love questions and live happily with them.
- ♥ what's required is always present, this i know.......
- ♥ i find myself in patterns of activity, and quietness, that bring revelation.
- ♥ answers come to me in a natural, unmistakable way.
  i understand the wisdom of discovered answers.
  i understand the meaning of answers that come-to-me
  i trust apparent obvious answers. simple answers are fine, too.
- ♥ i have an ever-expanding capacity to innovate.
- ♥ i have the power of engagement, being in creative process uncovering answers, movement occurs.
- ♥ i enjoy rich satisfaction, the answers i seek emerge in the form of my own process of change.
- ♥ i am happy and grateful!

ALL CONDITIONS CHANGE AND PASS

the process of life is my situation ...
        all conditions change and pass.
my feeling-intelligence guides me safely ...
        things appear, disappear, change and pass on.
i freely identify with life ...i am safe in life to grow and change ...
i give up holding back from life today ...
frustrations, emptiness and loss do not stop me ...
        all conditions change and pass.
discomfort, grief and confrontation do not stop me ...
        all conditions change and pass.
life instructs and transforms me ...
        all conditions change and pass.
life enlightens me ...i grow in wisdom
        all conditions change and pass.
life can be trusted to restore me....
        all conditions change and pass.

PATTERN SEEN EVERYWHERE

    Amazing to me, the patterns ...
    i used to sit for hours in the laboratory and twirl worlds, beneath
my fingers on the microscope ... watching cells, with nucleus and cytoplasm,
going thru their evolution from basal to superficial cell,
breaking up and disintegrating, washing away ...
    looking at an astronomy magazine ...
there is a star burnt out ... fading ... disintegrating.
just like what i used to see cells of bodies doing under the microscope!
    In the laboratory, in pathology sections there were layers and layers,
landscapes of all same kinds of cells stuck together in tissue ...
i saw the landstat pictures of earth later, taken from the sky
they were the same kinds of scapes ... same, seen in sections of rocks,
like sections of people, and sections of planet!
as above, so below.... far, far away ... little polka dots of planets,
stars, further out ... perhaps forever, merrily they roll along
                we are part of this
                we don't know what it is,
  out there or what it is that we are here, some kind of pattern.
we can participate deliberately in the pattern.
even though, we don't really know what anything is ...

THE IMPULSE OF LOVE DESIGNS MY FUTURE

    God is All in All... God's love is filling time and space...
Divine INTELLIGENCE is infinite, always present... so is love.
i am an expression of God's love. My real being is God's,
i am inseparable from God.
THE IMPULSE OF LOVE DESIGNS MY FUTURE.
i know and feel love with me, as me, in the midst of confusion,
i practice love. Large changes do not scare me.
People leaving do not upset me.
i RECOGNIZE THAT
DIVINE LOVE IS EVER PRESENT IN MANY GUISES,
AND IN EVERY CIRCUMSTANCE.
    Everyday in every way love is enriching my nature, magnifying,
purifying and elevating it....want and lack of any kind are dissolved.
DIVINE LOVE is not vague, distant or cold ...
DIVINE LOVE is concrete, tangible and warm.
    The impulse of LOVE is ever present, intelligent, with purpose, boundless and
eternal. There is a vast, invisible loving circuit between
Awakened God-Minded people, always attuned to
good news of the LOVE of GOD. We live inside the continuum of creation.
    We are in the Heart of the Divine ... heart speaks to heart joined with God
and each other. Love designs our future... this powerful mystical bond
               transcends space and every other seeming limitation.
THE IMPULSE OF LOVE DESIGNS FUTURES.
    New associations and interests, new friendships,
circumstances and events are always present ...i am inquiry in action.
Whatever is required is always present. i am guided by the Divine,
impelled to act and react by way of this guidance only ...
i weave the threads of understanding as i go......
i am grateful. Thinking and living proceed with affection,
increasing communication and great satisfaction.
THE IMPULSE OF LOVE IS DESIGNING MY FUTURE ...
i release these words of truth ... they do work ...
That's what so. THE IMPULSE OF LOVE DESIGNS MY FUTURE.

... Let us Be HAPPY NOW...

UNIVERSAL MIND ...

- ♥ to love is not a state, it is a process, a direction.
- ♥ i have the mind of universal intelligence.
- ♥ i remember, understand and accomplish all that is important to me each day.
- ♥ i have a continual supply of inner joy.
- ♥ i clear my mind of confusion and anxiety daily.
- ♥ i know what to do and i do it in this quiet time.
- ♥ intuitively i respond to what needs my attention.
- ♥ i call upon and use my vital universal mind.
- ♥ i remember more and more.
- ♥ joy is within all thinking this day.
- ♥ new joy is created , as i use intuition trustingly.
- ♥ i am open and receptive to the living spirit of truth.
- ♥ all situations are unfolding in perfect order.
- ♥ i am unfolding perfect pattern from within .
- ♥ i am aware of loving presence and power always with me.
- ♥ new levels of confidence and assurance are arising ,every need is met.
- ♥ i give thanks for new ideas, new growth, and new accomplishment.

I FOLLOW A HIGH CALLING:

God is All in All. Mind of God is my Mind.
The flow of Divine expression is with me.
AS i AM STILL, i HEAR DIVINE DIRECTION EVERYDAY.
i am charting new courses, ever perfecting experiences. i participate in the consciousness of unlimited good. The humility to trust the Divine providing for every aspect of my life is a quality that requires mental and emotional discipline. It takes practice to think and feel TRUST ... practicing quiet and peace. i am subject to the Divine, not to the voice of anxious mood. The basis for experiencing abundant good is to be still to realize Divine power right now, here. No loss can occur in trusting the power of the Divine.
i KNOW WHAT TO DO AND i DO IT.
Expression is never blocked or confused.
Infinite Intelligence reveals new good.
i FOLLOW HIGH CALLING. The Mind of God is my Mind.
The Spirit within is exhorting me forward. i am safe in the middle of anything everything. i have consciousness of unlimited good.
As i am still, i hear Divine direction guiding and upholding me.
EVERYDAY, IN EVERY WAY, i AM EXPERIENCING ABUNDANT GOOD.
i release these words now to work. They do.
i give thanks that this is so ...
The Mind of God is my Mind. I FOLLOW A HIGH CALLING.

WAITING WITH PATIENCE

> "all changes, even the most longed for, have their melancholy, for what we leave behind us is a part of ourselves. we must die to one life before we can enter into another."
>
> *- anatole france*

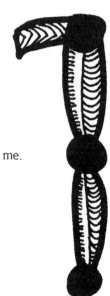

- ♥ what is whole, strong, and vital has had waiting first.
- ♥ increasing patience is mine... i enjoy waiting.
- ♥ life is a series of waitings, hopes and intentions.
  waiting is a feminine state, it is quiet gestation.
  the process of becoming, is feminine, in nature...
  i remember there is a program of subtle changes
  before bursting forward happens...
- ♥ forms of elimination are part of waiting
  wisdom comes with ripening...and patience.
- ♥ i am expectant in waiting.
  i know good will be brought forth for me, and through me.
- ♥ <u>instant-gratification</u> trivialize what is given...
  germinating is required, i am willing to have patience.
- ♥ when i wait, i am receptive
  to greet what i am waiting for...
- ♥ my practice of waiting, helps me to be grateful,
  watchful and appreciative
  of the changing
  that, what-i-wait-for, will bring to me...
- ♥ as life asks me to wait,
  i am initiated to an ever deeper
  experience of life's perfection. waiting is necessary in creation.
- ♥ patient waiting is more than delay, i see that...
  > i learn to allow,
  > i learn to trust,
  > i learn to accept.
- ♥ being grateful is an aspect of having been able to wait patiently...
- ♥ waiting is necessary to what is coming...
  i am willing to grow in waiting ....
- ♥ the tempo of haste, has it's time in life's circle.
  patient waiting, has it's time in life's circle too.
- ♥ i am wise to know when to wait and when to push...
- ♥ brewing, simmering and baking are active models of waiting.
- ♥ quiet incubation is innate in all transformations.
- ♥ movements of great value incorporate waiting
  there is new value to waiting periods in life.
- ♥ waiting first, is a wisdom of the winter.
  i am willing for the wisdom in waiting.
- ♥ i am expectant in waiting.

HAPPY WORDS ARE MY CHOICE

♥ happy words describe a happy world.
♥ i am changing words in my life.
♥ the words i speak, say how i am.....
♥ when i use new words, i create new life.
♥ words make ways-of-being, they are my choice.
♥ i use words to say, my chosen ways of being....
♥ vocabulary adjustments change the quality of my perceptions....
♥ disempowering words have left my sentences,
   i have replaced them with words of power and accomplishment.
♥ my choice of happy words develops a new level of satisfaction for me.
♥ i break out of unhappy habitual emotional states
   by altering word patterns. everything changes.
♥ i give up language that intensifies negative emotions.
♥ happy words change my emotional direction and feeling.
♥ what i say is what i am. i pay attention to words today.
♥ today my word choices, direct life to avenues
   of happiness and contentment.

LIFE EXTENSION

♥ i leave behind the idea of growing old.
♥ i declare the perpetual activity of life everywhere,
   at all times and under all circumstances.
♥ abundant life is mine at all times.
♥ life is ever active in and through me, now, right now.
♥ life is constantly and fully present in all of my body all of the time.
♥ i am attuned to the ever present activity of all life.
♥ life shows up in me powerfully and is increasing.
♥ accomplishments are increasing.
♥ life has no wane with me.
♥ i know what to do and i do it.
♥ i let go false appearances of worn-out, tired, run down countenance.
♥ the life force dances in me to the music of merriest moments.
♥ thinking is my living power and i use it to create enthusiasm and vitality.
♥ i dash forward joyously, and with vigor into new experiences each day.
♥ i participate fully in life, each moment, without exception.
♥ life power is ever active, expanding daily.
♥ i love being alive and vital, health is a function of participation.
♥ there is a perpetual inflow of new life in and with me all the time now.
♥ all obstruction gives way. obstacles dissolve.
♥ i have an unobstructed union with life's living power.
♥ freedom from age makes me younger each day!!

FREEDOM IS ALREADY MINE

♥ happiness is not a matter of seeking.
♥ truth is not a matter of seeking
   truth is, what is already so, with nothing added.
♥ i remove all contradictions today.
♥ i say goodbye to every trace of conflict...
♥ i leave behind opposition of any kind ...
♥ i leave behind division of any kind ...
♥ i leave behind desperate motivation of any kind ...
♥ freedom and joy are already mine.
♥ i am, at any moment, already free.
♥ i cannot become happy, by working for it.
♥ happiness is not a matter of seeking.
♥ i can only be happy, freedom is already mine.
♥ i embody lively happiness.

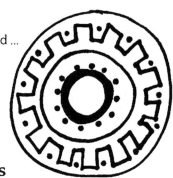

DECLARATIONS FOR ENLIGHTENING BEINGS

Today i am willing ...
   ... to enjoy miraculous displays.
   ... to have transformations and masteries occur.
   ... to grant new empowerments.
   ... to exercise new empowerments.
   ... to make untold offerings.
   ... to tame doubts and experience freedom.
   ... to observe right recollections.
   ... to penetrate untold truth.
   ... to see light appear.
   ... to know and practice untold generosity.
   ... to enter unspeakable spheres of action.
   ... to make promises, declarations, great vows & resolution.
   ... to be involved in the rigorous endeavors that bless me.
   ... to comprehend and distinguish refreshing new ways.
   ... to benefit all people with great compassion.
   ... to surrender my protective dispositions.
   ... to have all my deeds and results be "guided".
   ... to have clear comprehensive insights dissolve barriers.
   ... to be capable of deep concentration and comprehension.
   ... to cultivate courageous ability to teach truth.
   ... to praise virtue, wisdom, beauty and compassion everywhere.
   ... to overcome my tendencies.
   ... to expound teachings that call us to futures of greatness.
   ... to embody untold states of peace.
   ... to develop determination for enlightenment.
   ... to have unspeakable attainments.

WINTER HAPPINESS

♥ i am experiencing a sense of celebration.
♥ today i embody the power of feeling happiness.
♥ joy is the life force. today, i feel joy. i speak joy easily.
♥ power is always directed joyfully towards
   the happy service of all life, in all its seasons.
♥ in the circle of the seasons i can feel happy . . .
   opening my heart, in the face of all changes... happily.
♥ life shines for all, and in all, even in dark times ...
♥ songs without limit, everything lost is found
   again in a new arrangement, in another way.
♥ i dare to feel and speak happiness, no matter what ...
♥ there is a wonderful sense of close associations now.
♥ in the thread of seasons,
   all seeds will awaken in proper timing.
♥ life brings constant changes. endings bring beginnings.
♥ life links us with others, we gather. we are revivified.

CANDLEMAS:
LIGHT IN THE DARKNESS IS A HAPPY EVENT

♥ homes are filled with love this cold season.
♥ warmth, light and happiness prevail in the darkness.
♥ gratitude abounds, heralding a fruitful prosperous beginning.
♥ fallow fields have new seeds moving in the dark,
                    under melting snows.
♥ days turn upward into spring birth and beginning, before it can be seen ...
♥ the warming air is wonderful. increasing light is welcomed.
♥ winter is soon over, it's coming to completion.
♥ icy winter, brings welcome spring;
   we welcome return of the quickening of spring soon.
♥ time of rest and repose, rekindles new flame.
♥ there is more light, returning spring now coming ...
♥ we are grateful, warm winds are blowing stronger from the South.
♥ forest streams are breaking free of ice and snow.
♥ we can feel the coming bounty and richness of summer.
♥ soon trees are green again and flowers bloom.
♥ flowers that herald spring are on their way now.
♥ new life is ready to be seen again, soon. we are grateful.
♥ seeds are ready to call possibility into manifestation.

Seasons of Prosperity

I HAVE A NEW FRIENDSHIP WITH THE NATURAL WORLD

- ♥ everywhere is the green of new growth.
- ♥ everything flows, everything grows. prosperity abounds.
- ♥ there are amazing sightings of renewal everywhere.
- ♥ prosperity abounds, everything flows ...
- ♥ everywhere and always birdsongs, bushes, bendings, blendings, beautiful trees and ancient lively waters ...
- ♥ energies of life are everpresent, vitalizing, empowering.
- ♥ i dash forward to do what's mine to do today.
- ♥ i touch life.
- ♥ i am touched by life.
- ♥ i know life.
- ♥ i am known by life.
- ♥ i love life.
- ♥ i am loved by life.
- ♥ body, mind and spirit have a new rhythm .
  spring comes to me, thru me and life is recreated in me today ...
  i give thanks for new life.

WEATHER STORM DECLARATIONS

- ♥ we are grateful to have help in all stormy weather.
- ♥ we intend for direction each step of the way. we get it.
- ♥ we always master storms easily and fast.
  we have authority with thunderstorms today.
- ♥ we follow intuition about all weather patterns today.
- ♥ we look up at storms to predict what's needed next.
  we know what to do and we do it.
  we can tell what's next with accuracy.
  we do what's required.
- ♥ in stormy weather everybody rallies to stick their necks out for the others.
- ♥ electrical storms are now subdued in many ways.
- ♥ no loss can occur from trusting God's protection in storms.
- ♥ all uneasy weather is tamed and aimed away from people now.
- ♥ happy results are always the outcome in weather predicaments.
- ♥ our share of bad weather is always slight.
- ♥ miracles, regarding storms, are always occurring, we accept them gladly.
- ♥ oncoming disturbances pass us bye quickly.
- ♥ safety prevails. wise choice prevails. good company prevails.
- ♥ we have a rainbow in every storm. we see it.

WE KEEP EARTHWATERS SUSTAINING LIFE

> "Water brings about becoming and subsiding ... it is a balance point in natural process ... Water serves to maintain equilibrium ... it is the omnipresent, ever reestablished active element in life's freedom-zone. Water is present in everything alive."
>
> — **Theodor Schwenk**
> Water - The Element of Life

- ♥ today there are solutions for earth's water difficulties ... now we have openness and willingness to receive and act on local and worldwide water issues.
- ♥ re-enlivening waterways on earth increases life energies everywhere for everyone.
- ♥ today we are re-enlivening the earth's water supply.
- ♥ people are quickly entering right relationships with technology and waterways.
- ♥ ethical maturity is increasing in all human beings and industry.
- ♥ WATERS ARE NOW BEING RESTORED TO LIFE.
- ♥ death processes taking place in water are brought to a halt today.
- ♥ the continual restoring life force in water is now valued by all beings consciously.
- ♥ water is preserving and being preserved.
- ♥ water is sustaining and being sustained.
- ♥ water is renewing and being renewed.

Seasons of Prosperity

DECLARATIONS FOR A TREE

- ♥ everywhere, trees demonstrate the laws of nature's cycle.
- ♥ trees are wonderful symbols of stability and growth.
- ♥ this tree is vibrant with life energy.
- ♥ this tree is protected and protective.
- ♥ i see this is a perfect idea of a perfect tree.
- ♥ i extend my life giving attention to include this tree.
- ♥ blessings of praise and appreciation are now given this tree.
  as with this tree ...   MAY ALL TREES NOW RECEIVE
  MY THANKS AND BLESSING.
- ♥ this tree receives nurturance and light in
  all the required amounts to continuously thrive.
- ♥ in the ever ongoing union of nature and humankind, may this tree
  be loved, respected, and honored as an incredible gift of the Divine.

BLESSING FOR FLOWERS

Everywhere in creation, flowers demonstrate beauty, bounty and fulfillment. Flowers are easy-to-see simple symbols of successful completion. i am gratefully moved in the heart by the pure radiant beauty of these flowers. i praise and bless flowers, may they remind all who see them of Divine ideas. May they move hearts of observers to express love, the way they express vibrant life energy with color. Flowers are appreciated they generate more and more beauty.
we are ever grateful for flowers. we acknowledge blooming and blossoming activities all around us today.

HAPPY CELEBRATING NOTHING:

- ♥ i am getting out from under and getting back on top of nothing.
- ♥ i celebrate nothing, the source of all something.
  i am happy to have plenty of nothing.
- ♥ life is successful today. starting from nothing.
  nothing is where everything comes from....
- ♥ i give up aging concerns and sophisticated worries
  to laugh often and loud. everything goes back to nothing.
- ♥ morose viewpoints lose their power over me today.
  i celebrate the glory of nothing...nothing is potent to create everything.
- ♥ i give power and importance today
  only to thoughts that validate and empower.
- ♥ i have limitless inner resources...
  i am able to create possibility
  i create from nothing. i am happy
  i celebrate nothing as source of all something!

HUMAN BEINGS ARE A VIABLE SPECIES

"... of all the species that have existed it is estimated that less than one in a hundred exist today. The rest are extinct."
— John Seed

Human beings are making wise use of Intelligence today.
Rather than endanger the life of planet earth, they plan for its upkeep.
Humans are seeing where errors have been made ...
all errors are now being corrected.
  Young humans are being educated for planet maintenance.
People from all countries realize a common, concern for the human condition ...
an intimate connection with humans and nature is now seen and felt.
Empathy for the earth planet's ecosystems is now realized;
priorities for planet well-being are now defined;
patterns of consumption are now re-assessed.
Thankfully people can think like mountains and they are starting to.
  People all over are remembering that air is precious
and breathed by all creatures.
    Human beings are moved to: actions
                                 thinking
                                 speaking
                                 and feeling ...
... on behalf of earth, environment, and earth creatures today.
  The minds of human beings embrace all living things
as a mother cares for her only child, today.
Human beings are making wise use
of intelligence now.

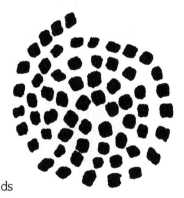

SIOUX PRAYER

Grandfather Great Spirit
All over the world faces
of living ones are alike.
With tenderness they have come
up out of the ground.
Look upon your children, they may face the winds
and walk the good road to the Day of Quiet.
Grandfather Great Spirit, fill us with light and wisdom
Give us strength to understand, and eyes to see.
Teach us to walk the soft Earth as relatives to all that live.

Seasons of Prosperity

SACRED SITE DECLARATIONS
- Tom Flynn

- ♥ i clear my mind of all grudges and ill intention.
- ♥ clearing mind leaves me in a relaxed unbothered state.
- ♥ i am now receptive to enduring power present at this sacred site.
- ♥ i am reverent and grateful for ancestor's spirit
  i am reminded of my modest spiritual beginnings.
- ♥ the spirit and vision of predecessors calls to me gently now...
  as an explorer of life i am drawn to the spiritual significance,
  timeless intelligence and ancient wisdom preserved here.
  i have come receptive, expecting nothing and prepared for everything.
- ♥ i am one in spirit with this sacred site ...
  today i am ancient and present at one with this place.
- ♥ at this sacred site, i am willing for constant rolling forward of life.
  i come here open to energetic influences .... willing for changes.
- ♥ i allow new views to occur ... i choose a future free from old conditioning.
- ♥ i freely release energy required to restrain emotional responses ...
  i stand aware and revealed in my feelings.
- ♥ on sacred ground, i give up conforming to my "already" history ....
  i now choose authenticity.
- ♥ i choose a willingness to "not know" already ...
  i allow paradox. i am allowing all the parts to show up,
  no matter what they look like.
- ♥ energies of this site, are allowed ...
  moving forward as a field of possibilities is what i do now.
  i give thanks to influences that brought me here.

THIS BODY IS A FIELD OF TRANSFORMATIONS

- ♥ i am an aspect of fluctuations and frequencies of emptiness itself.
- ♥ the full beauty of endless transformations is now unconcealed.
- ♥ this body is an infinitely flexible, dynamic field of all possibilities.
- ♥ i express full vitality everywhere.
- ♥ Intelligence lets go of what's no longer beneficial.
- ♥ i am an expression of Intelligence.
- ♥ i am a series of transformations in consciousness ... changing, faster and finer.
- ♥ i am Quick, light, bright... i am no longer encumbered.
- ♥ i sacrifice what's been for what will be.
- ♥ this body is a field of transformations ...
  i let go heavy concepts, ideals and beliefs.
- ♥ more able is how i am ...i am changing effortlessly. i am ever changing patterns
- ♥ evolution is upgraded ... old habit patterns are dissolved.
- ♥ internal dialogues are vitalizing, radiating simple,
  pure intelligence, in time eternal
- ♥ this body is an oscillating field of transformations.

BLESSING FOR SEEDS

"let your food be your medicine"
-Hippocrates

- ♥ we bless and appreciate the seeds of new life.
- ♥ seeds are formed in the breath of summer.
- ♥ seeds are valued and gathered spread to places that require them today.
- ♥ we bless those who have the foresight to protect seeds.
- ♥ plants were here before us.
  we honor plants and their seeds for the value they provide us.
- ♥ rather than use a small number of plants for foods, we grow, purchase and use diverse seeds to foster growth of deeper diversity in gardens today.
- ♥ we praise what is sweet, deep and within each seed that produces lush plants.
- ♥ life is a mysterious web of intricate interdependent relationships, diversity is its heart...gardens today express nature's diversity.
- ♥ we bless each seed everywhere which holds the recipe for growing, changing and blossoming.
- ♥ we acknowledge the great organic diversity of seeds which are grown without toxic chemicals.
- ♥ seed remind us of the capacity innate with us to unfold, express and achieve growth and outcomes.
- ♥ seeds are strong, sturdy and successful.
- ♥ seeds have all the sun, soil and water required to produce succulent vegetables and flowers.
- ♥ seeds represent freshness, off shoots and buds.
- ♥ seeds represent another opportunity again and again.
- ♥ we extend a great blessing thought to the hearts of all seeds. we bless the life and well being of all seeds today.
- ♥ may seeds easily root, off shoot and bud to recreate even more seeds for the next planting season.
- ♥ it is for all seeds we speak a blessing today.

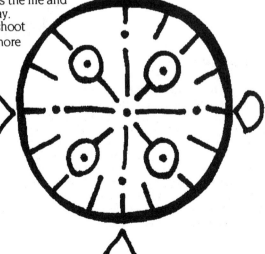

Seasons of Prosperity

BLESSING FOR THE BIRDS

- ♥ i love and appreciate feathered friends today.
- ♥ birds are beautiful outcomes of life's wish to fly lightly.
- ♥ birds are blessed by me now. they bring blessing to me often.
- ♥ when bogged down, embedded in my body
  i remember how easily attention could fly to what's next.
- ♥ birds remind me of how easy it is to fly on and be happy.
- ♥ birds sing for no reason...
- ♥ birds prove that life provides...
- ♥ birds find what's required wherever they are..
- ♥ birds show me a happy way to live.
- ♥ birds are brilliant expressions
  of life working benevolently.
- ♥ i am ever grateful for the joyful song and
  picture of birds.
- ♥ i am grateful for the beautifying
  idea that birds reflect
  all over EARTH.
- ♥ may all birds be blessed
  by all people today.
- ♥ may we always be grateful for
  beauty and playfulness
  of all the bright bird friends
  we have known.
- ♥ i declare that birds are cared-
  for, sheltered and nurtured
  by ever more people today.

NATURAL LAW

what we refer to as NATURAL LAW,
is an understanding of how human nature fits into the overall ORDER OF LIFE.
there is an intrinsic pattern of integrity in the order of life itself.
our culture, in contemporary times, keeps morality and truth separated,
to make morality more convenient. violations to the integrity of the intrinsic
pattern are re-worded. human reason, a function of egoic reactionary mind, tries
to create values that are convenient and impose them on life, but it doesn't work.
what works is to <u>discover</u> values that are inherent
in the order of life, as it has been created, already.
these values are real. everything in creation is organized
around these values. these ideals are Eternal

STREAMS COME ALIVE AGAIN AND FILL WITH FISH

♥ i put my attention to envisioning water, restored to its clean,
vibrant, crystal, clearness in all these earth waterways.
♥ i say water is attracting attention to its plight successfully .
♥ wetlands are a natural living filter to clean wastewater...
today more wetlands are being activated to help clean streams and rivers.
♥ inexpensive wastewater treatment ideas are manifesting all over earth.
goodhearted people are taking on the task of water cleanups.
♥ free design expertise is made available on water cleanup projects.
♥ restoring "deadened" waters becomes popular and successful everywhere.
♥ local military battalions are helping to make rivers come alive again.
♥ bulldozers, backhoes, trucks and shovels are put to work
to have waterways work again.
♥ materials, fuel and labor are attracted to environmental
waterway projects. success is imminent.
♥ people leave behind apathy and get into action on local
and national water issues now.
♥ military battalions become ecological task forces
whenever the need arises.
♥ ponds are being dug, channels are being installed,
cattails are being planted to help purify water.
♥ the U.S. annual military budget of $300 billion shares some resources,
to enliven earth's waterways, on which life depends today.
♥ environments improve as a direct result of value placed on this activity.
today i put attention and imagination to work for enlivening waterways.
♥ local, national and international streams are alive again
filled with fish and flowing free for the good of all.

THANK GOD FOR ANIMALS

i see God everywhere. God is with all things.

every single creature is fully LIFE, and is is a book about LIFE.

every creature is a word of God. every creature is a work of God
if enough time was spent with the tiniest creature...
a sermon would never need to be prepared.
so full of God is every creature. thank God for animals

they are happy companions for people, in many ways.
i appreciate animals and bless them today.
i extend kindness and compassion to animals.

adapted from Meister Eckhart

Seasons of Prosperity

THE ANIMAL BLESSING

(any species of animal can have this treatment used
on their behalf by changing the word "cat" to the animal who requires it)

this cat is life's perfect idea of a perfect cat.
right now, this cat is in harmony with the presence and power of God.
there is One God, One Life; that life is perfect, and that life is this cat's life too.
all creatures live and move and have their being in this One Life.
this cat releases any obstruction to Life's perfect flow now. this cat is light..
bright, happy and content to be expressing life perfectly, as a perfect cat!
this cat is blessed, renewed, invigorated...
with the possibility of expressing and experiencing life
as God's good idea, wherever this cat is ...
this cat is life's perfect idea of a perfect life form.
all of life moves to nurture and protect this cat.
this cat moves to nurture and protect all of life, too.
we give thanks for the perfect outpicturing of life
that this cat reflects.

COMMUNITIES REBUILDING

♥ communities are pulling themselves together to heal
  in this location; _____.
♥ the safety net expands, everyone is helping now.
♥ repair and rebuilding are everywhere present.
♥ TENDER CARE FOR ALL CREATION, EXTENDS TO INCLUDE EVERYONE.
♥ all creatures big and small enjoy widening care today.
♥ support that leaves no-one out, circles the neighborhood.
♥ love demonstrates an ever-widening circle of concern now.
♥ people reach out to include each other.
♥ people are sticking their necks out for each other.

♥ all ages of people answer the call of service.

♥ THE SUPPLY OF GOOD WILL NEVER STOP.
♥ there is a promise of good for all today.
♥ miraculous intervention is at work now.
♥ caring people everywhere continue to make a difference in _____.
♥ everyone in _____ acknowledges the Divine presence.
♥ VISION, COURAGE AND INSPIRATION REQUIRED ARE PROVIDED.
♥ there is a never-ending supply of inspired solutions.
♥ rebuilding takes place in a joyful spirit here.
♥ people in _____ are committed to
  community and conducting business in the world.
♥ everybody in _____ is standing on solid ground today.

DIVINE UNIVERSAL FAMILY DECLARATION

- ♥ Life, Truth and Love are here present on our globe.
- ♥ The family of humankind is amazingly blessed
    and prospered now.
- ♥ Today people are responsive to the rule of love
    and not destructive tendency.
- ♥ People are united as the loved creation
    of One Infinite Divine Source.
    One people, one globe.
    One family of humankind ...
- ♥ Love is inherent in humankind's true nature.
- ♥ Love is inherent in Divine Universal Family ...
  everywhere present beyond all galaxies seen and presumed.
- ♥ With a shift of thought that is peaceful, gone are divisions,
  injustice and appearances of animosity.
- ♥ The family of humankind and Universe
    are now more clearly in view
    for world leaders, groups and individuals.
- ♥ Relationships are no longer defined by race or culture ...
    we all belong to Divine Universal Family.
    We see, hear and feel this now.
- ♥ Throughout the galaxies and beyond, what's now seen ...
  we all belong equally to the Divine.
- ♥ We all have shared spiritual identity as Universal Family.

TODAY I AM A CITIZEN OF EARTH

- ♥ world evolution is my vision.
- ♥ the earth is a living moving being.
- ♥ i am a citizen of earth.
- ♥ i am a steward of earth.
- ♥ i make positive contributions to nature today.
- ♥ innovation and interaction are my tools.
- ♥ foresight and flexibility are my tools.
- ♥ we are human beings, in nature.

Seasons of Prosperity

ON EARTH TODAY

♥ We see and hear that ...
   ... the hearts of all world leaders
       are magnifying Divine compassion.
   ... people are perceiving peace-filled dialogues everywhere.
   ... countries all over this globe are ceasing warlike actions.
   ... nations stand for the goodwill in each other, year-round.
   ... creative circumstance-solving replaces war.
   ... peace is more evident in world news than it has ever been, all over the earth.
   ... peace prevails on earth as countries
      become "good neighbors" to each other.
   ... heartful communication happens everywhere.

WE HAVE PEACE PREVAILING ON EARTH

♥ appropriate peaceful outcomes are always apparent now.
♥ ALL WARS ARE DELAYED AND THEN CANCELED BEFORE THEY START.
♥ peace initiatives are accepted ... peace prevails.
♥ the overall peace process is divinely guided all over earth today.
♥ smooth transitions of power are now possible for peace
                       and they are happening this year.
♥ all places on earth are zones free of nuclear and chemical weapons.
♥ rights of human beings are protected successfully and permanently ..
  people everywhere are always guided to peaceful places and spaces.
♥ peace initiatives are accepted ... peace prevails.
♥ NON-AGGRESSION DEALS ARE SHOWING UP ALL OVER THE GLOBE.
♥ world leaders are following Divine directions today in all matters everywhere.
♥ peace settlements are being settled simultaneously in all countries now.
♥ all over the world, weapons manufacturers and dealers are being held
  accountable for injuries and deaths involving those weapons ...
  weapons are no longer required.
♥ everyday people are moved to intend peace each day.
♥ PEACEMAKERS ARE NOW IN POWERFUL POSITIONS all over the earth
  and peace is already prevailing in the minds and hearts of all people.
♥ ALL BATTLING HAS ENDED .. all challenges are subdued.
♥ those who once turned to violence to get a point across
  now turn to negotiation and mediation to resolve conflicts.
♥ feminine elements of character are now revealing themselves in world leaders
  all over the globe ... negotiation, compassion, listening, and minimizing
  differences is now showing up where conflict used-to-be.
♥ all conflicts in all relationships on earth, and in all countries on earth are now
  resolved for the HIGH GOOD of our SHARED GLOBAL PURPOSE.
♥ Divine Design is in our words, thoughts, circle and unfolding.

FOR EARTH THE TIME IS NOW

- ♥ Earth people are galaxy people now.
- ♥ Our perceptions create the combining realities we see.
- ♥ The time is now for a new vision of a new earth.
- ♥ Today we awake to enlightened thinking.
- ♥ Today we are willing for courageous actions.
- ♥ We see that on Earth, unity is manifesting. Growth is natural.
- ♥ We are talking and walking toward a bright future.
- ♥ Things are changing for the best around us now.
- ♥ We see spiritualization of value systems all around us today.
- ♥ WE ARE SEEING A NEW FACE TO THIS WORLD. we are grateful.
- ♥ There is global shifting of consciousness now.
- ♥ We let go the dictates of matter directing.
- ♥ We recognize mind as Source of matter. Mind directs.
- ♥ WE TAKE ON RESPONSIBILITY FOR GENERATIVE THINKING AND FEELING.
- ♥ Today all over the Earth, myriads of wonderful life forms are reviving and revitalizing others.
- ♥ The will of the Infinite is made manifest in the finite now.

> "... The WIND goes toward the SOUTH
> and turns about to the NORTH
> it whirls about continually.
> and the wind returns again
> to it's circuits ....
> all things are full of Labor
> we cannot say it ...
> the eye is not satisfied with seeing
> nor the ear filled with hearing.
> The Thing That has been
> it is That which shall be; and That
> which is done is That which shall
> be done: There is no NEW THING
> under The SUN ...
> nothing where it may be said
> SEE THIS IS NEW.
> ... it has been already in The
> Old Times which were before us..."
>
> — ecclesiastes

Seasons of Prosperity

WE DECLARE THAT PEACE IS PREVAILING ON EARTH.

1. We intend happiness and good fortune for all the people in _____.
2. In the face of any appearance, peace prevails and justice is served in _____.
3. the DIVINE force of order is at work today in _____

Afghanistan	Albania	Algeria	Angola
Antigua and Barbuda		Argentina	Armenia
Australia	Austria	Azerbaijan	Bahamas
Bahrain	Bangladesh	Barbados	Belarus
Belgium	Belize	Benin	Bhutan
Bolivia	Bosnia and Hercegovina		Botswana
Brazil	Brunei	Bulgaria	Burkina Faso
Cambodia	Cameroon	Canada	Cape Verde
Central African Republic		Chad	Chile
China	Columba	Comoros	Congo
Costa Rica	Cote d'Ivoire	Croatia	Cuba
Cyprus	Czechoslovakia	Denmark	Djibouti
Dominica	Dominican Republic		Ecuador
Egypt	El Salvador	Equatorial Guinea	Estonia
Ethiopia	Fiji	Finland	France
Gabon	Gambia	Germany	Ghana
Greece	Grenada	Guatemala	Guinea
Guinea-Bissau	Guyana	Haiti	Honduras
Hungary	Iceland	India	Indonesia
Iran	Iraq	Ireland	Israel
Italy	Jamaica	Japan	Jordan
Kazakhstan	Kenya	Kuwait	Kyrgyzstan
Latvia	Laos	Lebanon	Lesotho
Liberia	Libya	Liechtenstein	Lithuania
Luxembourg	Madagascar	Malawi	Malaysia
Maldives	Mali	Malta	Marshall Islands
Mauritania	Mauritius	Mexico	Micronesia
Mondova	Mongolia	Morocco	Mozambique
Myanmar	Namibia	Nepal	The Netherlands
New Zealand	Nicaraua	Niger	Nigeria
North Korea	Norway	Oman	Pakistan
Panama	Papua New Guinea	Paraguay	Peru
Philippines	Poland	Portugal	Qatar
Romania	Russia	Rwanda	St. Kitts and Nevis
St. Lucia	St. Vincent and the Grenadines		San Marino
Sao Tome e Principe		Saudi Arabia	Senegal
Seychelles	Sierra Leone	Singapore	Slovenia
Solomon Islands	Somalia	South Africa	South Korea
Spain	Sri Lanka	Sudan	Suriname
Swaziland	Sweden	Syria	Tajikistan
Tanzania	Thailand	Togo	Trinidad and Tobago
Tunisia	Turkey	Turkmenistan	Uganda
Ukraine	U.S.S.R.	United Arab Emirates	United Kingdom

United States	Uruguay	Uzbekistan	Vanuatu
Venezuela	Vietnam	Western Samoa	Yemen
Yugoslavia	Zaire	Zambia	Zimbabwe

and all regions of the World not listed here.

THE COMMUNITY PRAYER

... for the perfect outworking of the MOST
  HIGH ALL WISE WILL

Holy Spirit keep guiding us.
Holy Spirit keep illumining us.
Holy Spirit continue to sanctify us.
Holy Spirit lead us, we will go.
What is forbidden, we renounce
What is commanded, we will do
           enforced and empowered
           by your strength.
MAY THE LIVING SPIRIT OF TRUTH
keep us in the path
of appropriate choices as we yield
           to grace and protection.
           Guide us to the end
           of this decade
           in divine order.
                    SO MAY IT BE.

Seasons of Prosperity

AWAKE TO THE NATION

- ♥ service to my country begins in my community.
- ♥ in my community local people become peacemakers .
- ♥ in every dimension of modern life
  people of this nation are sticking their necks out for each other.
- ♥ as the world grows smaller my role in it gets bigger.
  i make a difference in wider and wider circles now.
- ♥ people are at their best helping each other
  to keep lives on track progressing upward.
- ♥ projects to improve global education, in my community,
  are happening now. everyone is a global citizen.
- ♥ ways to develop confidence and become responsible
  are now being taught, in this nation, in all its many schools.
- ♥ all communities, in nations, teach the courage-of-conviction to children.
- ♥ plans for successful fulfilling futures are set in place
  for nations and communities. everyone helps.

HELP EACH OTHER

EMERGENCY COMMUNITY AFFIRMATIONS

- ♥ Providence moves to support the people in _____.
- ♥ miracles abound and _____ inspiring actions
  are everywhere in this location now.
- ♥ today all people in _____ community demonstrate caring
  and concern for the others.
- ♥ help is on the way, essential support is forthcoming in _____.
- ♥ people are willing to help each other and they do in the _____ area.
- ♥ each person acts with courage to bring remedy and resolution.
- ♥ delivering what's required is easy and quick.
- ♥ food and supplies are in abundance for the people of _____.
- ♥ measures of assistance in _____, are implemented quickly...
  everyone helps everyone else.
- ♥ purposeful action happens fast for the people of _____.
- ♥ wherever evacuation is called for, provision is made.
- ♥ wherever change is required, it happens without obstacles.
- ♥ wherever safety measures are called for, they are enacted.
- ♥ Divine sublime order is now at work in the location of _____,
  people feel assured, they gather to help each other.
- ♥ peace prevails, safety prevails in _____ today.

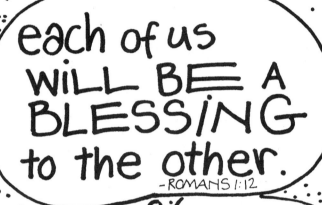

BEING FREE OF UNWORKABLE WAYS

"to understand is to see the way things belong together,
to see why they are together . understanding relates to underlying patterns,
relationships, meanings...the urge to understand ourselves
and the world is one of the noblest and most powerful motivations..."
-J.G. Bennett

- ♥ in the space of wisdom and quiet, i can see how far i've come.
- ♥ i notice what worked in its time and what didn't work very well.
- ♥ i am grateful for high perspective of the North to see the whole circle.
- ♥ power of observation is at work, i gather strength from the deep...
- ♥ informed by light of understanding, i am set free of unworkable ways.
- ♥ wisdom of quiet overview is mine to use...understanding prevails.
- ♥ life potential gathers here with me, i am free.
- ♥ a world of possibility opens to my view, being free ....
- ♥ excellence on new horizons is possible
- ♥ now, in the North i am free of unworkable ways.

BLESSED BE

Blessed be hands helping life.
Blessed be hands that gather seed.
Blessed be hands growing life.
Blessed be hands that water and watch over life.
Blessed be hands embracing people.
Blessed be hands that write uplifting words.
Blessed be hands pointing to promise of rainbows.
Blessed be hands that dial to communicate encouragement.
Blessed be hands turning pages so we can see.
Blessed be hands that reach out dependably.
Blessed be hands responding to reaching out.
Blessed be hands that point to possibility, wherever it is dark.
Blessed be hands wiping away tears and sorrow.
Blessed be the hands of people loving all people.
Blessed be hands that serve and serve.
Blessed be hands that heal and spread faith.
Blessed be hands motioning to God.
Blessed be all hands helping
                each and everyone.
Blessed be the hands of our CREATOR
                holding us in blessing.

Seasons of Prosperity

MERRY MAKING AT THE WINTER SOLSTICE

warm love pervades the days, peace prevails
WE ARE GRATEFUL
good company is certain, holiday lights burn bright
WE ARE GRATEFUL
going inside to gather, people give to each other
WE ARE GRATEFUL
carols play merrily
WE ARE GRATEFUL
evergreens remind us life goes on for ever
WE ARE GRATEFUL
washed of dark propensities
we have bright pictures of a happy world
WE ARE GRATEFUL
light shines in the darkness, days are getting longer
WE ARE GRATEFUL
we celebrate the community of humankind,
burning bright fires of the heart
in the midst of whatever cold seems to be outside.
WE ARE GRATEFUL

GOD IS THE COMPANION OF MY HEART

- ♥ i persist in love moment to moment today.
- ♥ God is the companion of my heart.
- ♥ the condition of surrender to God is the condition of my life.
- ♥ everything i see reflects God...truth...beauty...goodness...love.
- ♥ gestures of emotional dissociation
  as reactive disposition, no longer are required.
- ♥ everything is an extension of my own looking.
- ♥ God is not elsewhere in relation to me. God is here now.
- ♥ my obligation is beyond small insular self now.
- ♥ emotional withholding in each moment is given up.
- ♥ reactive dispositions of being "unsatisfied" are now given up.
  satisfaction of serving and loving others takes its place.
- ♥ obsessive dramatic patterns of reactive mind fade away today.
- ♥ i give up terms of limitation and emotional reactions,
  today i allow spontaneously happiness.
- ♥ God is my intimate heartfelt companion today...
  a cure for loveless hearts.

declare His GLORY among the heathen HIS WONDERS among ALL PEOPLE

— PS 96:3

© toni acker 82

WE YIELD TO THE LEADING EDGE OF DIVINE WILL

today
may UNITED WISDOM
of all worlds, seen and unseen,
come to us, and thru us
in full force
upon earth planet....

we yield to the leading
of HIGHEST INTELLIGENCE.
may our FATHER MOTHER GOD
guide us with grace and in protection
to the end of this decade
                  in perfect
                  outworking
                  of the all wise
                  DIVINE WILL
                  we yield to
                  the leading edge.

THANKSGIVING:
WE GIVE THANKS TO CREATION FOR ALL THIS....

these fruits of life constantly presenting to us;
        WE GIVE THANKS TO CREATION FOR ALL THIS...

blessing on the food we eat
blessing on the people we share it with
blessing on the gifts life is always providing
especially the good company of like minded others
        WE GIVE THANKS TO CREATION FOR ALL THIS...

blessing to our parents for the gift of life
blessing to all our relations for what they teach us
blessing to our enemies for what we've learned from them
blessing to all the generations that follow us down to the 7th generation
blessing to all who came before and prepared this way
        WE GIVE THANKS TO CREATION FOR ALL THIS...

may the world we leave
be a better one than was left to us
        we say this will be so.

Seasons of Prosperity

RESPONSIVE YULE RITE

Invocation of the Four Directions to begin.

LEADER: welcome, we celebrate Winter Solstice, the shortest day.

ALL: YULE is our time of beginning the sun will shine
from this point on for a longer period each day.

East reader:	YULE: a turning point
South reader:	YULE: a beginning
West reader:	YULE: a hope of the return, of Light and Life
North reader:	YULE: a time of rejoicing and gathering

LEADER: people living close to earth understand with
increasing light, earth soon awakens
to bring a green world about again.

ALL: this is a sacred time,
at this point in the circle we rejoice in happiness
and merriment for urging-forth the
sun's longer shining...into the new year.

LEADER: the birth of the SUN and the birth of the SON
coincide here in the circle...
the emergence of each human's CHRISTOS possibility is
<u>relighted</u> every year, at this most sacred time, in the circle.

ALL: our singing, praying, contemplations and the joy we
can't really explain remind us of what we've always known:
<u>OUR OWN POSSIBILITY</u> as higher humans.

East reader:	the evergreen shows promise of life everlasting
South reader:	increasing light and strength bring hope and push back the night
West reader:	in the middle of what is barren and cold radiance grows and grows and grows...
North reader:	the wheel of cycles turns and turns and turns..... what is frozen and fallow, becomes green and blossoming. what is green and blossoming, will again freeze and be fallow.

LEADER: we give thanks; all things change and pass
we are no longer diminished
by the nature of cyclic changing.

ALL: we expect, what we know comes next...
we are ready for increasing brightness
a most new year to come.

LEADER: we will each say goodbye to what
we leave in the dark now and declare
what is lighting up for this new year.

The Direction of North

ALL: inner radiance can shine forth now... we lay claim to the faculties and qualities we bring forth.

NEW YEAR CEREMONY in the burning bowl

Start in the EAST
Each person approaches wreath candle with votive candle
- ♥ announce <u>three ideas being left behind</u>
  (paper with these items is introduced to flame, quickly set down into sand to burn out.)
- ♥ declare <u>three qualities being called forth</u>!
- ♥ light candle now, return with lighted candle to sit in circle give attention to next speaker. a quiet mood of contemplation until everyone has acted and spoken.

LEADER: kindled before us, flames of life
are sparkling for possibility we bring to this new year.

take five minutes of quiet time to contemplate the possibility of this next year. (music may be used)

LEADER: we open our minds in radiance.
we are called forth by our future.
we trust, with faith unshaken,
that no shadow has power to darken our intentions.

each: start in the EAST each person speaks; that they know these intentions can come into manifestation, as reality in the next year.

ALL READ: WE CELEBRATE THIS YEAR
(or other mind Rx for the year, as selected)

East reader:	we use the sight of these flames to rekindle the desire to share light with all people.
South reader:	light blesses each of us, each of us, blesses all of us.
West reader:	as light, has passed, to each of us from the evergreen candle, may we expand light.
North reader:	weariness is replaced with strength we stand firm in knowledge, that everything will reawaken, and be green again.

LEADER: light and life all over the cosmos, is always being regenerated. we give thanks, this is true.

ALL: "we have finished our year like a sigh,
we are willing to be taught to number these days
so that we present finally A HEART OF WISDOM"
         - **Psalms 90 : 9-12**

CAPRICORN DECLARATIONS

i declare that through the power and mighty presence of the Divine within, i am a great contribution to people around me ... i am power of organization.
i have many accomplishments.
i am a steady surefooted troubleshooter.
i am never deterred by anything standing in my way.
working and planning are easy for me.
i find solutions to difficult problems easily.
i have great faith in practical solutions.
i put everything in good working order.
i represent conscientiousness.

i am successfully learning

- ♥ generosity
- ♥ appreciation and acknowledgment
- ♥ determination with humor
- ♥ to follow my excellent intuition
- ♥ everything isn't "sensible"
- ♥ to voluntarily step back sometimes
- ♥ de-emphasizing security
- ♥ depending on and with others

i am leaving behind

- ♥ melancholy
- ♥ isolation
- ♥ frugal instincts
- ♥ excessive details
- ♥ dogmatic "positions"
- ♥ overbearing discipline
- ♥ thinking about worries
- ♥ using people inappropriately
- ♥ being methodical all-the-time
- ♥ having "to get something" in return

AQUARIUS DECLARATIONS

i declare that through the power and mighty presence of the Divine within, i am a great contribution to people around me ... i bring spiritual energy to people. i stand for the vision of all people as one family on the globe. With unswerving loyalty i encourage free expression with everyone.
i know that security comes from being in the company of others, and helping everyone to see with universal vision. my presence empowers people to rise above differences. i promote worldwide exchange of ideas. i am a tireless worker. i see that all people are treated fairly whenever i am around. i am a true humanitarian.

i am successfully learning:

- ♥ teamship
- ♥ supportability
- ♥ balancing extremes of my nature
- ♥ patience when misunderstood
- ♥ to let go of unprincipled companions

i am leaving behind:

- ♥ anxiety
- ♥ apprehension
- ♥ stubbornness
- ♥ being opinionated
- ♥ exaggerating problems
- ♥ unpredictable behaviors
- ♥ stirring up opposition
- ♥ temperamental outbursts

PISCES DECLARATION

   i declare that through the power and mighty presence of the Divine within, i am a great contribution to the people around me ... i have great compassion. i initiate healing. i perceive difficulties in people's lives through intuition. i embody faith that moves mountains. i am loyal. renunciation can be easy for me.
i have exceptional understanding of people's feelings.
my emotions are extended to all life in the global family.
i am ambitious on behalf of all people.
i am always aware of the subtle undercurrents of human interactions. the power of devotion is what i represent.

i am successfully learning:

- ♥ strong willpower
- ♥ to talk to people about my projects
- ♥ that i matter to other people
- ♥ to be careful with other people's things
- ♥ to attract happy, uplevel friends
- ♥ to do things despite changes of mood
- ♥ to be open and revealing
- ♥ letting people help me
- ♥ i am not chained to any destiny unchosen
- ♥ to face self realistically
- ♥ to listen to the still small voice within

i am leaving behind:

- ♥ staying by myself
- ♥ stubbornness
- ♥ tired feelings
- ♥ having "hurt" feelings
- ♥ overactive imaginings
- ♥ unfinished business
- ♥ being disoriented
- ♥ morose considerations
- ♥ being too easily influenced

EXPECTATION IS IN PLACE

- ♥ i thank, praise, acknowledge. i claim highest good. i follow intuition.
- ♥ serving-the-future guides what's happening with me. syntrophy prevails.
- ♥ my feelings are receptive to taking on what's required with life purpose.
- ♥ i take the appropriate actions necessary. vision is directed.
- ♥ i give up what's useless. i take on what's necessary.
- ♥ i am directed and effective in acting for my future.
- ♥ i move into action serving the future today.

MERRY DAYS ARE BEHIND AND IN FRONT ...

- ♥ what was behind us in the past, is behind us now
  as into the holy holidays, we go ...
- ♥ we have the anticipation of meeting with friends and family.
- ♥ we plan gifts for heart, mind and bodies together.
- ♥ we convey happy thoughts in words and gestures.
- ♥ we have traditions, rituals and gatherings to go to ...
- ♥ we have the inspiration and spiritual understanding of rejoicing.
- ♥ we have something certainly worth celebrating!
  we have heaven within us ...
- ♥ we have the time honored traditions of expressing wonder and happiness.
- ♥ we affirm harmonious relationships with each other all along the way.
  what was behind us in the past is behind us now.
  we keep our holidays merry still.

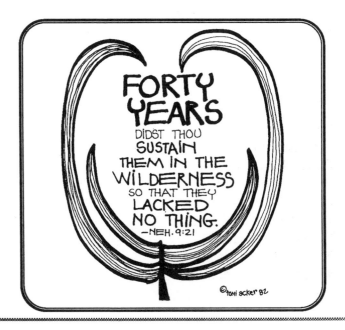

Intentions for all Seasons

TO PRAY FOR THE EARTH

HER CREATURES, PLANTS AND PEOPLE ARE OUR DAILY RESPONSIBILITY

Seasons of Prosperity

Intentions for Children

1. exceptional opportunities exist for all children.
2. children take on being powerful and able today.
3. children move from love, through love and to love today.
4. children appreciate each other and all creatures this season.
5. children live as a commitment and a purpose, to serve the future.
6. ancient sacred ways are being taught to young children in all countries.
7. children harvest abundantly all forms of good, all over the world.
8. people and children play together today, giving permission to imagination.
9. children turn their gaze in the appropriate direction and walk that way today.
10. children are giving up selfishness and fear in their relationships with other children today.
11. teachers are producing heartful <u>results</u> with children.
12. parents in the U.S. play a more active role in selecting music and play things for children
13. teachers help children to develop an early understanding of the Laws of Nature.
14. all teachers-of-children express harmony and wisdom in each circumstance, in each classroom.
15. religious freedom is restored. parents retain their right to give religious instruction to their children, as they choose.
16. small children influence grown ups to care more for animals and insects by speaking about how they see life.
17. young people take risks to act for the continued safety of animals, plants and people in their local living environments.
18. adolescents are seeing beyond limited opinions to have lives that make a difference for good.
19. young people give up faulty thinking to talk straight instead of avoiding confrontation.
20. parents have the courage to exercise options with children; they no longer shrink from leading offspring for fear-of-unpopularity.
21. children leave behind reactive emotions, head-on-love is the circumstance with parents and children.
22. children of today's world feel happy contributing and being contributed to. . . . .
23. women of the world are accepting and exercising authority to guide morals and standards for children and adolescents.
24. america's inner city youth problems turn around. individuals work to create programs for kids-at-risk in community services.
25. kids-in-cities are finding inspiration to resist bad role-models, to chart their own upward course and stick to it.
26. more young people are moved to have less doubts about self and more desire to do things which benefit their neighborhoods.
27. teenagers give up getting attention by being "a problem"; instead, they discover problems,
solve them, and get recognition for making-a-difference in their communities!

Intentions for all Seasons

Intentions for All People

1. people act. their actions make a difference today
2. miracles abound as people continue to stick their necks out for each other.
3. people realize the joy that loving brings.
4. people act to help each other everywhere.
5. night and day meet in a mutual hug, and we all do, too.
6. people all over the globe, become valentines to each other.
7. people, replace thoughtlessness with thoughtfulness.
8. justice and good will extend to people of all races, colors and creeds.
9. people have perfect appropriate transportation for all exchanges.
10. people remain open, giving love, and receiving love in all actions.
11. people are perfectly-at-peace each morning all over the earth.
12. people cultivate in each other, what is beneficial and generous.
13. people practice great-kindness, compassion ,and generosity.
14. people develop past, the road post they rest at now.
15. miracles abound at all public events... people take care for each other.
16. people walk together today being lights, in the darkness of flesh and logic.
17. people give thanks to the influences that brought them to where they are.
18. people notice risking is necessary to create new outcomes
19. women have breakthroughs-in-understanding that vastly elevate,
their quality of life.
20. whole families find satisfactory ways to relate and keep up communication.
21. there are no secrets, what is hidden is revealed and everyone notices.
22. earthquake participants realize what's required is always present,
they are grateful.
23. mothers have new-perspectives that turn all their "problems" into projects.
24. human beings know that their true nature includes love, health and wisdom.
25. all journeys are completed in absolute safety.
the way is made joyful for travelers.
26. people who contribute, prosper exceedingly
and enjoy bountiful blessings today......
27. people are guided, provided for and richly
supported in all their decisions, to serve-the-future.
28. people replace anger with joy; hopelessness
with faith, and pride with cooperation.
29. people are enlivened and empowered by affiliation.
30. people notice good-is-everywhere. people trust life...
satisfying results are forthcoming.
31. new ideas light the way for people to take risks
and accomplish works that benefit everybody.
32. our brothers, sisters and parents are protected and helped.
safety is always the circumstance. success is apparent.
33. people take on honesty .
speaking straight prevails anxieties cease.
34. sisters, aunts, uncles, cousins and grandparents. . .
are walking in protection today.
35. people are filled with joy realizing how great
their lives really are...they spread the good news in their communities.

Seasons of Prosperity

36. everyone uses impending-cold-seasons to restore ability to gather, give thanks, celebrate...good company and shared love.
37. people help each other. whenever a need arises, what's required is always present.
38. women all-over-the-world take on being powerful, nurturing, compassionate and able, today it makes changes.
39. people are calling forth, truth, intelligence and wisdom in all their WORLD ACTIONS today.
40. emergency response vehicles bring food and water relief to all those who need it. morale is lifted, people have plenty of what's required.
41. for every climate and every geographic locality...there is an <u>answering type of humanity</u>; today, everyone is in their perfect auspicious place.
42. all those who are departing embodied-life-on-earth have perpetual light guide their choices, and plenty of people holding good intention, on their behalf.
43. ...men have realizations of the structures that determine values and action. vital effectiveness increases with men. more men live like heroes in their communities.
44. people of earth practice the power of continuous-affirmative-intention. it works wonders in their lives and in the lives of all those around them.
45. people are sticking their necks out for each other. more americans take caring, courageous actions for the betterment-of-the-world all around them.
46. all people are free from burdensome debt, financial affairs move harmoniously and with ease.
47. messages of peace, justice, and love are being delivered in movies, books and songs all over the world today.
48. high influences continue to pass ideas to people, for the evolution of Humankind... they are received as uplifting intelligent thoughts to be acted on.

Intentions for Elders

1. elders give thanks for all of their past.
2. older Americans are no longer limited to living only a history.
3. elders bring the spirit-of-divine-creation into their everyday life.
4. older adults lay hold of growth and good company, to increase lively feelings.
5. thoughts are filled with certitude, assurance, peace and plenty for all elders.
6. elderly people celebrate life in this wonder-filled world.
7. grandmothers and grandfathers choose to create happy endings to all past memories.
8. good health and certainty are present, for all grandparents and elders, today.
9. elders see the plan and the design, that informs their life. they live it happily.
10. charming havens appear for elders seeking-quiet-spaces-to-think about life pathways.

Intentions for all Seasons

11. each hour holds chances for new beginnings....
    elders everywhere are vitalized by changes and serindipity events.
12. older people have discoveries
    which increase exuberance and insightfulness.
13. intergenerational experiences increase so that people of all
    ages and stages appreciate contributions the others bring. . . . .
14. elders live in accord with what they understand of
    spiritual reality. they find spirit in everything they do.
15. parents thoughts today are filled with health and wealth.
16. more people the world over, turn the aging process around and
    create ever exuberant vitality and well being. renewal is everywhere.
17. wise elders are honored and influential in today's world...
    direction is accepted, a spirit-of-co-operation is everywhere.
18. energies-of-life are present with grandparents; they are
    vitalized and fully known with great appreciation by all
    the people around them...in their neighborhoods.
19. senior citizens have plenty of affordable housing in their neighborhoods.
    people who have worked hard and contributed much, are able to live-in-dignity and security.

Intentions for People Health

1. wholeness of outlooks creates new healing outcomes.
2. the separation between medicine and botany has ended.
3. peoples thoughts are free from anxiety today. well being abounds.
   every disease in the world never occurs again.
4. health care professionals use good judgement based on divine guidance.
5. all nurses in America are cheerful, orderly, patient and full of faith today.
6. perfect peace and essential harmony are in place for miraculous healings
   everywhere.
7. people with health challenges engage in research and practices that vitalize
   and heal them.
8. more and more people are giving up drugs and alcohol as ways to veil life's
   possibilities.
9. restaurants all over the world see a new potential for
   "meat-free" meals.
10. more elder-people become promoters of natural health
    and healing all over earth today.
11. consumers refuse to eat irradiated chicken. authorities
    revoke the okay for irradiating foods for human use.
12. people who are overworked or under high stress restore the
    balance of their systems in natural, timely ways.
13. profiteering is disappearing from the health care professions...
    people are able to pay what they can afford. it's acceptable.
14. U. S. health care reforms are enacted. insurance companies are
    stopped from denying coverage to people with pre-existing conditions.
15. people with health challenges are inspired. and fully encouraged to keep
    up victory over all appearances.

Seasons of Prosperity

16. people who have received deadly diagnosis discover power over their bodies and successfully challenge the medical models.
17. cures for disease become more important than money to be made on disease. real help becomes apparent to those who want it.
18. intellectual and physical vitality, as optimism and enthusiasm, is extended and accepted, by people with health challenges.
19. americans choose to see freshly all memories of what they thought of as hurt or betrayal. they forgive and love by choice now.
20. people who have experienced frightening incidents,
experiences or expansions
find teachers within and without to bring stabilization back to their body, emotions and souls

Intentions for Americans

1. winter roads are dry and safe for all travelers.
2. in cities, new explorations and new patterns of good are emerging.
3. cultural barriers and prejudices are evaporated in all cities across America.
4. jobs, peace and justice are available to all Americans without reservation.
5. native americans remember their work
is to teach people ancient sacred ways.
6. downtown revitalization plans get plenty
of available funding in cities everywhere.
7. railroads are making quick recoveries, easily building
future tracks in America.
8. Americans are healing whatever needs redemption in their lives today.
9. everybody in the Americas is able to enter good mind
and undertake the great work of serving the future.
10. highest vigor, energy and best health are available to
all Americans today, in all cities, towns and countries.
11. happy resolutions are available in our vast American interactions.
12. in South America there is resolution for all political crisis
without armed soldiers.
13. U.S. and Canada enjoy mutual benefit from accords and
affinities that make co-operation prosperous and inviting.
14. change is trickling up and out from individual US citizens
making things better wherever they are all over the country.
15. congress cuts off money used for excessive road building
... .and unwise timber sales in national forests.
16. the USA studies war no more...instead people use
vitality to assure futures for trees, rivers and people.
17. negotiations to carve out a territory for Canadian and American native indians is progressing for the highest good of all concerned quickly.
18. people who are in the habit of complaining, give it up for today...
19. American actions, resolutions and attainments are for the good of nations.

Intentions for all Seasons

20. backlogs of cases for asylum seekers are processed right away.
    at US immigration services.
21. life moves ahead. people end despair and polarization in USA cites.
    people take on accepting challenges in their communities.
22. qualified people trying to enter the United States are treated fairly with generosity.
23. Americans seek truth and establish what's so with genuine certainty.
24. in America, human rights groups monitor refugee screening processes.
    those who qualify
    for political asylum are welcomed.
25. creeping christmas commercialism loses its hold on Americans.
    the journey of the three kings takes priority over the journey to the mall.
    people put spirit back into their celebrations this year.
26. Americans have a huge shift in thinking.
    they take on willingness to make-a-difference.
27. in the style of dismantlement in the USA where 5 out of every 7 nuclear weapons has already been retired............................ America continues to retire the remaining 19,000 nuclear weapons in divine order.
28. Americans
    recover their purpose,objectives and intentions
    for making a difference in the whole world today.

Intentions for Nations

1. bombs are safely found and defused today.
2. more nations cooperate to solve common problems.
3. peace is possible, probable and achieved everywhere.....today.
4. integrity in all countries knows no compromise today.
5. all elections bring the highest good to the most people.
6. countries extend gratitude to each other in serendipity ways.
7. interdependent progress happens for all nations.
8. soviet people work together to create a free nation that works.
9. in compliance with United Nations resolutions. Peace prevails.
10. politicians represent authentic ideals and wisdom in all exchanges.
11. nations say goodbye to: strikes, crimes, upsets and delinquency.
12. more nations apply wisdom of discrimination, in thought and action.
13. this is a planet at prayer, missiles are transformed into messengers of peace.
14. all warheads, are given up with negotiations for peace.
15. countries respect the social and religious value of other peoples.
16. the best imagined good blesses situations
    and circumstances in all CITIES today. . .
17. cooperation and mutual understanding increases among the United Nations.
18. Canada finds a plan to keep their countries
    union in place, beneficial to all the people.

Seasons of Prosperity

19. United Nations acts to create a War Crime Tribunal....
acts against humanity have appropriate consequence.
20. building weapons and arsenals is no longer attractive
or efficient. peace prevails.
21. understanding eliminates faulty thinking in
human negotiations ...especially in the family of nations.
22. refugees are being received in friendly ports. they have
plenty of food and water for traveling to safety.
23. methods of warfare which cause widespread damage to
natural environments have now been ended.
24. weapons plants cut back on programs to expand nuclear power. \
safety prevails in all radiation matters.....
25. all nations are able to sit in a single circle of assembly
and become practicing benefactors of the world.
26. now integrity is apparent in the actions of politicians, journalists,
and public serving officials all over the globe.
27. economic and humanitarian help is carefully applied for
highest good in nations all over the earth.
28. nations replace cynicism with sincerity,
in thinking about the whole world.
29. the soviet commonwealth creates stable agriculture.
there is peaceful progress in soviet transformation.
30. what to do with peace time plutonium is discovered...
toxic substances are put to good use. weapons are dismantled.
31. more nations leave positions they've become accustomed to... forging
ahead and confronting the unknown, to follow heart-centered-goals.
32. voice of america, radio free europe, and radio liberty receive global
funding necessary to continue broadcasting essential news.
33. United Nations councils act with equanimity-to-all-nations.
they do not favor some and demand meticulous implementation from
others. justice prevails.
34. people recognize nature creates union thru diversity and multiplicity.
nations now do....what nature does....
35. understanding and negotiation replace
adolescent "power struggle" monologues between nations.
36. harmony and accord are happening.
conflict-resolution replaces war today.
37. people in the former USSR take responsibility
for hard-work-required to establish freedom.
they communicate and cooperate, to have this happen.
38. people have outgrown war. war is unattractive and degrading.
people refuse to kill, or be killed. everyone celebrates life. there is dancing
on the streets.
39. people from all countries are making friends with each other.....
everybody prospers. boundaries and borders loose their importance.

Intentions for all Seasons

Intentions for World Leaders

1. the United Nations is prospered and it's finances work.
2. world leaders leave behind small, narrow, local thinking.
3. world leaders have the strength to stay with intended outcomes.
4. for world leaders negatives are filtered out. what's positive is reinforced.
5. powerful blessings to leaders are created and received all-over-the-world today.
6. the stress and storms of experience have no power to slow world leaders down today.
7. world leaders intuit and act for the ever increasing uselessness of nuclear weapons in real life.
8. leaders hear great TEACHINGS today and they are able to work innumerable miracles.
9. world leaders abandon assumptions, notions, and imaginations that keep them stuck-in-the-past.
10. the nations leadership is competent-in-action and ready to take on world-opinion, for the highest good of all.
11. spiritual leaders are in good spirits and excellent health, constantly inspired to do their work with people...
12. the mythic traditions of culture are rediscovered and embraced by all who are awake, leading the nations today.
13. world leaders remember "when you know the notes you sing, you can do most anything", they move to accomplish.
14. leaders become willing to trust. nothing is hidden that shall not be revealed.....there are no secrets.
15. more people are making things happen by taking the lead.
16. ...instead of being advised by polls, leaders persist in doing what quiet analysis says is best for nations and generations.
17. talents and leadership are being called forth from new groups of people in emerging countries.
18. disheartening perspectives are quickly dissolved for world leaders today.
19. people in leadership foster a love of life and act accordingly.
20. leadership convinces people it will not tolerate corruption, the common man's well being is in full view and acted on.
21. feminine elements-of-character are now revealing themselves in world leaders all over the globe. negotiation, compassion, listening and minimizing differences is now showing up where conflict used-to-be.

Intentions for Business

1. ethical maturity in industry is increasing today.
2. managers steeped in competition, learn to cooperate.
3. the disciplines of entrepreneurs are strengthened today.
4. all conversations of strife disappear thru no attention given to them.
5. ethical maturity increases in all human beings, countries and industry.
6. business people cultivate in each other what is beneficial and generous.

Seasons of Prosperity

7. Christian Science Monitor prospers and has great influence in our world.
8. service providers prosper exceedingly and enjoy great blessings easily today.
9. people preserve forests, enrich forests and make them economically viable.
10. people leave making confusion together
    and make peace together all over the world.
11. increasing world trade agreements pave the way
    for "one-world-one-people" thinking.
12. countries focus less energy on arms races
    and more energy on economic development.
13. praise and genuine thanksgiving are increasing
    everywhere today in business workplaces.
14. environmental whistle-blowers continue to turn
    in companies who violate pollution guidelines.
15. manufacturers are again producing quality goods
    that last beyond a decade of service.
16. people in communities across the nation choose birds
    and trees instead of malls.
17. electronic vehicle manufacturers prosper and generate
    great demand for non-polluting transportation.
18. all over this world a continued series of events
    establishes right order at nuclear plants.
19. home buyers choose homes in a spirit of gladness,
    all financial transactions are fair and joyful.
20. many therapists are moving to engage clients
    in an active role, taking charge of their own transformations.
21. reverence for, and intimacy with all life, calls forth
    an ecological ethic beyond consumer society thinking.
22. airports are reducing congestion without raising airfares.
    everything moves smoothly.
23. executives have humility to reform their styles, meeting
    the challenges of running business effectively in foreign cultures.
24. all over the globe people are helping each other, giving money,
    time, ideas, inspirations, and strengths to noble causes.
25. all airplanes, buses, cars and trains are piloted with care and love...
    reaching their destinations in divine order.
26. everyone who wants to own their own business is empowered to act
    and begin work immediately to manifest that result...
27. around the earth workable political agreements are reached,
    war becomes extinct, armies are used for humane errands.
28. fast food chains continue to offer vegetarian burgers and sales increase,
    vegetarian fare increases, people are glad.
29. world popular newspapers now employ truthful reporters who express
    what's so for the good of all people.
30. living wilderness is measured in the value it provides for all of life systems
    and not in terms of : dollars, lumber, barrels of oil and tons of minerals.
31. unemployed people move forward in their ability to provide.
32. businesses the world over, become happy about changing...
    a global way of looking replaces small local thinking.

Intentions for all Seasons

33. newspapers devote more space to stories describing love and compassion in our world. good will increases everywhere as a result.
34. owners of property are guided and act only in perfect right order to extend the Divine Will. anything else is prohibited and stopped immediately
35. more business owners recognize they influence life for all people around them...they act to create a world that works for everyone.
36. movie companies reflect on and respect values of human culture... they make movies that inspire truth, beauty, goodness and love. readjustment is now taking place in the world of film-making.
37. all over the world, restaurants remember they have a real stake in the health of the planet, in the future of farmers, and producers. they act to support small organic farmers and community markets.
38. retailers offer more that is environmentally friendly. they pack shipments in recycled paper. they do what serves the planet's future.
39. newspapers exercise spiritual as well as intellectual perspectives. solid quality reporting is the immediate result. reports of prophecies are dispersed. world view replaces the only-local way of looking.
41. changing from war-economy-production to peace-time-prosperity requires giving up havens-of-military-bases...people use base-closings to create effective entrepreneurial endeavors.

Intentions for the Green World

1. life giving air is de-smogged.
   trees and plants gratefully respond with new growth.
2. there is plenty of rain to keep crops vigorous and healthy.
3. people preserve forests, enrich forests and make them economically viable.
4. every year people all over rejoice in the fruits, of the green EARTH!
5. farmers grow food without polluting the land.
   national leadership encourages these options.
6. people are able to enter the forest and live in it
   as easily as they sit in front of city computers.
7. all over the world new policies create ancient
   forest reserves in regions and reduce timber sales.
8. every creature and circumstance is aligned with the law of high good and only good prevails in green spaces all over EARTH.
9. the order of nature is made manifest to the minds
   of people in receptivity and revelation.
10. american farmers go back to nature. reduced chemical use and appropriate organic soil conservation methods are in wide use.
11. people everywhere today are planting trees, living in harmony with all creatures restoring EARTH where they are.
12. PEOPLE CALL FORTH BEAUTY AND ORDER EVERYWHERE THEY ARE AND EVERYWHERE THEY GO in the natural world today.
13. life in the forest is a universal school. people participate in "forest" projects creating greater love instead of fear of the natural world.

Seasons of Prosperity

14. appreciation for all life is
    experienced by people, growing things and creatures today.
15. people are willing to be dressed in peace, singing songs of nature...
    whose design exceeds technology, by a billion years, at least.
16. great blessing is provided to the 191 million acres of Americas' national
    forests. the natural beauty and habitat they provide is certain to survive.
17. richer perspectives are now widely available for understanding
    our world. people have reverence for all life around them today.
18. oil grants, chemical companies, timber mills and industrial fishing fleets are
    challenged and HELD RESPONSIBLE for destruction in EARTH
    environments.

Intentions for the Weather

1. weather is in accord with the highest good of all people everywhere.
2. stormy weather passes bye populated areas...
   peaceful weather prevails all over the EARTH.
3. the influence of weather-trends-and-cycles, advises "sensitive people"
   to be where they feel safe in all weather conditions and circumstances.
4. extreme weather is tamed and aimed away from people now.

Intentions for the Ecology Environment

1. massive programs of reforestation are happening.
2. the environment remains a public and international issue.
3. laws of divine principle are at work in the creation of ecology cleanups
4. there is an on going response to environmental problems. resolution occurs.
5. birdsongs, breathable air, ancient forests and clean rivers are being
   preserved.
6. people are putting ethics in and making a safe sane
   environment for the next seven generations.
7. the wilderness society is helped and successful
   in stopping the destruction of national forests.
8. all parties stay engaged to restore damaged regions to
   former levels of environmental beauty and usefulness.
9. each of us realizes manifestation, action, and direction
   in re-establishing the planets eco-system.
10. social and environmental challenges are being resolved today
    through deeper caring in our world.
11. national parks are held in the highest regard...
    everyone who visits there is prospered.
12. government enforces laws which protect national forests.
    smart management of public lands is always the case
13. the green mountain power company in Vermont builds a successful system
    of windmills, a model power project for all of America.

Intentions for all Seasons

14. the U.N. resolution "to strengthen international cooperation in monitoring, assessing and anticipating environmental threats" is implemented today.
15. U.S. forest service knows how to do it's job;
they preserve wildlife habitat, protect watersheds, provide recreation, manage wise timbering practices, and have all the
accountability and resources to get the job done.

Intentions for the Ocean & Waters

1. earth waters are being restored to life.
2. ocean pollution becomes ocean revitalization.
3. all nations join the international whaling commission and stop whaling.
4. all whales and dolphins are regarded with wonder and treated with honor.
5. Greenpeace exposes, confronts, and stops decimation of the world's oceans.
6. for seaports worldwide, dockside improvements are keeping regional economies vitalized.
7. people enhance human commitment and resources for preserving life in oceans all over the EARTH.
8. all polluted rivers have people working for their cleanup and further protection. these projects are successful.
9. nations stop using plastic high sea driftnets.
dolphins, seals, whales and marine birds have freedom prevail.
10. commercial fishing off the BERING SEA in ALASKA is limited to allow sea lions return to normal quotas.
11. GREENPEACE is supported to keep up nonviolent, direct actions to protect marine animals and preserve ocean ecosystems.
12. the safety and well-being of all GREENPEACE staff is established in their risky missions to uphold justice...all over the watery world.

Intentions for Animals

1. herds of birds are healthy and active all over forests today.
2. people motivate sustained action on behalf of all animals.
3. birdsongs, breathable air, ancient forests and clean rivers are being preserved.
4. gray bats, red kangaroos, brown bears, and antelopes abound easily all over this planet.
5. swamp deer, sea otters, monk seals, gorillas, and sand gazelles are being preserved in our land.
6. swallow-tailed butterflies, gray wolves, blue whales, and marsh mice are no longer endangered species.
7. restaurants all over the world
see a new potential for "meat-free" meals.

Seasons of Prosperity

8. we widen our circle of compassion to embrace all living creatures, the whole of nature and all it's beauty.
9. around Amsterdam breeding grounds are successfully established for storks, geese, cranes, and otters.
10. children influence grown ups to care for animals and insects.
11. EARTHLINGS rise up and create a world centered on true love and compassion for all living creatures.
12. all creatures of heaven and EARTH are animating happiness at wildlife sanctuaries and in open wild places all over the world.
13. people take risks to act for the continued safety of animals, in their neighborhoods.
14. people understand how deeply lives intertwine, they agree not to harbor ill will toward any plant, animal or human being today.

Intentions for the Earth World

1. peace on earth, good will to all people is always going on.
2. this globe works towards leaving behind borders and boundaries.
3. earthlings today remember we cultivate a flourishing garden of life.
4. all countries have an important function in the Global Village of Earth.
5. the spirit of peace, prosperity and good company prevails in today's world.
6. all over the world... the Holy Spirit helps with everything.
7. cooperation happens everywhere and today the world works for everyone.
8. people see beauty of the world, zest of life and the mastery of love bound together in infinite possibility.
9. levels of financial exchanging increase miraculously. one-world-one people thinking prevails.
10. angels, nature spirits, and forces-of-nature, are able to evoke a spirit of co operation with humankind.
11. the uranium/plutonium "hearts" of nuclear weapons all over the globe become subject to the Divine Heart... love only is expressed. miracles abound. weapons disappear.

Intentions for the Future

1. guns disappear from city schools. . .
2. understanding increases, happiness happens.
3. illegal drug trade is over forever, everywhere.
4. there is great intention for the EARTH'S future.
5. generosity-in-serving-the-future replaces self concern.
6. cooperation and communication take the place of conflict.
7. politicians are unable to hide the depth-of-damage done with war. wars end.
8. WHATEVER APPEARS TO END, HAS A HAPPY ENDING

Intentions for all Seasons

9. elected officials work for the good of the next seven generations...
10. all thoughts and actions are of benefit to the next seven generations.
11. human beings call forth planetary-minds and global-compassions
12. people are magnets, recognizing great progress, and attracting new good.
13. more people pray, watch and work for the-future-of-humankind.
14. high influence prevails. peaceful-ways-of-thought are popular.
15. people everywhere are willing for **BIG CHANGES** to take place in their lives
16. people come to understand, everything they see is a reflection of how-they-are-being.
17. the world we leave, to the next generations, is a better one than what was given to us.
18. all people are guided, provided for and richly supported in all decisions to serve-the-future.
19. courage-for-changing is available to all who choose avenues into futures, unlike their past.
20. all entrepreneurs are getting work done ahead of time and serving-the-future in all actions.
21. more and more people capture a moment of light on the hills, and keep flowers and music, in their work space.
22. self doubt, self pity and low esteem are replaced by zeal-for-living and intentions-for-serving.
23. life brings understanding and guides human beings unerringly into the future.
24. more and more people take time to intend for other human beings and circumstances, only the highest good.
25. people use the past to create possibilities for a future that's new...all people serve-the-next-generations.
26. nations successfully work together to prevent demands of human population, from destroying earth's ability-to-sustain-life.
27. people in cities no longer accept violence as inevitable; they teach each other that peaceful-conflict-resolution is a better choice
28. Divine assistance is given those afflicted by fire, flood, earthquake, storm and drought. this includes every living thing.
29. discord of every name and nature, is heard no more...the harmonious sense of life is present now in human consciousness.
30. at holidays people see and act to create uplifting celebrations that perpetuate good will for the whole human family.
31. ancient songs, beautiful trees, sacred spaces, rainbows and sunshine establish traditional teachings deeper in the minds of men today.
32. students of philosophy take on "living experiments", creating new realities for humankind today.
33. we are always reminded of our responsibility to ACTIVELY BRING FORTH WITH OUR THOUGHTS what is good for all the people, this moment, and in future generations.
34. people everywhere are looking deeper at what they see, no longer settling for surface prevailing ideas. they establish deep grounded ideals, for serving the future.

Seasons of Prosperity

Intentions for the Universe

1. human beings receive currents that carry the insight of eternity.
2. the source of ALL LIFE is eternally maintaining what's to be relied upon.
3. people recognize CREATIVE INTELLIGENCE at work in universe.
4. wonderful blessings are happening everywhere in galaxies.
5. peace pervades the reaches of the cosmos.
   what is required is always present.
6. HUMAN WILL IS IN ALIGNMENT WITH DIVINE WILL...
7. ...people, take an active part in ongoing unfoldment of the universe.
8. megaliths built by ancient people begin to reveal
   messages today to contemporary society.
9. the purpose of the universe guides accomplishment of people.
10. people realize that the universe is a series
    of VIBRATIONS HELD-TOGETHER BY INTENTION!
11. people realize humankind;
    is an evolutionary function of the earth.
    (this is now what is so.)

Intentions for all Seasons

Index by Subject

Subject	Pages
abundance	28, 169, 176, 177, 179, 180, 184, 188, 189, 190, 191, 240
acceptance	32, 49, 52, 62, 63, 160, 613, 165, 173, 231, 236, 251, 253, 256, 258, 260, 281
accomplishing	10, 11, 15, 16, 38, 39, 44, 46, 92, 105, 106
accountability	16, 29, 106, 134, 204, 205
action	8, 27, 32, 37, 40, 41, 61, 62, 63, 245
ancestors	28, 248, 268, 285
animals	270, 271, 272
appreciation	29, 206, 227, 285
Archangels	5, 83, 151, 223
change	32, 65, 126, 137, 160, 174, 176, 190, 191, 192, 200, 205, 247
cooperation	106, 109, 205
courage	6, 12, 52, 140, 188, 200, 245
creativity	155, 210, 212, 213
death	165, 167, 234, 235, 236, 237
family	64, 109, 155, 156, 157, 158, 206, 273
fear	29, 35, 45, 48, 56, 64, 65, 66, 103, 105, 159, 165, 191, 205

Four Directions

East	2, 5, 6, 8, 9
South	80, 83, 84, 85, 86, 87
West	148, 151, 152, 153, 154, 155
North	220, 223, 224, 225, 226, 258, 261
health	118, 119, 121, 122, 124, 125

Seasons of Prosperity

holidays	207, 208, 209, 295, 286, 289, 290
love	109, 112, 167, 251, 253, 256, 273
money	96, 168, 172, 174, 175, 179, 180, 183
mystery	254, 255, 256, 264
partnership	110, 114, 115, 133
patience	109, 135, 206, 258, 264
peacekeeping	55, 156, 158, 234, 246, 247, 274, 277, 278
plants	264, 269
playfulness	22, 24, 29, 66, 259, 261
Psalms	101, 209, 232, 234
renewal	32, 36, 37, 39, 49, 58, 105, 138, 233
renunciation	32, 43, 65, 66, 94, 160, 165, 247
Sun Signs	73, 74, 75, 142, 143, 214, 215, 216, 292, 293, 294
Thanks	206, 208, 209, 289
tithing	180, 183, 184, 189
traveling	55, 67, 68, 69, 70, 262
waiter/waitress	177, 183, 206
weddings	116, 117
worry	66, 232, 244, 246, 247
yule	207, 208, 290, 295

Quotations

Baba, Meher	109
Bach, Dr. Edward	125
Bennett, J. G.	285
Berry, Thomas	205
Brizendine, Dana	23
Brooks, Phillip	237
Emerson, R. W.	37
Einstein, Albert	248
Erhard, Werner	100
Ford, Henry	55
Fuller, Buckminster	99
Gibran, Kahil	129
Hammarskjold, Daj	29
Hippocrates	269
Homes, Oliver W.	101
Lincoln, Abraham	39
Lindsay, Karen	173
Paulsen, J. Sig	46
Plato	129
Rabinowitz, Mark	56
Rilke, Rainer Marie	254
Roosevelt, Theodore	53
St. Francis	234
St. John of the Cross	43
St. Thomas Aquinas	211
Schwenk, Theodore	263
Seed, John	267
Seneca	134
Seng-Ts'an	234
Spaulding, J. L.	165
Whitman, Walt	177

Index by Intentional Prayer

Intentional Prayer	Page
a declaration for the work place	89
a human being is part of the whole	248
about bad habits	140
about being supportable	203
about breakthroughs	36
about challenges	30
about communicating	18
about creativity	212
about enrolling	127
about friends	205
about good use of time	40
about leaving worry behind	66
about relationships	126
about results	15
about winning	54
about the flow of money	168
abundant thinking	169
achieving leadership	103
action begins today	27
affirmation: conscious creative speaking makes things real	76
affirmations for today in the city	57
alive and alert each morning	50
all conditions change and pass	255
always there is increase	177
an ancient proclamation of forgiveness from China	156
answers are always available	254
appearances are powerless over me	43
aquarius declarations	293
aries declaration	73
attention to successful results	16
attraction increase decree	240
autumn - west	152
awake to the nation	282
beauty is a way of looking	127
beauty is expressed	122
beauty is expressed	19
beginning in confidence	58
beginning today everything insures my success	44
being free of unworkable ways	285
being fully beginning	63
being pregnant is a happy experience	22
being responsible	95
blessed be	285
blessing all people	206

Seasons of Prosperity

blessing for flowers	264
blessing for seeds	269
blessing for the birds	270
bodhisattva vow	248
breakthrough to beginnings	37
cancer declarations	142
candlemas: light in the darkness is a happy event	261
capricorn declarations	292
celebrating life with my family	64
change is the heart of my being	191
changing continues to bless me	192
commitment	112
committed	104
communities rebuilding	272
complaining is a thing of the past	126
conditions for intentional prayer	233
constantly remember death	237
courage: we are no longer avoiding what is new	62
creativity	210
Dana's birth declarations	23
day of transcendence	51
dealing with death	236
dealing with disorder in body	119
decisive, i choose my next plan of action	245
declaration for prosperity teachers	195
declaration of divine order	246
declaration: to command a thing to be so	245
declarations for a tree	264
declarations for enlightened beings	260
decree of perpetual health	124
Direction of the East	2
direction of the west	148
divine universal family declaration	273
don't worry no matter what anything looks like	232
East is a time of	6
east thinking	8
east: i accept plenty of help	52
emergency community affirmations	282
end the old: autumn process	159
entrepreneurial affirmations	90
esteem	58
expansiveness	21
expansiveness	239
expectancy treatment	241
expectation is in place	295
expecting good	15
extending beyond	49
for earth the time is now	277
freedom is already mine	260
freely and happily i forgive	157
friday going forward	176
gathering power in risking	45

gemini declarations	75
generosity affirmations	186
getting back to work	10
giving up being afraid and conflicted	165
goals are achieved	40
God great spirit, i see you with my heart	250
God is God....is God is....	252
God is greater than chaos	48
God is the companion of my heart	286
good is assured	243
good is certain	243
good will for all, wherever we are....	242
goodbye anger	135
goodbye obstructions to getting the job done	91
goodbye self-pity	163
goodbye small world	251
goodbye to enemies	156
goodbye to fear	64
goodbye to fear of the future	65
goodbye worry	66
goodbye: remember me as loving you	167
goodwill	20
growing to more good	134
happy celebrating nothing	264
happy words are my choice	259
healing is always available	125
health today	118
healthy thinking is mine	124
here approaches autumn of the circle	153
heros are just like us	37
holiday declaration	207
holiday times together are events of celebration	208
human beings are a viable species	267
i accomplish despite appearances	46
i am a prosperity teacher	198
i am a universe creature	250
i am associating with people who empower me	204
i am awake and fully conscious now	130
i am decisive	43
i am determination	87
i am determined	39
i am discipline	139
i am expansive	20
i am free to prosper in my business	179
i am guided to go forward	244
i am integrity	94
i am leaving behind	174
i am loved and appreciated	227
i am of God therefor sustaining perfect partnership	133
i am open and receptive to miracles	24
i am purposeful	41
i am transcendence	49

Seasons of Prosperity

i am willing to act quickly	29
i am willing to be contributed to	188
i am willing to think further than i've been before	32
i am working hard, no matter what	92
i assess myself as competent	56
i begin now in the east	12
i choose changing	200
i choose prayer as a foundation	228
i communicate breaks in my sense if integrity	129
i complete what i start	141
i create congruence	97
i enjoy animating happiness right now while beginning	29
i establish certitude of plenty	176
i express praise easily	206
i follow a high calling…	257
i give up scare scarce thinking by giving	183
i grow in closeness with God	232
i have a clear space to work	213
i have a new friendship with the natural world	52
i have a new friendship with the natural world	262
i have entrepreneurial spirit	92
i have what it takes in integrity	86
i have what it takes in the autumn	154
i have what it takes in the spring	8
i have what it takes in the winter	224
i know	175
i know how to be with people	128
i know how to work	88
i know what to do and i do it	45
i know what to do and i do it	138
i know when to hold and when to fold	165
i leave behind, i accept and i am willing	173
i let go	174
i let go of problems	159
i live as a success story today	134
i move in new ways	63
i must be what i was created to be	52
i promise today…	199
i realize	175
i recognize and release resistance to changing	160
i release the past to move forward now	62
i say yes to good	32
i see	174
i speak prosperous results	211
i speak true. i take a stand on myself	100
i thank God	253
i tithe effortlessly and i prosper	184
i trust that everybody prospers me	189
i work effectively	10
i work hard today	94
i work successfully with others helping me	205
in the east this is how i work	16

The Index by Prayer

increasing generosity	187
increasing income	183
integrity is congruence	99
intimate with everything	161
it takes many new actions	61
it's possible	103
Jason's best thought	237
leadership	200
leo declarations	142
letting go	236
libra declarations	214
life always responds	233
life extension	259
life is created with thought	190
life is good	120
life is no longer a popularity contest	101
listening	228
listening to life	231
living the mystery	254
love: affirmations and denials	112
men affirmations	188
merry days are behind and in front	295
merry making at the winter solstice	286
mighty presence of God within	166
mind treatment: we are already connected with perfection	76
monday declarations	50
more affirmations for the city	56
more money affirmations	172
my giving makes me rich	180
my heart is true	101
my heart reveals love, i surrender	251
my own nature can be heard in quiet	244
my speaking resolves breakdowns	55
myself: a hero	36
natural law	270
new affirmations	46
new year mind treatment	240
north is a time of	224
nothing is where everything comes from	166
oh south spirit	84
on death	234
on earth today	274
order is apparent	19
order perfectly outworking	245
our activities together help us know ourselves	111
parents daycare treatment	24
partnership	110
partnerships help me serve my purpose	114
partnerships serve human community: declarations for partnership	115
patience for today	135
pattern seen everywhere	255
peace with my parents	158

Seasons of Prosperity

perpetual light - declaration for the dead	235
physical well being	121
pisces declaration	294
practicing love in everyday life	109
practicing transcendence	48
prayer of a dedicated teaching life in the company of others	196
prayer of appropriate choices	247
prayer of peace	234
prayer treatment for divine guidance	246
prelude to forgiveness	155
prosperity attitudes	170
prosperity mind treatment	173
prosperity prevails	179
prosperity teacher covenant	194
prosperous declaration	171
prosperous doing	96
prosperous provision has been made	190
prosperous thinking	170
providing power is always with me	52
pumpkin harvest	193
purposefulness	38
purposefulness: gathering power in risking	41
powerful purpose is mine	105
qualities to call forth in the east	9
qualities to call forth in the north	226
qualities to call forth in the south	87
qualities to call forth in the west	155
reactive responses no longer run me	130
ready to relocate declaration	192
reflection	233
release decree	160
relinquishment	165
renewed: we seek to draw new circles	22
renunciation decree	247
responsive yule rite	290
sacred site declarations	268
safety prevails	67
safety: i move in good sequence	68
sagittarius declarations	216
saturday goodbye tensions	131
saying no	94
scorpio declarations	215
self-talk for an advisor	197
sioux prayer	267
something new is beginning	248
south is a time of	84
spirit of the west	152
spring equinox	9
spring-east	6
Standing in the east	5
standing in the north	223
standing in the south	83

The Index by Prayer

standing in the west	151
start out with thanksgiving	208
stay coherent	98
streams come alive again and fill with fish	271
summer in the spirit of the circle	86
summer-south	85
sunday in an opulent universe	191
sunshine morning	28
supportability looks like this	204
taurus declaration	74
teacher's proclamation	197
teaching affirmations	199
thank God for animals	271
thanksgiving: we give thanks to creation for all this	289
the animal blessing	272
the buck hollow declaration for surrender	163
the circumstance of this car is safety	70
the community prayer	281
the decision for quietness	226
the direction of north	220
the direction of south	80
the great way isn't difficult	227
the high laws	252
the impulse of love designs my future	256
the litany of dissapointment	137
the power mightily with me....of perfect pattern	233
the serious thing	100
there are no mistakes	66
thinking language	128
this body is a field of transformations	268
this body is in perfect submission to Universal Intelligence	132
this is completely good	105
thoughts like i want to have	231
thursday: self concern gives way	166
to go beyond limits	27
to practice death	234
to truly dare	55
today i am a citizen of earth	273
today is the day	11
today: i accept good	242
traveling declaration	69
treatment for a peaceful passing	235
true creativity	213
true satisfaction of together	106
truth song	239
universal mind	257
universal prayer	253
up,up, and away: broken open	253
virgo declarations	143
waiter/waitress affirmations	177
waiting with patience	258
we are the same as heros: the author's breakfast	53

Seasons of Prosperity

we celebrate this year	54
we declare that peace is prevailing on earth	278
we give thanks for life	209
we give thanks for protection	69
we give thanks for this marriage day	117
we have a healthy peopled peaceful world	249
we have authentic speaking	97
we have peace prevailing on earth	274
we keep earthwaters sustaining life	263
we yield to the leading edge of divine will	289
weather storm declaration	262
wedding convocation	116
wednesday declarations	50
well being decree	122
west is a time of......	154
what is in error in unreal	70
what's eternal?	238
what's mine to do is done today	106
winter - north	225
winter happiness	261
without fear	35